THE INTERPRETATION OF BELIEF

Also by David Jasper

IMAGES OF BELIEF IN LITERATURE (*editor*)

COLERIDGE AS POET AND RELIGIOUS THINKER

THE INTERPRETATION
OF BELIEF

Coleridge, Schleiermacher and Romanticism

Edited by

David Jasper

Fellow and Chaplain
Hatfield College, Durham

St. Martin's Press   New York

First published in the United States of America in 1986

Printed in Hong Kong

ISBN 0–312–42401–9

Library of Congress Cataloging-in-Publication Data
Main entry under title:
The Interpretation of belief.
Includes index.
1. English literature – 19th century – History and criticism –
Addresses, essays, lectures.   2. Religion and literature –
Addresses, essays, lectures.   3. Coleridge, Samuel Taylor,
1772–1834 – Criticism and interpretation – Addresses, essays,
lectures.   4. Schleiermacher, Friedrich, 1768–1834 – Influence
– Addresses, essays, lectures.   5. Romanticism – Addresses,
essays, lectures.   I. Jasper, David.
PR469.R4I58 1986   820'.9'145   85–26204
ISBN   0–312–42401–9

Contents

Preface   vii

Acknowledgements   x

Notes on the Editor and the Contributors   xi

1 Utopianism around AD 1800   *Ulrich Simon*   1

2 Coleridge's Theory of Imagination: a Hegelian Solution
   to Kant?   *Kathleen Wheeler*   16

3 Coleridge's Religious Thought: the Search for a Medium
   John Beer   41

4 Inside without Outside: Coleridge, the Form of the
   One, and God   *James S. Cutsinger*   66

5 The Impact of Schleiermacher's Hermeneutics on
   Contemporary Interpretation Theory   *Werner   G.
   Jeanrond*   81

6 Schleiermacher: True Interpreter   *T. H. Curran*   97

7 Romanticism and the *Sensus Numinis* in Schleiermacher
   Robert F. Streetman   104

8 On Reading Nature as a Romantic   *Stephen Prickett*   126

9 Wordsworth and the 'Mystery of Words'   *Michael
   Edwards*   143

10 Wordsworth and the Credo   *J. R. Watson*   158

11 Changing Sensibilities: the Puritan Mind and the
    Romantic Revolution in Early American Religious
    Thought   *T. Mark Ledbetter*   176

12 Tennyson, Newman and the Question of Authority
    Michael Wheeler   185

13 Contrary Imaginings: Thomas Hardy and Religion
    Ian Gregor   202

14 The Impasse of Coleridge and the Way of Blake
    Kevin Lewis   225

Index   235

Preface

In 1808, Caspar David Friedrich exhibited his altarpiece *The Cross on the Mountains* in his studio in Dresden. Commissioned for the chapel of Count Thun's castle at Tetschen, the painting provoked a debate over the suitability of landscape for religious purposes. One critic, Freiherr von Ramdohr, declared it sacrilegious to make 'landscape creep on to the altar'. In his radical approach to the conventions of landscape composition, Friedrich posed questions for the relationship between art and religion, the secular and the sacred.

Some of the questions posed by German and English Romanticism are explored in this book. Friedrich was careful to paint a scene which might actually exist in the forests and mountains of his own land, with its fir trees, its rocks and its wayside crucifixes. This realistic picture is not, as Ramdohr described it, an allegory, which Coleridge called 'a translation of abstract notions into a picture-language which is itself nothing but an abstraction from objects of the senses'. It is rather symbolic in the sense described by Coleridge, quoted by Stephen Prickett in his essay, when 'the other great Bible of God, the Book of Nature, become transparent to us, when we regard the forms of matter as words, as symbols, valuable only as being the expression, an unrolled but yet a glorious fragment of the wisdom of the Supreme Being'.

The landscape, with its disturbing realism, presents a series of contrasts or ambivalences which prompt reflection: not simply the perception of the sacred in the real world, but the stark contrast between the central image of the Cross and the background of the twilight, between the massive created earth and the sun-shot sky, within one of whose beams rises Christ crucified, interceding between earth and heaven.

These ambivalences in artistic representation provoke reflection and lie at the heart of the hermeneutic task – that business of interpretation between two realms, whether between God and man, the Bible and the present, or the Greek and German languages. Schleiermacher's pioneer work in hermeneutics is explored here by Werner Jeanrond and Thomas Curran. The reflection which the ambivalences of the painting promotes exemplifies the creativity in the processes and evolution of human perception and consciousness which Kathleen Wheeler examines in Coleridge's theory of imagination, and Stephen Prickett attends to in his discussion of metaphor and its meanings in Romanticism.

Finally, Friedrich's *Cross on the Mountains* raises the question of the relationship between the sacred and the secular, and the association of religious images in a secular, 'realistic' context. J. R. Watson, in his essay on Wordsworth's poetry, explores the problems presented by the poet's use of the language of Christian devotion in contexts often remote from the protection of assumed and accepted doctrine or conventional piety.

The aesthetician Karl Solger (1780–1819), an enthusiastic reader of Schleiermacher, was convinced of the necessary unity between philosophy, art and religion. They are, he wrote, 'the three necessary parts of a harmonious culture: Philosophy without art is means without purpose; art without philosophy is end without beginning; and both without religion are utterly debased, vile and godless: philosophy becomes insolence and violence, and art arrogant amusement'.

The essays in this book in various ways seek to substantiate Solger's conviction, focusing on the work of Coleridge and Schleiermacher. The last four essays trace the development of some of the themes in Romanticism through the nineteenth century in America and England. Ian Gregor's study of Thomas Hardy and religion returns firmly to Coleridgean language, the language of contraries, symbol and metaphor, as the 'absolutist' conclusions of Victorian language of scepticism and belief are rejected by Hardy the poet and novelist. Kevin Lewis concludes the book with a question. Are we right, after all, in our contemporary struggle with religious belief, to look back to Coleridge for help and guidance? The discussion remains open.

James Cutsinger wishes to acknowledge the help given to him by Mr Owen Barfield in the preparation of his essay. An earlier version of Stephen Prickett's essay was published in the *Papers and Synopses from the Twenty-Second Congress of the Australasian Universities Language and Literature Association, Canberra* (1984). My thanks are due to Mrs Frances Durkin, who typed the final script.

All the essays were first presented as papers at the Second National Conference on Literature and Religion in Durham, September 1984. The Conference met to commemorate the 150th anniversaries of the deaths of Coleridge and Schleiermacher in 1834.

DAVID JASPER
Hatfield College

Throughout the following abbreviations are used:

BL Samuel Taylor Coleridge, *Biographia Literaria*, ed. J. Shawcross, 2 vols (Oxford, 1907)

CL *The Collected Letters of Samuel Taylor Coleridge*, ed. E. L. Griggs, 6 vols (Oxford, 1956–71)

CN *The Notebooks of Samuel Taylor Coleridge*, ed. Kathleen Coburn, 3 parts in 6 vols, 1794–1819 (London and New York, 1957–73)

Acknowledgements

The editor and publishers wish to thank the following for permission to reprint copyright material:

John Knox Press, a Division of the Presbyterian Publishing House, Atlanta, Georgia, for the extracts from F. D. E. Schleiermacher's *On Religion: Addresses in Response to its Cultured Despisers*, translated by Terrence N. Tice, copyright M. E. Bratcher 1969;

Princeton University Press, New Jersey, for the extracts from E. L. Griggs's *Wordsworth and Coleridge: Studies in Honor of George McLean Harper*, copyright 1939, © renewed 1966 by Princeton University Press.

Notes on the Editor and the Contributors

John Beer is Reader in English at Cambridge and a Fellow of Peterhouse

T. H. Curran is a Research Fellow of Hatfield College, Durham

James S. Cutsinger is Assistant Professor of Theology, University of South Carolina

Michael Edwards is Reader in Literature, University of Essex

Ian Gregor is Professor of Modern English Literature, University of Kent

David Jasper is Chaplain and Harris Fellow of Hatfield College, Durham

Werner G. Jeanrond is a Lecturer in the School of Theological Studies, Trinity College, Dublin

T. Mark Ledbetter is a member of the Graduate Institute of the Liberal Arts, Emory University, Atlanta

Kevin Lewis is Assistant Professor of Religious Studies, University of South Carolina

Stephen Prickett is Professor of English, Australian National University, Canberra

Ulrich Simon is Professor Emeritus of Christian Literature and Dean Emeritus of King's College, London

Robert F. Streetman is Professor of Religious Studies, Montclair State College, New Jersey

J. R. Watson is Professor of English, University of Durham

Kathleen Wheeler is a Fellow of St John's College, Cambridge

Michael Wheeler is Head of the Department of English Literature, University of Lancaster

1 Utopianism around AD 1800

ULRICH SIMON

I

When it was my lot to teach undergraduates about Schleiermacher nothing irritated me more than the lack of background knowledge. One was supposed to ignore the complex development of the man himself, who naturally enough shared all the influences of, and reactions to, Herrnhut pietism, the Enlightenment and the rationalism of the eighteenth century, the political enthusiasm and the disenchantment caused by the French Revolution, the Terror, and soon Napoleon. But even more annoying was, and, I think, still is, the presentation of Schleiermacher out of context, without so much as mentioning the poets of the *Sturm und Drang* and their own reaction to these events and to the formidable voice of Kant. True, this grave omission ought to have been remedied when Karl Barth's famous and brilliant *Protestant Theology in the Nineteenth Century* appeared at last in its English translation in 1972, but even in this monumental work there are gaps. Barth is more interested in the roots of liberal Christianity than in the utopian strands of religion and secular movements, and, as he himself came to regret, time was not found to complete the grand design with a chapter on Goethe. Hölderlin only receives one mention, and that in company with Schelling and Hegel. Barth eschews references to Coleridge and the English-speaking world. No wonder, because European thought and creative genius reaches an apex of such dimensions that no one book can do justice to what was going on at about 1800. Mozart was dead, but Haydn was still gloriously active and twice visited England with huge success. Beethoven's *Eroica* (1804) celebrated

1

the coming glory. Turner and Friedrich were to turn painting upside down.

It is commonplace to assert that the wave of enthusiasm and the fervour of idealism broke upon the rock of French terror. The advent of Napoleon afterwards annulled for many the expectations and illusions created by Rousseau and nourished by a belief in the goodness of man. Beethoven's disenchantment has become famous: he deleted his original dedication of the *Eroica*. The Emperor had for him ceased to be the Hero. He saw intuitively that heroism did not belong to the upstart from Corsica. Beethoven's gesture was in defence of a utopian hope shattered soon by war and destruction.

But more than a gesture is at stake. Schiller showed in his life an amazing development which may be held to be typical. In his early masterpiece *Die Räuber* he could still portray anarchism as an idealistic movement. These Robin Hood characters are free and even admirable, without ties and property. But they undermine their utopian destiny from within by whoring and murdering. This drama, though highly critical of Utopia, was considered dangerous and forced Schiller to flee from Stuttgart in 1782 – '*Die Räuber* took from me family and fatherland.' But, despite straying in need, Schiller never contemplated the clerical profession once thought fit for him, and via work in Dresden he arrived as a professor in Jena in 1789 and married in 1790. However, illness soon took its toll physically and Kant mentally. Yet for ten years, from 1794 to his death in 1805, Schiller could collaborate with Goethe in Weimar and profit from the work in the theatre.

Schiller's Utopianism matured without loss of his glowing longing and the heroic ideal. He paid tribute to two worlds: naïvety or nature, on the one hand; sentiment or the ideal, on the other. The former exists; the latter seeks harmony after conflict. But this higher synthesis is still to be achieved in obedience to the moral postulate (Kant). The Christian faith is 'only an aesthetic religion' (to Goethe in August 1795) but the notion of God's Fatherhood vanishes, since Man must create God in himself so as to fulfil his destiny of God-likeness. Clearly *Sturm und Drang* did not fizzle out for Schiller when he created the tragic *Don Carlos* in his maturity. The prince and his friend Posa must give their lives for the cause of freedom, but this concept owes nothing to irresponsible enthusiasm. Tyranny must end and responsible statesmanship serve as a bastion of freedom.

This theme is finally developed in *Wilhelm Tell* when the free consensus of representative leaders only reluctantly sanctions the act of rebellion. Schiller distances force from immoral violence and he envisages in this drama social enlargement, continuity and benevolence. This Utopia of a new society (the Swiss Federation was still to come) is designed to be acted upon, not only on the stage but also in the political world and practice. Schiller's translation no longer requires any religious sanction or cultic loyalty. He ranks as one of Schleiermacher's foremost 'cultured despisers' who frees the political ideal from transcendental authority, unless, with Kant, the Practical Reason may be accepted as just that – namely, apprehended within the conscience and in the cosmic order.

When Schiller met Goethe, and before their intimacy could inspire both, the young genius from Frankfurt had long ago grown out of the pubescent craze, so as to fulfil a lasting role. But in his retrospective *Dichtung und Wahrheit* Goethe by no means dismisses his mad enthusiasm as worthless. The twenty-two year old could cry in the vein of Rousseau 'Und ich rufe Natur! Natur! Nichts so natürlich als Shakespeares Natur' ('And I call out Nature! Nature! Nothing as natural as Shakespeare's Nature!) at the celebration of the Shakespeare *Tag* of 1771. He came to learn from his own experience that *Natur* is not only elemental but also destructive. Despite Goethe's debt to pietism he clearly identified, as some pietists had done, with all kinds of protest. Goethe displays *Auflehnung* in every context: alienation in the family, sexual passion, rebellion against authority, social dissension and political scepticism. But he never became a moralist. In 1774 he set the European world ablaze with his *Werther*. In the form of letters he builds up the timeless drama of an impossible devotion, passion set against marriage and home, which must end in the hero's suicide. Goethe drew his material from the real world and he also affected the real world: many potential Werthers were to fire a bullet into their heads and thus complete their individual Utopia. Not so Goethe himself, who describes this episode later at a distance and with the irony of aged wisdom. As he presents himself in *Dichtung und Wahrheit* he had by the turn of the century left behind him Promethean ecstasy, revolutionary wildness, and the utopian fire, still found in the early dramas *Götz* and *Egmont*. He demonstrates most touchingly his almost conscious *Abkehr* (turning-away) in his poem 'Ilmenau' of 1783, a time when general Utopianism was still a heady wine. But even then Goethe mastered the titanic feeling at enormous cost. He joined his princely employer and benefactor in Weimar. Thenceforth he projected the demonic groundswell into the ocean which was to become *Faust*.

Goethe was and remains *sui generis*, if only because Kant did not trouble him. By 1805 Schiller was dead and for Goethe idealistic Utopia had altogether died with him. He came to abhor it, for he loved order and worked for the civilised life. Thus he turned from false expectations to scientific investigations, especially to geology and optics. For years he wrote about light and colour in fierce opposition to Newton. *Faust* might have been abandoned since there was no Schiller to urge him on. But after Napoleon's downfall Goethe's so-called second puberty, a miraculous revival of poetic force in the aged Olympian, led him to 'redeem' Faust. The tragic modern man, embroiled in seduction and violence, is granted something higher than Utopia. Goethe took up the cherished strands of the Christian tradition (free from all clerical ties), especially the imagery of Dante's *Paradiso*, to place Faust ascended in eternity and cosmic glory. Faust in his striving for Utopia is accepted despite his criminal past.

Goethe's *Faust* has received and still requires endless comment, though it is now fashionable to deride secondary literature, the 'talk about' the primary text.[1] Admittedly Goethe is not a didactic poet who theologises. Nevertheless Goethe is the unique interpreter of the diabolical strain in human progress within the divine plan. He relates the Christian deposit, which includes Jewish Messianism, prophetic and apocalyptic Utopianism, to the classical world view. In modern terms he envisions the titanic drive and power of science, technology and industry within a harmonious and universal whole. In and around 1800 such an optimistic estimate was still possible, perhaps because the unholy alliance epitomised in Faustian energy was still in its infancy. Some Utopians had their instinctive suspicions and wanted to resist. Blake was not alone in divorcing the false Jerusalem or Babel from the true, for how could an innocent Utopia succeed in pacific simplicity?

The danger of generalising confronts us acutely when we speculate about the mental climate at around 1800. Christians and non-Christian secularists seem to have lived on a different planet. There was no uniformity of belief in Western Europe.

But the old world, which Goethe describes in such detail, of small towns, high walls, professional guilds, formal elections, grand ceremonies, horses with golden spurs and saddles of brocade, heralds with bugles, wigs and pearls, was vanishing rapidly. Moreover, the new world across the Atlantic was fulfilling the role of the mythical Utopia, of More's ideal Bermuda. Goethe realised sooner than most that the future must lie in America.[2]

As we have stressed, Goethe is neither typical nor normative. There are not many human beings who retain the extravagances of youth and blend these with scientific work. Goethe had to learn to stand apart from the world and its immediacy of stress and strife. He was helped in this too by certain weaknesses, such as his mathematical obtuseness and his dislike of Kantian philosophy.[3] He came to create his own personal Utopia, which only became popular after his death. During his lifetime and later he has been criticised for distancing himself from anything to do with *Liberté, Egalité* and *Fraternité*; His almost servile, unnecessarily decorous welcoming of Napoleon to Weimar still shocks many who abhor the military aggressor. But Goethe is not typical of the period around 1800. Neither, perhaps, was Schleiermacher, though he joined the nationalistic protagonists for freedom against Napoleon. Goethe and Schleiermacher had little in common,[4] except perhaps the instinct to advance positively and creatively in new directions. Both abandoned the pietism and dogmatism in Protestant belief. Goethe at that time is not far from, though not to be identified with, his Faust, who translates the *Logos* of the Johannine Gospel's prologue as *Deed*: 'Am Anfang war die Tat' ('In the beginning was the Deed').

Utopianism around 1800 is rampant and complex, perhaps elitist, and its influence on Christian theology is far from clear. Goethe's temperament opposed the French Revolution not out of love for a decadent court but owing to his conviction that society like nature must evolve gradually. Insane pathos disgusted him, and the atrocities sealed his hatred for violence. Thus he describes his feelings during the military campaign of the allies in France which he attended in 1792. This operation was a complete fiasco and Goethe's interest focused less on the battle of Valmy on 20 September than on the physical effects of the bombardment on the surroundings. Yet he muses on the absurdity of war and military expectations, and when asked for his

verdict on the defeat he gives a somewhat utopian prophecy:
'From today a new epoch of world history emerges, and you may
say that you have been present.'[5] In this he was right. Utopianism had to take a new turn.

This development can best be gauged through Goethe's own
works. In 1797 he could look at the misery of refugees and the
terrible losses caused by the invading armies by transforming
this dreary theme. In a miraculously short time he composed the
unsurpassed *Hermann und Dorothea*. It is a classical epic of domestic charity and salvation, celebrating in hexameters the triumph
of goodness and nobility over savagery and suffering.

The plot is simple enough. Hermann, the rich landowner's
only son, a youth with melancholy feelings of isolation, rescues
the outcasts and marries the maiden who owns nothing except
inward virtue and outward grace. This sacred union, presented
with humour, is not utopian; it is a religious achievement in
secular terms. The smiling and urbane pastor interprets the
drama as Resurrection, for the terror of death is defeated in this
life and in the life to come.

Thus Goethe converts Dionysian Utopianism into Apollonian
order, though he keeps his innermost secret to himself. 'Ilmenau'
was written in 1783 and marks the great change, but it was only
published in 1815. Then the wild and inspired extravagances of
the youth had long been overtaken by serious endeavours in the
promotion of agriculture, cottage industries and mining. Though
retired from official business (except the theatre) Goethe supported the good state of the land. Even Napoleon could not upset
Goethe's dedication to the good life. He had greeted the 'great
man's' *coup d'état* in 1799 as necessary, remained in Weimar as a
sober realist after the Prussian defeat in 1806, and used the
confusion to marry his Christiane to normalise his own domestic
irregularity. But Goethe's acceptance of conventions, of duty, of
the limitations of expectations, must not be read as a faltering of
genius. His *Entbehrung* – 'renunciation' is a poor rendering – is
neither a Stoic act of acceptance nor a Christian act of resigna-
tion.

Goethe, then, secularises and heightens the pietistic tradition
of Christian service. He surrenders the loved, romantic, fantastic
world of *As You Like It*, in his own Forest of Arden, the gypsy-like
world of nightly revels, for a mature devotion to the *Herzog*, his
house, his government. He gives in exchange for what he re-

ceives – namely, an earthly condition which is not Paradise, which does not warrant endless happiness, but which enables him to work. But it is not a bourgeois contentment which succeeds to the early enthusiasm, nor a compromise. Rather it is the classical style, a hierarchical or architectural harmony of dimensions which in some way still reflects the cosmic order. In Eckermann's entry for 23 October 1828 Goethe looks back and evaluates not only the *Herzog*'s great qualities but also considers the future of mankind. Calling for a bottle of wine and in high spirits, he envisages a future and a relative consummation of ideals and progress in millennia after millennia. In this he does not exclude the possibility that God may sicken of the whole spectacle and make a new beginning. All this *Stirb und Werde*, coming-into-being after dying, is reflected in physics, astronomy, biology, morphology. And looking back to 'Ilmenau' Goethe acknowledges the madness of his youth, the irrepressible energy, and the romanticism of camp-fires; they yielded to the higher purpose of responsible government, and in a remarkable passage he anticipates the unification not only of Germany, but of the whole of Europe, with monetary stability and cultural prosperity, flourishing universities and theatres. A note of ironic doubt remains, of course; but clearly Utopia is contained within and fuels the forward drive of humanity, both in rational pursuits and beyond, in realms of poetry and music — stretching into the Hereafter, where Providence is obliged to offer consummation and entelechy.[6]

II

Not so with Hölderlin! Born later than Goethe, in 1766, he lost two fathers in early youth: his own, who died suddenly in 1772, and his mother's second husband, of whom he was very fond, who died in 1778. He was a boy most happy in the stillness, the giver of gracious joy, musical and highly competent on the piano and the flute, privately educated, schooled in reverence and piety, an enthusiast for the Old Testament and classical mythology, confirmed in 1784 and a pupil of the Klosterschule Denkendorf, highly regarded by the authorities, but privately already conscious of religious problems and with his head full of poetic fancies, emotions beyond his control which fuelled utopian ambitions in the youth in his twenties. The triad of Hegel, Schelling and Hölderlin symbolises for posterity the galaxy of genius assembled then to promote utopian idealism. But genius overworks and suffers; youthful infatuations cause alienation and at times a melancholy sickness unto death. Political troubles also induced in Hölderlin anger and hatred, when he swears vengeance against the people's enemies. But more stirring for him and all that generation than the Fall of the Bastille is the contact with Kant; from 1790 onwards heads spin and a passion for philosophy lessens or eliminates the pietism, the desire to study theology and to become a parson in some Swabian village. Cicero's *De Natura Deorum* is perhaps found more interesting than the Gospels. But Hölderlin speculates also on metaphysical themes, such as immortality and human destiny, truth and cosmic harmony. Overarching these endless mental activities stands the pantheistic motto ῾Εν χὰι Πάν, the One and the All.

In 1791 Hölderlin is in Switzerland, rowing a boat on the Lake of Zürich, wandering at night over the passes, visiting the cloister of Einsiedeln. The utopian heart beats to the peaceful huts, the sacred monuments of freedom, the martyrs' blood which flowed to achieve it. He denounces superficial self-indulgence and celebrates a future life free from sorrow and shame. Splendour and beauty give the frame to greatness. But the Utopian pays the price with headaches and indigestion. Isolated in his fight for freedom, in 1792 Hölderlin sides with the French Revolution in the war against Austria and Prussia. Patriotism and revolution now go hand in hand; just like Hegel, Hölderlin joins a political club as a 'tough Jacobin'. At the end of May the first reference to *Hyperion* appears and soon the constellation darkens, with the French occupation of Mainz and the advent of the Terror. At the first reading of parts of *Hyperion* his friends toast the sacred freedom. Though not without some funds, Hölderlin complains of his sick finances, and political and military concerns aggravate his spirit. Tyrants and despots threaten everywhere and theology is but an empty galley. Commenting on reading Schiller's *Don Carlos* Hölderlin proclaims his love for mankind, the generation of coming centuries, when freedom and virtue will flourish in the holy and warming light freed from despotism. When Hegel leaves for a post in Berne, the slogan of their farewell, which has become famous, is simply 'Reich Gottes' – *Regnum Dei*, the Kingdom of God. But then contact ceased; the successful Hegel never again referred to Hölderlin, nor to his influence – a typical dénouement of utopian friendship.

By 1793–4 Hölderlin preaches sermons and looks for a job. He leaves his mother and travels, at first on foot. He becomes tutor to a young man, recommended for this somewhat isolated post by Schiller. The solitary reads Kant: the challenge of the Critiques overspills into a feverish mental activity. The tutor and his boy, who seems to fare none too well, visit Jena to see Schiller; a stranger completely ignores Hölderlin. This is Goethe. In 1795 Hölderlin loses his position. His mother is prepared to support him. A new friendship with Isaak von Sinclair begins in March, the 'radiant and lovable ideal', a revolutionary with a strong influence. Hölderlin flees from all contacts, even from Schiller, who wants to promote him. A new position is on the horizon for the ill-humoured wanderer; he drowns his emotional paralysis with more Kant. At last he arrives, after a difficult journey, in Frankfurt, to teach the eight-year-old Henry Gontard. His first impressions are more than favourable: thus live the blessed gods, in the still land of beauty. The peace outside the city is heavenly, and to hell with the sordid muck of German and European politics! But the French armies cross the rivers towards Frankfurt in 1796, and, with the exception of Mr Gontard, the small family and the tutor flee eastwards to Kassel. The quiet life returns despite the armies and the worries and soon the family can return to Frankfurt. Hölderlin begins to compose rhymes about his emergent central concern, neither of armies nor supplies: Susette Gontard, his Diotima. Schiller comments on an early draft, 'Avoid philosophical themes, stay close to the world of the senses!'

It pertains to the Utopian of genius to combine and, if possible, exploit all the contradictions of the external world and the inner life. Hölderlin is the exponent of all those who suffered from the immense weight of rational philosophy, prescriptive ethics, and a lyricism of the heart. Hence his 'soldiering' under the stress of abstract thought and his attempt to rid himself of its enslavement. How can you think logically and feel sincerely, warmly, with enthusiasm – *Be-geisterung* – and emerge unscathed? Again, how can you translate utopian enthusiasm into action?

Yet it is the intolerable burden of irreconcilable forces which gives utopian genius its unique hour of splendour, such as Hölderlin was to experience around 1800. Externally the world seemed to have quietened down; the horror of the French Revolution passed into the stable conditions of the Consulate. Many hopes were left unfulfilled as normality returned. Domestically Hölderlin enjoyed temporary bliss with Diotima. The first part of *Hyperion* had already appeared in 1797. Yet there is no resonance. Goethe, for example, remains patronizingly cool, shows little understanding of him, no doubt numbering him among the 'half savages'. His advice to Hölderlin consists of a brisk and unhelpful 'Write shortish poems!'

Hölderlin seeks Utopia in a different world. Not for him the Court; only the attainment of the highest will suffice. Exposed to destructive reality, sickly, tired, plagued by headaches and discouragement, he approaches the catastrophe. On 25 September 1798 his employer, the banker Gontard, fires his son's tutor. Diotima and Henry lament his departure. Faith, hope, and love vanish at a stroke. The ideal wanes, for how do you recognise the All in the One, or place the singular in the All? The utopian ideal of total, intense, inward, close, tender, intimate, gentle union, the fervent and the lyrical 'Innig eins' dissolves, disintegrates, dies.

Hölderlin embraces his ideal of perfectionism in the manner of Empedocles. He identifies with the sacrificial hero, ready like 'a living corpse' to emulate his example. He will be a mediator and reconciler in and through death. His Mount Etna opens up to receive his dedication, in which form and content blend uniquely. Political hopes ended when Napoleon became 'a sort of dictator'. The time has come for Hölderlin 'to praise the more exalted' in the completion of his *Hyperion*.

No reader of *Hyperion* will agree with another in a reading of this masterpiece of prose poetry. The mythical sun god serves as a symbol which retains much of biblical and classical pathos. The work takes the form of a series of letters addressed to 'Bellarmin'. He is a cryptic figure whose name alludes to a *bellum* (war) as well as to *bellus* (beautiful). Arminius, the German hero who fought against the Romans, also hides behind the cryptogram. Bellarmin never answers and remains a shadow of the utopian past and future. His heroic presence remains strikingly integral to Utopia. *Hyperion* is a renewed and heightened appeal to German idealism, even to German action, but its utopian perfectionism makes direct political action impossible. Fifteen years later such action could have been identified with the struggle against and victory over Napoleon. But by 1800 Hölderlin could not fulfil any role, Messianic or liberating. He refuses his mother's advice to accept a regular post. He meets his Diotima secretly and engages in exhausting and probably disastrous travels to Bordeaux and back. Soon Diotima dies of consumption and despair. There remains a deep void, an incurable pain, and a realisation of the transitory nature of all things, events, and meetings. The poet turns from all kinds of manifestos to elegies, for in the elegiac form the heart can still hold fast to its faith, hope, and love. After 1800 a veritable flood of inspiration buries utopian expectations under the order of classical metres. At length Hölderlin reaches his Patmos, where the poet–servant finds God in absence, salvation in peril: 'Nah ist – und schwer zu fassen der Gott. Wo aber Gefahr ist, wächst das Rettende auch' ('Near is – and hard to hold is God. But where danger lurks the saving power also grows').

Hymns followed the elegies, and they may be hailed as the last word, the climax, of utopian creation, of perfect harmonisation of all discords, of the unification of the Many in the One. The external world must now be ignored and surpassed. But the price to be paid cannot be gainsaid; a total mental breakdown leads to a mild form of insanity, an entry into a night of nothingness. To talk here of schizophrenia is an easy way out and very misleading. Rather this is the tragic principle of greatness, which the utopian knows from within. But the insanity also takes different forms. Whereas Nietzsche from 1889 to 1900 must have railed against the hated Christ and screamed against God in the pitiless isolation imposed upon him by his sister, Elisabeth Foerster-Nietzsche, Hölderlin, tenderly looked after by Ernst Zimmer, a joiner in Tübingen, can still enjoy the river and the vista of fields and hills. This sick man is visited by friends with whom he cannot properly or rationally communicate, but he can love childhood to the end. He achieves Utopianism in his love for the innocence of infancy.

All this ended a long time after 1800, for against all medical foresight the invalid lived until 1843; he died as one 'of whom the world was not worthy' (Hebrews 11:38). Nor did his utopian purgation and achievement survive in anything except poetry. The Word stands for ever, perfect, inviolable. But this Word could not influence the world that was not worthy of the poet. Nor would one deem Goethe's redemption of Faust to provide the answer to utopian demonism. Faust, too, sublimates the groundswell of madness and ecstasy. If *Faust* is called a tragedy, as it is, the tragic may be found in uniqueness and the failure to move the world by means of, and for the purpose of, pity. Terror, and not compassion, was to win the utopian dream.

By 1800 *le jour de gloire* of the Marseillaise had ended. In France it was 'a prodigious spectacle as the new society was being replaced in its turn. Here was confusion to turn heads as nothing was stable and nothing lasted.'[7] Even in England this was felt as a challenge: 'Not in Utopia – subterranean fields, – Or some secreted island, Heaven knows where! / But in the very world, which is the world / Of all of us, the place where in the end / We find our happiness, or not at all.'[8] In other, prosaic words, something non-utopian remained to be done. In Germany the future lay with Fichte and Hegel.

Hölderlin goes a different way and *Hyperion* remains the lasting monument to Utopia, beyond place and time. His prose poem, the author insists, is not a plant to be smelled or to be plucked. He is no teacher with didactic ethics. Reflection and pleasure cannot answer to the joy and the pain which take the reader to a heroic Greece where the One is united with the All, freed from science and reason. In these gardens of Nature the longing is stilled with laurels and roses, with gorges and marble. Here the child gathers stones and the ears of the corn in the fields. There are no riches unless we renew the old world in ourselves with loving freedom. At Homer's grave the soul contemplates its destiny and the miserable cup of unheroic sustenance for such a thirst. There are imperatives which are personal: learn to be patient, choose the best, move forward, walk over the land, climb the rocks, listen to the birds and the animals, and let your heart glow from the holy fire. The poet becomes Hyperion, comrade and friend with men.

Everything will become different, but it is no joke to better the world, for trusted and familiar allies turn out to be traitors. There is a serpent in Utopia. Love cannot survive distrust. The gardener tears his hands at the rose he has planted. Hunger, anxiety, darkness and death wait to celebrate their feast. Hence

Hyperion exiles himself. On Salamis, the island of Ajax, the rains have freshened the tired soil. It is cool and green, light and full of mirth. This is not to be confused with Romanticism. The pathos is ecstatic as well as restrained. Hyperion drinks from the past in the pure air. The divine bursts through the prison and Elysium is open for the perfect, with Diotima the queen of unending beauty. But what flower adorns the world without decay? The death of Diotima seals Utopia and the grave is the surviving heart. Those who win all must lose all. Forgetfulness and re-membrance fill the mourning breast.

How did Utopia end for Hölderlin? Outwardly in the political field. Hyperion against Diotima's will goes out to fight for Greece against the Turks, only to be defeated by his own men, who murder and plunder. This horror reflects the terror not only of the French Revolution but also of Germany. The famous penultimate chapter is an indictment of the Germans: 'I asked not for much and I was prepared to find even less.' His home-coming differs from Oedipus's arrival at Athens: Hyperion finds only barbarians from the start, made more barbarous by dili-gence, science, and even religion, bereft of every grace, sherds of a broken vessel, who may be artisans or priests but not *Menschen*. He piles up the accusations against the degraded and unnatural slaves. In this waste no poet is at home. He pronounces a woe, which Nietzsche took up later, and Hitler fulfilled.

Hence Utopia is lifted beyond the catastrophe through an epic form that in its pathos transcends classicism and Romanticism. I have read Marxist and Freudian theses to explain what has happened here, as if Hölderlin merely condemned the market economy or himself suffered from the Oedipus complex.[9] Noth-ing could be further from the truth. The political and the religious Utopia of perfection cannot operate, because perfection is not within our reach. Just as Keats was to find some twenty years later, the Old and the New, the Titanic and the Apollonian order, remain irreconcilable because power is its own destroyer. Only beauty can intimate the One-which-differs-in-itself, the τό ἕν διάφερον. Only the poet can achieve perfection in poetry. Thus Utopia is transformed into the aesthetic order which is both tragic and all-transcendent, ecstatically blessed but tinged with black despair.

By 1800 a new Utopia had emerged which no longer looked

for perfection in action and institutions. Hyperion's Song of Destiny seals a transcendent exaltation, in the blessed light of divine air and to the sacred chords, comparable to the breathing of the sleeping infant, chastely kept in modest bud, but blooming in spirituality towards eternal clarity. Suffering mankind has here no resting-place but blindly falls like water from cliff to cliff into the Unknown. Kleist's suicide in 1811 sealed perfection with despair.

But this extreme pessimism should be balanced by the music of that age, even of 1800. Then Haydn was creating his *Creation*, surely the greatest mimesis of divine Creation on earth, and Beethoven was completing his Opus 18 quartets, in which all the utopian strands of external stress and lyrical inwardness meet, making the Unknown heard and realised by those who have ears to hear – as if there could also be an ascent from cliff to cliff.

Hölderlin himself takes Utopianism beyond the limits of optimism and pessimism. These banal evaluations are beside the point. He appeals to the Soul, to the beauty of the world – both indestructible. What are death and woe measured against eternal youth? He ends *Hyperion* with the reconciliation of dissonances: in the midst of strife all the separate opposites find one another in unity. He ends on a note of glowing life, or, rather, he interrupts his thinking and promises 'More next time'. What this 'More' might have been no one can say. Scholars are divided. But there is little doubt that it is the Word, the word of poetry, the perfect poem. Perhaps the last lines of 'Patmos' are to be treasured even in 1984: the Father who reigns above all loves most of all that the 'feste Buchstab' (the firm letter) be cultivated and that Tradition be well interpreted. Song, German song, but surely also all proper, sacred, inspired, true song celebrates and eternalises the longing of genuine Utopianism. Poetry is not a message to, but a model for, society; it is already *per se* what society has become. The poets' task is achieved when they create what endures. Such a poet can sing 'Jetzt aber tagts! Ich harrt und sah es kommen, und was ich sah, das Heilige sei mein Wort' ('Now day has come. I was waiting and saw it come, and what I saw, let the Holy be my word'). The term 'realised eschatology' hardly rises to the claims such Utopianism fulfils here and now.

NOTES

1. Structuralists and deconstructionists have certainly freed the reader from dipping into 'talk about' primary texts. But denunciations, such as George Steiner's, are tinged with irony, since he and most of us derive our living precisely from 'commenting'.
2. In Conversations with Eckermann on 15 February 1824 Goethe thanked Heaven that he was no longer young: 'I could not stay here. Nay, if I sought refuge in America, I should come too late, for there is now too much light even there' (*Conversations of Goethe*, trs. John Oxenford (London, 1883) p. 59).
3. See esp. Ilse Graham, 'Kant-Goethe-Kleist: Of Knowing and Relating', Inaugural Lecture, King's College, London, 1976. Cf. also Emil Staiger, *Goethe*, 3 vols (Zürich and Freiburg, 1952–) *passim*. Eckermann remembers Goethe's words on 11 April 1827: 'Kant never took any notice of me, though from my own nature I went a way like his own' (*Conversations*, p. 243).
4. Note the total absence of reference to Schleiermacher in Goethe's works and accordingly in secondary literature.
5. See *Goethes Campagne in Frankreich, 1792*, ed. G. Roethe (Berlin, 1919).
6. Eckermann's entries for 4 February 1829 and 1 September 1829: restless activity 'obliges' nature to assign to Goethe another form of existence or being, but 'we are not all, in like manner immortal; and he who would manifest himself in future as a great *entelecheia*, must be one now' (*Conversations*, pp. 360, 412).
7. See J. D'Ormession, 'Mon dernier rêve sera pour vous', *Une biographie sentimentale de Chateaubriand* (Paris, 1982).
8. William Wordsworth, *The Prelude* (1850) XI.140–4.
9. Cf. Stephan Wackwitz, *Utopie und Trauer um 1800. Studien zu Hölderlins Elegienwerk* (Stuttgart, 1982). For the opposite view see Martin Simon, 'The Theory and Practice of Religious Poetry. Studies in the Elegies of Friedrich Hölderlin' (unpublished PhD thesis, Durham, 1982).

2 Coleridge's Theory of Imagination: a Hegelian Solution to Kant?

KATHLEEN WHEELER

I INTRODUCTION

Coleridge's theory of imagination has all too frequently been misunderstood throughout its history, with a few notable exceptions.[1] Both recent critical works and, lamentably, the new edition of the *Biographia Literaria* perpetuate the past misunderstandings, in spite of the well-charted pitfalls of previous interpreters. The problem arises from a lack of attention to the import of Coleridge's numerous, if scattered, statements related to the theory, combined with a tendency to undervalue the significance of the philosophical context of his theory, as well as its origins, inspiration and aims. The theory of imagination lies at the heart of Coleridge's aesthetic and philosophical projects, situating Coleridge clearly in relation to rationalism, empiricism and idealism. For it cuts through many of the pseudo-problems of philosophy, based as they were upon unexamined assumptions, often couched in terms of dualities or reified entities inherited from earlier philosophy. A closer examination of the intellectual context within which Coleridge was formulating his discoveries and answers to traditional problems helps us to clarify his theory and its contribution to an understanding of processes of perception and knowledge.

Surprisingly, misinterpreters of the theory, as in the new *Biographia* edition, suggest that the primary–secondary imagination distinction is an analogy of the copy–imitation distinction. The primary imagination is unconsciously confused with the

16

memory and the fancy in these accounts, which say that primary imagination merely repeats and copies what already exists in nature or is created by other individuals. Originality, or 'true imitation', is denied to the primary imagination,[2] yet, curiously, primary and secondary imagination are said to be of one kind. A moment's reflection reveals the contradiction in such an account: primary imagination cannot merely repeat and copy; it is not memory or fancy with a glorified title. Imagination, primary or secondary, is in Coleridge's words the *'very power of growth and production'*; it is originality *par excellence*. An unexamined assumption leads to such mistaken accounts – namely, that the primary imagination is supplied from without with its 'raw material', which it receives and then presents to the secondary imagination to refashion. I. A. Richards sought to expose this assumption in *Coleridge and Imagination*, but without making explicit the context of the theory that would have given his account more force and clarity. As Richards makes clear, the primary imagination is not even in a modified sense a *vis receptiva*; rather primary imagination originates, creates, unifies, and synthesises. Coleridge offered us in the concept of primary imagination an account of perception which completely rejects the passive accounts of mind as a repeater or copier of an already or even partially constituted objectively conceived world of real or external objects independent of perception and imagination. Perception itself, like secondary imagination or artistic creativity, is for Coleridge originative and constitutive. If by 'perception' we mean an even partially passive receptivity, a repeating or copying of an objective world, then for Coleridge such 'perception' simply does not exist. This is not, however, to say that Coleridge espoused either an idealist position or any theory of knowledge that sets the knower, subject or observer up over against a world of objects, and then describes knowledge as a transcript of the real nature of that world. On the contrary, Coleridge's efforts to resolve such dualities and emphasise that all experience, including knowledge experience, occurs within a context inclusive of all dualities, is a rejection of the basic epistemological assumptions of rationalism, empiricism and idealism alike. Moreover, this 'context' is not reified into a fixed, determined, static entity, nor is it a metaphysical 'presence'. Rather, it is a means of insisting upon the interactive, non-subjective nature of experience, such that 'reality' is understood to reside neither in an absolute

subject nor in the object, but in the experienced interaction
between the two. While for Coleridge the concept of reality itself
suggests variety, growth, development and change, as well as
relative stability and permanence, the theory of imagination
excludes the metaphysics that is often said to re-emerge to some
extent in Coleridge's later writings, where there is a tendency to
tolerate what can be construed as a reified concept of Reason.
Even there, though, 'Reason' is spoken of as an evolving, developing experience, and not as a predetermined absolute, gradually 'revealed' by history. Reason, in reasoning, evolves itself
into being, and continues to evolve.

II   KANT AND THE SYNTHETIC REASON

Coleridge's encounter with Kant's writings in the late 1790s
focused the issues of perception and knowledge in terms of
'synthesis', and provoked what we might call a Hegelian attempt
at correction, inspired by Coleridge's experiences as a creative
writer *and* by his readings of Plato, Plotinus and others. This
attempt (the outcome of which was the theory of imagination)
went very far in avoiding the errors and assumptions of Coleridge's predecessors.[3] Coleridge came to Kant out of a dissatisfaction with Cartesian and empiricist accounts of experience and
philosophic method.[4] He complained, in a comment descriptive
of the difficulty entangling rationalists, idealists and empiricists
alike, about the unsatisfactory situation that these philosophies
place us in:

> Our Senses in no way acquaint us with Things, as they are in
> and of themselves: . . . the properties, which we attribute to
> Things without us, yea, . . . this very *Outness*, are not strictly
> properties of the things themselves, but either constituents or
> modifications of our own minds.   (*CN*, III, 3605, f. 121)

Nevertheless, Coleridge seemed to have found an implicit
assumption in Descartes at least, if not in the empiricists, that
thought could not only *analyse* but also *synthesise*. This assumption of a creative faculty was contained partly in the form of
conceptions pre-existing in the mind. Note the idea here of a
proper perceptive faculty, when Coleridge comments, 'Des Cartes

seems indeed to attribute a *proper perceptive faculty* to the Soul; but still not the things themselves are the Objects of this perception, but certain material ideas, modifications of our own subjective being' (ibid.; emphasis added). The *'proper* perceptive faculty' means for Coleridge that perception is not a *vis receptiva*, but 'a species of this Power' – namely, of imagination. The 'soul' has the capacity *not only to analyse, but to synthesise as well*. But this assumption, only implicit in Descartes, was not adequately integrated by him into an account of perception, philosophic method and the criterion of truth. In the empiricists' account was to be found, however, the same impossibility of moving from thought to existence[5] as in Descartes, but without his 'proper perceptive faculty'. Coleridge early recognised the confusion and contradictions of Locke's model of mind as a mirror of nature. Mind was assumed by Locke not even to supply the synthetic connections and relations to perception that constitute knowledge.[6] Rather, they must already exist as necessary connections in the ideas of sensation or reflection that come to mind. For Locke, the relations that constitute knowledge are given to the mind by natural connections.[7] Coleridge knew this confused account to be contradicted by Hume and Berkeley. According to Hume, for example, simple sensations are the ultimate source of experience. They cannot admit of analysis or necessary connection,[8] or indeed any connection except accidental ones of, for example, time, thus revealing the contradiction in Locke's account.[9] Empiricists and rationalists alike failed to explain either the synthesis (relations) that constituted knowledge, or the means of bridging thought and existence. Coleridge complained of the sensationalist's atomistic account of perception as a matter of simple, single sensations, here in relation to Hume's inability to account for self or unity of consciousness:

> How opposite to nature & the fact to talk of the one *moment* of Hume; of our whole being an aggregate of successive single sensations. Who ever *felt* a single sensation? Is not every one at the same moment conscious that these co-exist with a thousand others in a darker shade, or less light. (*CN*, II, 2370)

A more vivid rejection of Hume is Coleridge's description of 'the *streamy* Nature of Association, which Thinking = Reason, curbs and rudders' (*CN*, I, 1770; emphasis added). Thus Coleridge unveils and challenges one of the basic assumptions of empiricists and rationalists alike: namely, atomism. Kant brought home to Coleridge what the latter had imbibed from Plato and Plotinus and had seen implied if not explicitly developed in Descartes: namely, that the problem of knowledge and philosophic method is how to explain the synthesis which creates the relations and connections in the mind constituting experience in general and knowledge in particular. First, Kant showed how *synthetic a priori* judgements were possible, thus focusing upon synthesis rather than analysis in knowledge.[10] Second, Kant also showed the faculty of reason to be synthetic (actually creating and constituting relations) as Descartes implied and the empiricists assumed.

III LOGICIAN *VERSUS* METAPHYSICIAN

Coleridge read Kant as having elaborated systematically in the *Logic* the (itself synthetic) idea that thought or reason is in its nature *both* analytic and synthetic. Thus, as a logician, Kant exposed the earlier errors of empiricism. Coleridge insisted that Kant's 'Transcendental Logic' was one with Plato's dialectic, and he included Lord Bacon in this relation, as 'The great Restorer of the genuine Platonic Logic – viz – Progress by Induction' (*CN*, I, 457–8; see also *CL*, V, 15).

As a logician, Kant gave an account of philosophic method and the criterion of truth that emphasised knowledge as synthesis and reason as synthetic. That is, according to Kant, the reason acts synthetically through its unified system of categories which form experience. The categories have objective validity because no experience is possible without them. The system of categories, then, provides the criterion of knowledge experience, and yet the criterion of the categories is that very experience. No reference is made to any external given or foreign material or substance. Logically, Kant makes knowledge independent of the transcendent 'Substance' of empiricists and rationalists alike, that external 'Reality' or 'Given', or Presence which the mind is supposed to copy and repeat, an assumption that creates the unbridgeable gulf between mental copies and 'Reality', or real objects. Kant avoids the Cartesian overemphasis upon analysis. *Logically*, there is no break between thought and existence in

Kant, nor any difficulty in accounting for synthetic ideas of, for example, causality.

Coleridge discovered, however, that, as a metaphysician, Kant seemed to have reintroduced the rationalist-empiricist assumption that made it impossible to bridge the subsequent gap between thought and existence. That is, in the *Aesthetic* Kant assumed that for reason to be synthetic it needed a material external to it, a 'noumenon', a Presence. This assumption is exactly repeated in the misinterpretations of Coleridge's own theory of imagination: they assume that, in order to act, the primary imagination, like Kant's reason, must receive material from some source external to itself. This assumption becomes necessary (but unintelligible) only on a theory of knowledge that presupposes the duality of subject and object, such that reason, imagination, memory and all the faculties of the mind pre-exist in a 'realm' distinct from the 'realm' of objects upon which the perceiving, knowing mind gazes. If mind is set apart from the world, then of course a world external to it, and never truly known, becomes necessary to explain 'experience'. But, if mind is understood as simply a part of the world, a type of object related to other objects, then experience can be understood not as something arising from independent nature and independent mind, but, as Coleridge puts it, as something, *upon reflection*, distinguishable into subjects and objects. It is not inherently dualistic, but rather is distinguishable only upon analysis; synthesis must reunite the analysed elements to describe experience intelligibly. In Kant's terms, through the synthetic activity of its own categories, reason (or, analogously, imagination), could fashion this noumenon into phenomena, as they are known in actual experience. But Coleridge's emphasis upon the distinction between Kant as a logician and Kant as a metaphysician reveals his penetrating insight into Kant's borrowed assumption of a 'Given' (see *CL*, V, 421).

This most fundamental error, of the assumption of a 'noumenon', caused Coleridge early to question Kant:

> The perpetual and unmoving Cloud of Darkness that hangs over this Work to my 'mind's eye', is the absence of any clear account of – Was ist Erfahrung? What do you mean by *fact*, an empiric Reality, which alone can give solidity (inhalt) to our conceptions? – It seems from many passages, that this

indispensable Test is itself previously manufactured by this very conceptive Power – and that the whole not of our own making is the mere Sensation of a mere Manifold – in short, mere influx of motion, to use a physical metaphor. – I apply the Categoric forms to a Tree – Well! but first *what* is this tree? How do I come by this Tree? – Fichte I understand very well – only I cannot believe his system.[11]

In this passage Coleridge exposes the heart of the inconsistency between Kant's *Logic* and his *Aesthetic*. Coleridge objects to the noumenon, or 'naked Ding-an-sich', that alone is supposed to give content (intuition) to our concepts, and in so doing he reveals the complete falsity of any account of his own theory of imagination that relies on such a noumenon. In the Kantean scheme, he complains, 'all that we can conceive, or perceive as existing are no more than ein Begriff-spiel, while the sole objective Reality is a naked Ding an sich O, which a Vernunft-glaube is to raise into a + /0, not for the *truth* but for the *interest* of the Position!'[12]

In speaking of Spinoza, Coleridge states the assumption of Kant and of the misinterpreters of his own theory of imagination in another, related way:

> The πρῶτον ψεῦδος of Spinoza is . . . one in which all his Antagonists were as deeply immersed as himself . . . [it] consists in the assumed idea of a pure independent Object – in assuming a Substance beyond the I; of which therefore the I *could* only be a modification.   (*CL*, IV, 849).

Kant, in his aesthetics, had brought in the same erroneous assumption as Descartes, Locke, Spinoza and others before him, an assumption that was 'the common principle of [their] Philosophical System' (*CN*, III, 3605, f. 121). The assumption of 'a pure independent Object – in *assuming* a Substance beyond the I' (emphasis added) means first, that the subject–object relation, which ought to be relative only and a product of reflection, is made transcendent, or a character of primary experience, and is 'posited of the absolute'. Consequently, Reason is made the absolute Subject, noumenon the absolute Object, and Coleridge's conclusion is one with Hegel's: 'The Subjectivity of Reason is the great error of the Kantean system.'[13] The grounding

principle of philosophic method – self-consciousness or reason
– must rather, says Coleridge,

> be found therefore neither in object nor subject taken separately . . . it must be found in that which is neither subject nor
> object exclusively, but which is the identity of both . . .
> This principle . . . manifests itself in the SUM or I AM; which I
> shall hereafter . . . express by the words spirit, self, and self-
> consciousness.   (*BL*, I, 182–3)

That externality supposedly necessary for reason to be synthetic
(or for Coleridge's imagination to act) turns out to be reason
manifesting itself, the very position assured in Kant's *Logic*, but
apparently abandoned in the *Aesthetic*. It is reasserted by Coleridge in his theory of imagination as the only consistent account
of the criterion of knowledge.

The further confusion that arises in Kant's account, and
which is implicit in the misinterpreters of Coleridge, is his
distinction between subject and object in the process of knowledge. Kant seemed to identify the perceiving organism, the
individual mind, as the subject of knowledge, and the objects of
its perceptions with the objects of knowledge, instead of realising
that, according to his own *Logic*, both the individual perceiver
and the things experienced are objects arising within the single
realm of experience or 'self-consciousness' when it subjects itself
to its categories. Only this realm of self-consciousness, of experience, that 'unity of apperception', can properly be called a
subject in the process of knowledge; but it must equally be called
an object, for it makes itself its own object through its categories.
Thus, the comment 'the Subjectivity of Reason is the great error
of the Kantean system' has two applications. It applies to
making reason only or merely the subject, while the noumenon is
the object. And it applies to making the individual reasoning
mind, the empirical ego, the subject in the process of knowledge,
instead of recognising that it too is, *logically* speaking, an object of
knowledge. For, like things, it too is constituted by the categories. Thus Coleridge's astute remark, 'I feel assured there is a
latent sophism in the Kantean argument.'[14] For the transcendental unity of apperception, self-consciousness, is made purely
subjective in relation to the noumenon, and then the individual
subject of knowledge is virtually identified with this subject, thus

contradicting all Kant's careful deductions in the *Logic*. The common misinterpretation of Coleridge's theory of imagination is based on this same assumption and sophism. The individual mind is taken as the subject in the process of knowledge, opposed to known objects supposedly different in kind from itself, and at the same time the subject is experience, self-consciousness, or the infinite 'I AM'.

Coleridge's insistence on a distinction only, not a division, between thoughts and things reaffirms from another position the error of assuming two absolutely different types of existences, the subjective (knower) and the objective (thing known), and is another way of formulating his rejection of all philosophic dualisms. On Coleridge's accounts, the 'subjective' and 'objective' exist only within the realm of reason itself. First, he astutely points out that 'the law of casuality holds only between homogeneous things, i.e., things having some common property; and cannot extend from one world into another' (*BL*, I, 88–9). More explicitly, he writes,

> Even so as thoughts, from Images even up to ideas, are distinct but not divided Existences of the Mind, [quasi proles semper in utero,] so are the Products of Nature, which we call things or *Fixes* (res fixae, intellectiones coagulatae) are never really producta jam et vere fixa; but themselves portions of the act of producing. (*CN*, III, 4351)

Elsewhere Coleridge insists that to think absolutely or indefinitely is impossible, for a finite mind at least ('thoughts without content are empty'), and in a pithy penetrating remark he says, 'To think (Ding, denken; res, reor) is to *thingify*' ('intuitions without concepts are blind') (*CL*, IV, 885). Reason, 'thinking' or acting by means of its categories, 'makes' things, including thinking things, who also 'thingify'. This organic unity of experience and self-consciousness insisted upon by Coleridge gives the activity of the categories its significance and validity. Kant's error had been to posit the validity of the categories, and, consequently, the knowledge they produced, by reference to a material alien to them and external to reason, because reason is construed as subjective (therefore in need of an object) just as Coleridge's critics have done in relation to the imagination. But this reference to an alien material immediately makes the categories themselves subjective in relation to that objective material. Hence, all the knowledge they were supposed to supply is a mere relative, subjective knowledge, a 'knowledge' only for beings equipped with our particular capacities. Moreover, their role becomes purely analytic as they no longer synthesise but analyse received material. Both Coleridge and Hegel insisted, on the other hand, that the categories are valid not by reference to an external material, but rather by virtue of each being an integral part of a single organic system of experience or self-consciousness. The categories are limited, not by reference to an external noumenon, as Kant supposed, thinking thereby to retain their objective validity. Rather they are limited in themselves; but Coleridge makes it clear that this limitation does not mean that the consequent knowledge they supply is merely subjective. Kant had confused, he said, 'Limit by Negation, or defect, and Limit by Position and as an essential Perfection'. The 'perfection' of limitation resides in the position of the categories in a unified organic system of self-consciousness.

IV REASON AS WILL

Consequently, the noumenon that makes possible reason's synthetic acts is part of reason, experience, and self-consciousness itself, as Kant everywhere implied in the *Transcendental Logic* and the other Critiques. According to Coleridge

> The I = Self = Spirit is definable as a Subject whose only possible Predicate is itself – Ergo, a Subject which is its own Object, i.e., a Subject–Object. . . . The Spirit . . . cannot be an Object ['object' means necessarily dead, inert], . . . it becomes an Object through its own act. . . . The Spirit is Power self-bounded by retroition on itself, and *is* only for itself . . . in it subsists the primary Union of Finity and Infinity . . . absolute Co-presence of the Infinite and Finite. . . . However, we yet do distinguish our Self from the Object, *though not in the primary Intuition* – now that is impossible without an act of abstraction – we abstract from our own product – the Spirit snatches itself loose from its own self-immersion – . . . . But this is absolutely impossible otherwise than by a free Act – (*CN*, III, 4186)

Another notebook entry functions almost as a gloss to this passage. Speaking of spirit Coleridge writes,

> As an absolute Principle it can be neither Subject nor Object . . . but the identity of both. . . . And yet to be known, this Identity must be dissolved – and yet it cannot be dissolved. For its Essence consists in this Identity. This Contradiction can be solved no otherwise, than by an Act . . . the Principle makes itself its own Object, [and] in and thus becomes a Subject. The Self affirmative is therefore a Will; and Freedom is a primary intuition, and can never be deduced. . . . All Truths therefore are but deductions from, or rather parts of the History of Self-Consciousness. (*CN*, III, 4265)

These two passages state in subject–object terminology the essence of the definition of imagination:

> The IMAGINATION then, I consider either as primary, or secondary. The Primary IMAGINATION I hold to be the living Power and prime Agent of all human Perception, and as a repetition in the finite mind of the external act of creation in the infinite I AM. (*BL*, I, 202)

The finite acts of creation occur *within* the infinite 'I AM', – experience, self-consciousness, or reason (as Coleridge defined it), with no reference to an external substance. Moreover, for Coleridge perception itself *is* synthesis – a finite act of 'creation'; and it is a 'living Power', not a *vis receptiva* of an independent subject which provides materials to the secondary imagination by repeating and copying them from nature, the independent object. Perception *is* primary imagination. That is, perception is the *context* for a distinction between perceiver and perceived, not the product of that duality.

In these passages is implied a further development of Coleridge's solution to Kant's assumption that a noumenon external to reason was needed in order for reason to act synthetically. Coleridge criticised Kant for his separation of 'the Reason from the Reason in the Will or the theoric from the practical Man'. He then queried 'whether the Division of Reason into Speculative and Practical, amounting to the Assumption of two Reasons, different in function and extent of jurisdiction, was not arbitrary, and an hypostasizing of mere logical entities'.[15] Thus a 'barren dualism' affects Kant's account of reason which Coleridge criticised still more fully in a marginal note:

> even Kant makes the fundamental error of . . . 'the derivation
> of ideas from the Speculative Reason *entirely*, for the *behoof* of
> the practical Reason and the Active Principle, but not by
> *means* thereof, or in conjunction therewith; which latter is
> nevertheless the true and Platonic theory of Ideas . . . according to which the Reason and Will are the Parents . . . and the
> Idea itself the transcendent Analogon of the Image or die
> Spirituelle Anschauung'. (*CN*, III, 3802, f.102n)[16]

By reuniting the pure and practical reason into a reason that involves the will by definition, Coleridge makes the reason 'neither Subject nor Object', but something whose essence consists in an act. The reason 'makes itself its own Object [and] in and thus becomes a Subject'. Coleridge avoids Kant's subjectivity of reason and his 'barren dualism' in insisting that reason (like imagination) is self-sufficient and in need of no external 'somewhat in order to act synthetically. Reason, like imagination, is to be understood as at once both distinguishing and differentiating (or analytic); *and* as reuniting, relating and unifying (or synthetic) within its own being, and hence in no need of any external given.[17] Indeed, synthesis is itself knowledge (hence Coleridge's emphasis upon the 'act' in knowing); analysis can by itself furnish the mind with no knowledge. Distinction and analysis occur only as preliminary acts of synthesis, but both belong to the very nature of reason and imagination, whether primary or secondary; neither is dependent upon an external 'Somewhat'. Coleridge explains,

> The office of philosophical *disquisition* consists in just *distinction*;
> while it is the privilege of the philosopher to, preserve himself
> constantly aware, that distinction is not division. In order to
> obtain adequate notions of any truth, we must intellectually
> separate its distinguishable parts [analysis]; and this is the
> technical *process* of philosophy. But having so done, we must
> then restore them in our conceptions to the unity, in which
> they actually co-exist [synthesis]; and this is the *result* of
> philosophy. (*BL*, II, 8)

V OPPOSITION, NEGATION AND DIALECTIC

In marginal notes, letters and notebooks, Coleridge traced all
Kant's defects to the 'barren dualism of the Reflective system'.
Dualism is the consequence of the assumption of the noumenon
whether in relation to reason or to imagination: 'The assumption
of two Powers only, was the occasion of all the errors and
imperfections of his theory' (*CL*, IV, 808). 'Essential dualism',
'reconciliation of opposites' and 'polar philosophy' were indications that Coleridge, like Hegel, saw the necessity for an opposition or 'negative quantity' to occur within reason itself if there is
to be a world of representation and knowledge. The 'negative'
for Hegel and the analogous concept of 'opposition' for Coleridge
became the 'solution' to Kant's positing of a noumenon outside
reason, experience, and self-consciousness. First, Coleridge
points out a vital distinction: 'He alone deserves the name of
Philosopher, who has attained to see and learnt to supply the
difference between Contraries that preclude, and opposites that
reciprocally suppose and require each other' (*CN*, III, 4326).
The essential difference between opposites and contraries, he
says in chapter two of *The Constitution of the Church and State*, is
that 'opposite powers are always of the same kind, and tend to
union, either by equipose or by a common product'. He then
states what follows from quotations given earlier, that 'in the
Deity is an *absolute synthesis of opposites*'. Within experience and
self-consciousness as a unified organic system, the dialectic of
oppositions occurs which makes experience and knowledge possible.

Coleridge cautions us however on the danger of misunderstanding his Kantean critique on several fronts, one concerning
the meaning of synthesis: 'It is the object of mechanical atomistic
Philosophy to confound Synthesis with Synartesis, or *rather*, with
mere juxtaposition of corpuscles separated by invisible
interspaces.'[18] The proper understanding of 'Synthesis' is clarified by further statements on the nature of 'essential dualism' (as
opposed to the 'barren dualism' of Kant). Coleridge writes,

> *Every Power in Nature and in Spirit* must evolve an opposite as
> the sole means and condition of its manifestation; *and all
> opposition is a tendency to reunion*. This is the universal Law of
> Polarity or essential dualism, first promulgated by Heraclitus.

He then explains that matter is best understood as the product, or 'coagulum spiritûs, the pause, by interpenetration of opposite energies'. Coleridge further states that he holds no matter as real otherwise than as the copula of these energies (*CL*, IV, 774). The notions of copula, pause, interpenetration, identity and relation all become elements in a more complete understanding of the meaning of synthesis as occurring within experience and reason itself in order to produce matter, that 'coagulum spiritûs', as well as all other 'objects', including individual perceiving organisms. In formal terminology, Coleridge explained that the '*Identity* of thesis and Anti-thesis is the substance of all *Being*'; opposition, on the other hand, is the condition of all existence, or 'Being manifested'.[19] This distinction between existence and being is the cornerstone of his rejection of Schelling's misconceived account of polarity.

While there is then no proper opposition except within a single power, Schelling erred in actually 'establishing Polarity in the Absolute' – that is, making dualism absolute, a consequence of his making nature itself absolute (*CN*, III, 4449). Similarly, in the misinterpretation of Coleridge's theory of imagination, nature is made absolute. It is the source of material for a subjectively conceived imagination or perception. Coleridge explains further that

> Schelling who . . . had seen the inadequacy of Kant's *two* Powers as constituting Matter, and had supplied a third as the copula and realization of the two, has yet succeeded no better *in fact*: though by *stealing* – in the Law of Polarity he has counterfeited a more successful appearance.[20]

To Coleridge's mind, Schelling had both made nature absolute and the Absolute absolutely dual. And yet Coleridge placed the absolute in the Act, in the Reason as Will, and had kept unity and 'identity', not duality, as the nature of all being:

> The reality of all alike is the A and Ω, or rather that Ineffable which is neither Alpha separately, nor Omega separately, nor Alpha and Omega by *composition*, but the *Identity* of both, which can become an object of *Consciousness* or *Thought*, even as all the powers of the material world can become objects of *Perception, only as two Poles or Counterpoints of the same line*. (*CL*, IV, 688)

Reason (like being) *manifests* itself as the copula of opposition, opposition being the condition of any existence or reality. But 'being' for Coleridge, and reason, was not reducible to the juxtaposition or additive total of the two opposites.

VI   REASON AND IMAGINATION

We argue here, then, against the version of refined, Kantean rationalism offered by many as the meaning of Coleridge's theory of primary and secondary imagination; that the primary imagination (like the senses) supplies material, while the second-ary imagination (like the reason) works on that material extra-empirically to provide connections and relations. What Hegel and Coleridge insist is that this account presupposes, first, that the subject or perceiver is set outside and over against the real world of nature, rather than *in* it, as an organic part of it; and, second, that thought, reflection and connections or relations must be extrinsic to experience (since experience was assumed to be a mere sensory manifold of discrete particulars by rational-ists, empiricists and idealists alike) and supplied to it from outside by a superempirical faculty. Coleridge, like Hegel, re-jected both of these assumptions, insisting that thought and reflection are intrinsic to experience, which is full of relations and connections and in no need of an extra-empirical faculty (reason or secondary imagination) to supply those relations. Intelligence, reason or imagination has a real constructive role to play in experience; it need not be conceived, however, as extra-empirical. For Coleridge, the subject or perceiver is set within the real world of nature, which is the actual subject matter of experience, not some ultimate reality at the base of experience. Moreover, subject and object are relative dualities within experi-ence; experience itself is not to be conceived as subjective, related somehow to an objective world. Experience is not a private world of a perceiver outside the course of natural exist-ence. Experience is, rather, modes of interaction of natural objects, amongst which the perceiver happens to be one. His experience is not of ideas, sensations, or impressions arising from a 'real' substrate; it is of other real objects like himself. Thought, reflection, imagination, are all modes of interaction within ex-perience, not extra-empirical activities. The terms 'subjective' and 'objective' are relative only, and apply within the realm of experience, not one within and one without.

Rationalists, empiricists and idealists alike all assumed an absolute subject, knower or perceiver outside the material world of events, whose various faculties furnished man with a transcript of those events, more or less accurate. Experience was a mental, supernatural and private event set over against an objective, non-mental world. Coleridge insisted that this view makes it impossible to account for knowledge or to have any knowledge, and that the idealist solution is nonsensical, giving too much constructive power, or the wrong kind of power, to an externally conceived mind. Alternatively, we can see mind as a natural part of the course of natural events, with experience as neither subjective nor private nor mental, but the interactions and interrelations of natural objects, including minds. Imagination and intelligence are not, then, thought to 'create' the world of subjective experience based on some unknowable objective reality, thus denying the force of a natural world constantly at odds with, and pressing itself upon, intelligence. Imagination and intelligence are basic aspects of experience which can profoundly affect and alter experience for the better or the worse. When Coleridge described perception as imaginative, he did not mean that a subjective knower set over against an objective world creates the nature of that world as experienced. He meant rather that an intelligent organism continuous with its environment behaves and reacts not passively and receptively to that environment, but that it behaves in a fundamentally creative way that involves relations, connections and future consequences, from the most basic forms of perceptual activity to higher intellectual, cultural modes of interaction. All interaction, Coleridge says, is relational and creative, not just the higher, secondary cultural forms. These latter, secondary forms are not based upon a passively received primary particularism which is then imbued with relations by a supernatural faculty of secondary imagination or reason. The higher cultural and intellectual activities are homogeneous with the relational, intelligent activity of perception itself. Experience, even at the level of perception, is simply relational, connected, goal-oriented, or, in Coleridge's terms, imaginative. To ask what the 'real' substance of experience is over and above our experience is already to postulate a non-empirical element of experience, and to assume the

subjectivity of experience, such that, a non-empirical and inde-
fensible conception of experience being assumed, no reinte-
gration into an intelligible account is possible.

Coleridge's early use of the term 'imagination' takes on, then,
almost entirely the character of the later term, reason. The
imagination is 'that synthetic and magical power' (*BL*, II, 12);
'Imagination is the laboratory in which the thought elaborates
essence into existence';[21] it dissolves, diffuses, dissipates, *in order*
to recreate' (*BL*, I, 202; emphasis added); it is a sort of 'fusion to
force many into one'. Elsewhere Coleridge speaks of the 'philosophic imagination, the sacred power of self-intuition' (*BL*, I,
167); and of the 'imaginative Reason'; and, as the above quotations suggest, 'it is wonderful how closely Reason and Imagination are connected'.[22] The *eventual*, latterly developed distinction
between Coleridge's use of 'reason' and his use of 'imagination'
seems to consist in his applying and *confining* the latter term to
the aesthetic and perceptual activities of the finite, human mind;
'reason', on the other hand, is also *present* in the finite, individual
mind, but seems to refer more explicitly to the union of individual minds and nature into one Hegelian whole and to the more
general Act of causative generation, rather than specific acts of
aesthetic or perceptive powers. The term 'imagination' is used as
the 'repetition in the *finite* mind of the eternal act of creation in
the infinite I AM' (*BL*, I, 202; emphasis added). We can further
define Coleridge's eventual distinction between reason and imagination by noting that the former is, strictly speaking, the
source of ideas, while the latter,

> that reconciling and mediatory power, which incorporating
> the Reason in Images of the Sense, and organizing (as it were)
> the flux of the Senses by the permanence and self-circling
> energies of the Reason, gives birth to a system of symbols,
> harmonious in themselves, and consubstantial with the truths,
> of which they are the *conductors*.[23]

Imagination is the activity of embodying the ideas or truths ('the
eternal relations of things') of the reason into symbols. Symbols
are characterised by the 'translucence of the Eternal through
and in the Temporal'. A symbol 'always partakes of the Reality
which it renders intelligible; and while it enunciates the whole,

abides itself as a living part of that Unity, of which it is the representative'.[24]

We could conclude that the imagination is itself a symbol of reason, and, consequently, that it, while it 'enunciates the whole, abides as a living part of that Unity, of which it is the representative'. As such, it is reason embodied, manifested, or made finite: that is, imagination *is* the reason individualised into a finite perceiving mind. Thus each individual mind becomes potentially a symbol of experience and self-consciousness. Combined with the truth that 'to the Eyes of the Man of Imagination, Nature is Imagination itself',[25] we arrive at what Coleridge calls the Pythagorean 'view': 'the very powers which in men reflect and contemplate are in their essence the same as those powers which in nature produce the objects contemplated'.[26]

Correlatively, 'the spirit in all the objects which it views, views only itself' (*BL*, I, 184). If we relate the finite perceiving mind to the perceived world according to the above 'view', and remember that the essence of the *perceiving* individual mind is imaginative activity (while nature too is all 'Imagination itself'), then these two 'opposing' finite objects or forces are related to reason as symbols of it, and so partake of its 'intelligibility rendered Reality'. Nature *and* imagination, as reason individualised into relative object and relative subject, both inhere within experience and reason itself, not one within and one without.

VII   ORGANICISM

Coleridge's organicism emphasises an organic system of reason and self-consciousness whose essence is processes and acts, growth and productivity, not products, completion and stasis. He distinguishes the products 'of the mechanic Understanding . . . from the ποιησεῖς of the imaginative Reason . . . Products in antithesis to Produce – or Growths'.[27] He also remarks that the 'higher life of Reason is naturally symbolized in the process of growth in nature'.[28] That is, reason is best understood in terms of growth, production, activity and process, as opposed to statis, fixity, and predetermination. Furthermore, the essence of knowledge is *activity* (*CN*, III, 4265), while intelligence and imaginativeness are conceived as self-development, not 'qualities supervening' (ibid.); thus Coleridge denies any role to a noumenon or substance external to reason. Imagination and consequently perception, 'is essentially *vital*', as 'all objects (as objects) are essentially fixed and dead' (*BL*, I, 202):

> 'Eclectic Philosophy', 'Syncretism', . . . is the Death of all Philosophy. Truth is one and entire because it is *vital*. Whatever lives is contradistinguished from all juxtaposition – and mechanism . . . by its oneness, its impartibility; – and mechanism itself could not have had existence, except as a counterfeit of a living whole. (*CN*, III, 4251)

Like truth and imagination, reason must be understood to be one and entire; it is *vital*. That it is 'one', a 'unity', does not mean it is a dead, finished, totally determined whole. Coleridge concludes, 'in Kant's system there can be of course no intelligible Genesis, or real Production – in Heraclitus it is all in perpetual Genesis'.[29] The 'barren dualism' of Kant's philosophy, which allegedly introduced an element foreign to reason to explain synthesis, allows of no 'intelligible Genesis'. Moreover, any account which suggests that perception receives its materials from without reduces to a barren dualism. Structural 'organicism' is itself a disguised dualism. It mistakes structures and products, the 'familiar' form of processes, as different in kind from the processes and growth that are the essence of all products and objects. Or it mistakes the rules and powers of growth and production for *ab extra* instead of *ab intra* principles, and thus degenerates unwittingly into a dualism as barren, in fact, as the dualism of Kant's aesthetic.

The difference between true 'growth' (real 'generation') and the mechanism of 'fabrication' is that in the first case form is *evolved* '*ab intra*, the other *ab extra*, impressed – the latter is representative always of something not itself . . . but the former . . . of its own cause within itself, i.e., its causative self' (*CN*, II, 2444).

Through his organic, vital definition of intelligence as self-development, of perception and imagination as vital, of nature's products as processes, and of reason's educts as growths, Coleridge cleansed from his system the last trace of passivity and stasis and rejected any trace of a substance external to reason. He defined mind simply 'as a pure *active* and proper *Perceptivity*', rejecting the passive account of the object as an *affection* of the perceiving subject. Coleridge sought to redefine the word 'object' itself to reveal its truer, more essential nature as conceivable only in terms of growth: 'But / Observe! that in my system the *Object* is not, as in the Fichtean Idealism the dead, the substanceless, the mere *Idol*, but the absolutely free Productivity in the always perfected Product.'[30] Here he reveals that our conception of object and product is a natural consequence of a 'degeneration' of our imaginative vision, which if activated would reveal all objects and products (for example, artifacts) as themselves essentially living growths and processes. With this emphasis upon growth, productivity and *acts*, Coleridge concludes, 'God is . . . one eternal Act, in which all other Acts are comprehended. All else arises out of the Relations in which Finites exist to Finites.'[31] Later we shall see this become the definition of reason.

VIII *R*EASON AND REASON

Constitutive philosophy says that reason is in the process of elucidating itself *in and through the individual mind*, not external to it. Moreover, it gradually evolves ideas of itself that actually change it. Reason grows and alters in the process of knowing itself, for it is 'one and vital'. Reason, as Hegel and Coleridge agree, is not a fixed, determined, static nature gradually revealing itself to itself – either from the point of view of the individual or from that of history. Rather, reason is in the process of *making* itself. Knowledge is both its product and an influence upon it. Thus the 'constitutive' philosophy, the Pythagorean view, does not suggest that subjective ideas can be raised to an objective validity in the sense of giving us a glimpse of the structure or nature of an already whole, totalised Reason, Reality, or God. These ideas themselves are gradually evolving in significance and meaning for the individual thinker; they are not static, fixed and determined. The verbal formulations of these ideas are for ever being altered and re-expressed.

In *The Statesman's Manual* Coleridge writes,

> The Reason (not the abstract reason, not the reason as the mere *organ* of science, or as the faculty of scientific principles and schemes a priori, but reason) . . . reason substantiated

and vital, 'one only, yet manifold, overseeing all, going through all understanding' . . . the *Reason*, without being either the *sense*, the *Understanding*, or the *Imagination* contain all three within itself, even as the mind contains the thoughts, and is present in and through them all. . . . Each individual must bear witness of it to his own mind, even as he describes life and light . . . and it dwells in *us* only so far as we dwell in *it*. It cannot in strict language be called a faculty, much less a personal property of any human mind![32]

Later, in *Aids to Reflection*, Coleridge simply states, 'there is no such thing as a particular Reason'. This dynamic distinction between reason and Reason is, we must remember, not a division: 'there is no such thing as a particular reason'. Reason cannot properly be called a faculty, much less a personal property. 'Reason' designates a dwelling, an active participation in reasoning by an individual mind. Coleridge concludes, 'the whole human Species . . . may be considered as One Individual Mind' (*CL*, II, 701). He describes his '12 Lectures on the History of Philosophy as the gradual Evolution of the Mind of the World, contemplated as a single Mind in the different successive states of its development'.[33] Elsewhere, Coleridge designates Reason 'Supreme Reason'; he insists that its 'knowledge is *creative*, and antecedent to the things known'.[34] But one of the things known is reason – that is, Reason realised in so far as an individual dwells in it. Knowledge is not only a product of reason, but *creative* of it; 'the more we dwell in Reason, the more it dwells in us'. Reason reasons, and in reasoning realises itself. Yet in realising itself, it develops itself and creates itself further. Coleridge explains,

all Knowledge, I say, that enlightens and liberalizes, is a form and a means of self-knowledge . . . the whole of Euclid's Elements is but a History and graphic Exposition of the powers and processes of the Intuitive Faculty. . . . We learn to *construe* our own perceptive power, while we *educe* into distinct consciousness it's inexhaustible *constructive* energies.   (*CL*, VI, 630)

Instead of 'intelligence' we could say that 'reason is a self-development, not a quality supervening (*CN*, III, 4265); or, 'God is . . . one eternal Act.'[35] For Coleridge, knowledge too is 'essentially a verb active', and he concludes from these points that *'Truth* and *Being* are *correlative'* (*CN*, III, 4265). In the *Biographia* he elaborates this position:

> The term, Philosophy, defines itself as an affectionate seeking after Truth; but Truth is the correlative of Being. This again is in no way conceivable, but by assuming as a postulate, that both are *sub initio*, identical and coinherent; that intelligence and being are reciprocally each other's substrate. (*BL*, I, 94)

Intelligence, truth and knowledge are not qualities supervening to the fixed, predetermined substrate, Being. Their reality resides in Act, in active self-development. For Coleridge this means that intelligence, knowledge, truth and reason cannot be properly understood apart from the coinherence of the will,

> We (that is, the human race), *live by faith*. Whatever we do or know, that in kind is different from the brute Creation has its origin in a determination of the Reason to have faith and trust in itself. This, its first act of faith, is scarcely less than identical with its own being.[36]

The theory of the Imagination as primary and secondary in distinction from the fancy has carried us to the concept of Reason and experience as self-sufficient and in no need of an external ground for its synthetic–imaginative acts, whether primary (perceptual) or secondary (artistic). He adopted the essentially Hegelian solution that Reason and experience are not subjective, and therefore in no need of an object, an external. Reason is synthetic by virtue of making itself an object of itself, through an original 'Act'. There are scattered hints and indications in Coleridge however, of a further elaboration of his conception of Reason, which suggests anticipations of Heidegger's emphasis upon language and being – indeed, which suggests that Reason, when properly understood, is language, and that the emphasis upon language in modern theory is an elaboration of earlier insights in a new terminology.

Coleridge's remarkable insights into language are scattered widely throughout his published work, letters, notebooks and marginalia. Here we must conclude by mentioning only a few of his comments on the relation of language to Reason. In an early notebook entry Coleridge mused on the power of words to affect reason: 'Not only as far as relates to speaking but the knowledge of words, as distinct component parts, which we learn by learning to read – What an immense effect it must have on our reasoning faculties?' (*CN*, I, 866). Earlier it was suggested that reason develops and further creates itself by reasoning; but words, says Coleridge, are the tools and powers of thought. He repeatedly insisted that it was a mistake to think that words have significance because they refer to, represent, or correspond to things or thoughts (*CL*, VI, 630). Words, he explains, are 'learnt by us in clusters, even those that most expressly refer to Images and other Impressions are not all learnt by us determinately'. He then concludes,

> Words therefore become a sort of Nature to us, and Nature is a sort of Words. Both Words and Ideas derive their whole significancy from their coherence. The simple *Idea* Red dissevered from all, with which it had ever been conjoined would be as unintelligible as the word *Red*; the one would be a *sight*, the other a Sound, meaning only themselves, that is in common language, meaning nothing. But this [disseverance] is perhaps not in our power with regard to Ideas, but much more easily to Words. Hence the greater Stability of the Language of Ideas.[37]

The 'immense effect . . . upon our reasoning faculties' of words leads Coleridge to conclude, 'Reason, Proportion, communicable Intelligibility intelligent and communicant, the *WORD* – which last expression strikes me as the profoundest and most comprehensive energy of the human Mind . . . (*CN*, II, 2445). 'Word' is seen here to have been raised to an even higher power, a move that is naturally consequent upon the previous reflections. In *The Philosophical Lectures*, Coleridge takes a step further toward the goal when he equates 'Reason' with 'Logos', 'word', and 'nous'. Correlatively, he had insisted that, in early Christian times, λόγος was used to mean 'personal Being' (*CL*, IV, 850). And in a passage in *The Statesman's Manual* he had changed a quotation from John 1:4 to read 'in the Word [instead of 'in him'] was life; and the life was the light of man'. Here 'Word' seems to be equated with 'God'; in a late letter he equates not 'Word' but 'Reason' with 'God': 'in the Reason *is* God' (*CL*, IV,

689. In Greek, ὁ λόγος means both the word as expressive of thought, and the thought, and reason itself. Coleridge seems to have led us to the very brink of this crucial double meaning of ὁ λόγος as reason and language. It is not unlikely that Heidegger's meditations of λόγος and λέγω would have been a familiar kind of speculation to Coleridge, as would Heidegger's conclusion that 'language is the house of being'.

NOTES

1. I. A. Richards, in *Coleridge on Imagination* (London, 1934), and R. H. Fogle, in *The Idea of Coleridge's Criticism* (Berkeley, Calif., 1962), give a lucid account, but without a Kantian-Hegelian context.
2. Coleridge, *Collected Works*, VII: *Biographia Literaria*, ed. J. Engell and W. J. Bate (Princeton, NJ, 1983) I, xci.
3. I am deeply indebted in this portion of this article to John Dewey's 'Kant and Philosophic Method', *Journal of Speculative Philosophy*, XVIII (Apr 1884) 162–74. It was Dewey's analysis of Kant and Hegel that brought home to me the fuller implications of Coleridge's efforts to relate Kant's achievements to a Pythagorean–Platonic philosophy, and his theory of imagination as a compressed 'solution' to Kant.
4. See, *CL*, II, 677–703, for Coleridge's Locke–Descartes discussion.
5. Existence, said Kant, being no predicate or part of any conception, could never arise from 'pure analysis'. See *CN*, III, 3605 f.120–117; and see *CL*, II, 679ff., where Coleridge exposes the inconsistencies of Locke's exposition of the *tabula rasa* and the ideas of reflection. He also reveals the close connection of Locke to Descartes.
6. John Locke, *Essay Concerning Human Understanding*, I. i.
7. See ibid., II. iv.3–4.
8. Ibid., I. ii.2: 'simple ideas [are] the materials of all our Knowledge; David Hume, *Treatise of Human Nature*, I. i.
9. See Ch. 7 of the *Biographia* for Coleridge's criticism of associationists, who make time a law rather than the condition for association.
10. See, *CL*, IV, 852, for Coleridge on Kant's 'great merit'.
11. Marginal note to Immanuel Kant, *The Critique of Pure Reason*.
12. Marginal note to W. G. Tennemann, *Geschichte der Philosophie*. See also *CN*, III, 3725: 'when Pride will work up the φαινομενα into a system of *Things in themselves*, then they become most pernicious errors'.
13. Marginal note to Kant, *Metaphysische Anfangsgründe der Naturwissenschaft*.

14. Marginal note to Tennemann, *Geschichte der Philosophie*, VIII, referring to p. 765.
15. Ibid., VI, referring to p. 64.
16. Ibid., referring to p. 145; also quoted in Coleridge, *The Philosophical Lectures*, ed. Kathleen Coburn (London, 1949) p. 425.
17. See Shelley's *Defence of Poetry*, opening statements, for this characterisation of mind as analytic and synthetic within its own being, and for the further emphasis upon synthesis as knowledge and as the proper activity of the imagination.
18. Coleridge, *Collected Works IV: The Friend*, ed. Barbara E. Rooke (Princeton, NJ, 1969) I, 94.
19. Ibid.
20. Marginal note to Kant, *Metaphysische Anfangsgründe*.
21. *Anima Poetae*, ed. E. H. Coleridge (London, 1895) p. 186.
22. *Friend*, I, 203n.
23. Coleridge, *Collected Works*, VI: *Lay Sermons*, ed. R. J. White (Princeton, NJ, 1972) p. 29.
24. Ibid., p. 30.
25. William Blake, letter to Dr Trusler, 23 Aug 1799.
26. *Philosophical Lectures*, p. 114.
27. *Lay Sermons*, p. 29 n.1.
28. Ibid., p. 72.
29. Marginal note to Tennemann, *Geschichte der Philosophie*.
30. Unpublished notebook entry, British Library MS 36, 2.
31. *Friend*, I, 117 n.1.
32. *Lay Sermons*, p. 69.
33. Marginal note on Copy G of *The Statesman's Manual* (1816); see *Lay Sermons*, p. 114 n.2, and *CN*, III, 4265.
34. *Lay Sermons*, p. 18.
35. *Friend*, I, 117 n.1.
36. *Lay Sermons*, p. 18.
37. *CL*, II, 698. Here it seems that Coleridge may be using 'Idea' loosely, as if to mean 'impression', 'sensation', and so on, as Locke and others, about whom he is writing, used it.
38. *Lay Sermons*, p. 114.

3   Coleridge's Religious Thought: the Search for a Medium

JOHN BEER

In August 1802 Coleridge embarked on a short walking-holiday in the mountains of the Lake District, taking writing-materials so that he could make entries in his notebooks and write letters to Sara Hutchinson. The tour came to its climax when he found himself on the slopes of Scafell, from the summit of which he wrote a letter describing the splendour of the scene, at once beautiful and awesome. While there was a marvellous view back over Derwentwater, almost to his own house, he was more immediately impressed by the drop beneath him: 'But O! what a look down just under my Feet! The frightfullest Cove that might ever be seen / huge perpendicular Precipices, and one Sheep upon it's only Ledge, that surely must be crag!' (*CL*, II, 840). Next day he wrote again to Sara, this time about his descent from the mountain – which, he had to admit, had been irresponsible, particularly for one with a wife and children and 'a Concern'. He had moved away from the edge of the precipice, but had not looked round for a beaten track:

> The first place I came to, that was not direct Rock, I slipped down, & went on for a while with tolerable ease – but now I came (it was midway down) to a smooth perpendicular Rock about 7 feet high – this was nothing – I put my hands on the Ledge, & dropped down / in a few yards came just such another / I *dropped* that too / and yet another, seemed not higher – I would not stand for a trifle / so I dropped that too / but the stretching of the muscle[s] of my hands & arms, & the

41

jolt of the Fall on my Feet, put my whole Limbs in a *Tremble*, and I paused, & looking down, saw that I had little else to encounter but a succession of these little Precipices – it was in truth a Path that in a very hard Rain is, no doubt, the channel of a most splendid Waterfall. – So I began to suspect that I ought not to go on / but then unfortunately tho' I could with ease drop down a smooth Rock 7 feet high, I could not *climb* it / so go on I must / and on I went / the next 3 drops were not half a Foot, at least not a foot more than my own height / but every Drop increased the Palsy of my Limbs – I shook all over, Heaven known without the least influence of Fear / and now I had only two more to drop down / to return was impossible – but of these two the first was tremendous / it was twice my own height, & the Ledge at the bottom was so exceedingly narrow, that if I dropt down upon it I must of necessity have fallen backwards & of course killed myself. My Limbs were all in a tremble – I lay upon my Back to rest myself, & was beginning according to my Custom to laugh at myself for a Madman, when the sight of the Crags above me on each side, & the impetuous Clouds just over them, posting so luridly & so rapidly northward overawed me / I lay in a state of almost prophetic Trance & Delight – & blessed God aloud, for the powers of Reason & the Will, which remaining no Danger can overpower us! O God, I exclaimed aloud – how calm, how blessed am I now / I know not how to proceed, how to return / but I am calm & fearless & confident / if this Reality were a Dream, if I were asleep, what agonies had I suffered! what screams! – When the Reason & the Will are away, what remain to us but Darkness & Dimness & a bewildering Shame, and Pain that is utterly Lord over us, or fantastic Pleasure, that draws the Soul along swimming through the air in many shapes, even as a Flight of Starlings in a Wind.

The terms in which he expressed his relief are worth attending to, since they show with curious precision the point to which his thinking had brought him at this moment in 1802. Coleridge is amused by his own calmness in the face of a terrible danger, by contrast with the feelings which he knows he would have if such a situation were to come on him in a dream. Daylight reality permits the operation of reason and the will, whereas in a state where they were not able to operate the whole mental experience would be of darkness, pain and shame. Coleridge, who was a vivid dreamer and knew such nightmare states well, finds it a relief that in spite of the danger he is in he is experiencing nothing of their paralysing hold.

There is an oddity at the end of his account, however, which occurs elsewhere in Coleridge's writing – though not perhaps so often as in Blake. That is, an argument which seems to be pointing firmly in one direction turns out to contain within itself a statement which acts as a counter-current, suggesting some-where an alternative motion of the mind. For, while it was natural enough to welcome the distancing of himself from dark-ness, pain and shame, the disparagement of what he describes as 'fantastic Pleasure that draws the Soul along swimming through the air in many shapes, even as a Flight of Starlings in a Wind' is a different matter – particularly when we remember the event which gave rise to that particular metaphor. Late in 1799, when he had just met Sara Hutchinson, Coleridge had been riding in a stage coach into London in the early morning and had scribbled into his notebook a description of the behaviour of flocks of starlings:

> Starlings in vast flights drove along like smoke, mist, or any thing misty [without] volition – now a circular area inclined [in an] arc – now a globe – [now from a complete orb into an] elipse & oblong – [now] a balloon with the [car sus-pended], now a concaved [semi] circle & [still] it expands & condenses, some [moments] glimmering and shivering, dim & shadowy, now thickening, deepening, blackening!- (*CN*, I, 582, cf. 1589)

The experience was one of considerable delight, and he would still be recalling it a year after the Scafell adventure:

> My spirit with a fixed yet leisurely gaze
> Following its ever yet quietly changing Clusters of Thoughts,
> As the outward Eye of a happy Traveller a flock of Starlings'
> (*CN*, I, 1779).

Looking back over the years immediately preceding, one can see that two movements had been proceeding simultaneously in his mind. One of these (related to the starlings) was an attempt to create a new vision of nature in which human beings might be brought through particular experiences of delight and fear to understand their own human nature more fully, and perhaps also to see it as a faint model of the divine. This enterprise, which had originated in his early reading in mystics such as Boehme and the Neoplatonists, and which had been given early expression in 'The Eolian Harp', had been strongly reinforced when he came into contact with Wordsworth. With him he observed nature in some of her subtler and more unusual forms, and wrote works, including the major meditative poems and supernatural poems such as 'The Ancient Mariner' and 'Kubla Khan', which explored further what was involved. His own explorations had been encouraged by seeing at first hand the relationship between William and Dorothy Wordsworth – which was in a sense extended further when he fell in love with Sara Hutchinson, Wordsworth's future sister-in-law. This seemed a form of human love which could transcend ordinary physical and social attractions: the kind of love which he felt binding them together was more like a participation of being – linked in turn to his own religious sense.

At the same time Coleridge had been trying to work out his own moral and religious position; this too was a continuous and developing process. Even in the case of 'The Eolian Harp' he had no sooner developed an interesting theory of the workings of nature than he was invoking Sara Coleridge to condemn such unhallowed ideas (lines 49–64). Many critics dislike the move – understandably in terms of the decline in sensuous quality at that point in the verse – but one cannot ignore it, since it turns out to herald what was to be a continuing back-and-forth movement in Coleridge's mind. As William Empson used to point out, twenty years later he was still introducing further heretical thoughts for his youthful bride to reprove;[1] that does not mean however that the original reproof lacked genuineness. It indicates rather that, despite Coleridge's permanent awareness of the moral thought, he was unwilling to deny the validity of either. In his account of his attempts to work out a position for himself in Nether Stowey just before he became intimate with the Wordsworths, he records his basic conviction that religion *must* have a moral origin (*BL*, I, 135). Talking to Hazlitt in 1798, at a time when he had just been writing his finest nature poetry, the same point emerged. The conversation turning to Joseph Butler,

Coleridge praised his work: not, however, as might have been expected, the *Analogy of Religion* but the *Sermons at the Rolls Chapel*; he presumably had in mind Butler's discourses on the sovereignty of conscience.[2]

This strain in his thinking took a new strength from his reading of Kant after he returned from Germany, for in Kant the role of the moral will was paramount. Reason and Will were, after all, the pillars of Kant's universe: to read him was to find the double strain in his own thinking powerfully reinforced. In the *Biographia* he spoke of Kant as having taken hold of him 'with a giant's hand'.[3] But the nature of Kant's arguments could not fully satisfy Coleridge's needs, since he was looking for something more than a regulative nature in the mind: indeed he came to believe that Kant had been inhibited perhaps by timidity from drawing out the further possibilities inherent in his speculations. He criticised Kant also in his Notebooks as a 'wretched psychologist';[4] in 1801 he was reading various books bearing on the nature of the human mind as part of his plan to attack the theories of Locke and Hume. Among others he visited the cathedral library in Durham, borrowing books by Aquinas, Suarez and Aristotle.[5] The implication is that his researches had brought him to a point where he was considering the nature of the divine itself, and exploring those previous writers who had written subtly of the divine being and of the kind of knowledge which was available to finite human beings. The Durham reading in fact took place while he was staying with the Hutchinsons and enjoying the platonic love between himself and Sara, later described in the verse letter of 1802 which became 'Dejection: An Ode'. He seemed still to be at a promising moment in his career. His philosophy of nature and of Christianity told him that he could not hope to consummate his love with Sara or turn his back on his wife and children, but the philosophy he was developing offered a way forward in which he could still persevere, morally, with a disappointing marriage while exploring the implications of a higher love and higher philosophy. There were of course darker elements in this, especially the suspension of his creative powers, and the verse letter to Sara in April 1802 acknowledged them; but he still believed it possible to carve out a way in which he might flourish as a thinker and enjoy, at least vicariously, the happiness of the Wordsworth household – including, of course, that of Sara herself (see *CL*, II, 796–8).

In the event those hopes were not to be realised. Words-worth's marriage to Mary inevitably led to some diminution of Dorothy's status in relation to him, which she must have felt; the death of John Wordsworth was a bitter blow after hopes that he would come back and form part of the small community; and eventually Sara Hutchinson, finding the strain of her situation in relation to Coleridge intolerable, withdrew. But in July 1802 all this lay in the future, and Coleridge, writing to Sara, could put his faith in the dominion of Reason and Will as a guiding principle.

Yet despite the nobility of this position it involved a certain degree of self-falsification – at least so far as the whole self which included the creative Coleridge was concerned. I have already mentioned an example of this: the so-called 'fantastic' pleasures of dreams had always been a rich source of imaginative life for Coleridge, linking readily to the pattern that he found in nature. He could hardly now dismiss them in favour of reason and will without suppressing vital elements in his own psyche.

Oddly enough, moreover, this sense of a self-falsification is reinforced when we look at what he later did with the experience at the summit of Scafell, when he had been filled with delight and awe at the vista of nature which lay around him. For instead of writing a poem of his own directly about it he raised his sights. 'I involuntarily poured forth a Hymn in the manner of the *Psalms*', he wrote to Sotheby, 'tho' afterwards I thought the Ideas &c disproportionate to our humble mountains – & acci-dentally lighting on a short Note in some swiss Poems, concern-ing the Vale of Chamouny, & it's Mountain, I transferred myself thither, in the Spirit, & adapted my former feelings to these grander external objects' (*CL*, II, 864–5). There is a touch of afflatus here: the Lakeland mountains are no longer good enough for Coleridge's conception – and indeed his very language suggests that he is moving into the prophetic role of St John the Divine: 'And he carried me away in the spirit to a great and high mountain, and showed me that great city, the holy Jerusalem, descending out of heaven from God' (Revelation 1:10). Cole-ridge's aspiration to the sublime, it will be noted, reverses the biblical priorities: 'I transferred myself in the spirit', instead of 'he carried me away in the spirit'.[6] Meanwhile there was falsifi-cation of another kind, for as has often been noticed the 'Hymn before Sunrise' draws very heavily on a German poem by

Friederike Brun. The degree of plagiarism should not be exaggerated: Friederike Brun's poem runs to twenty lines, Coleridge's to seventy-eight. There is much which is Coleridge's alone – and much of that the best. But the fact remains that in the moment of afflatus he also takes over quite directly the hymn form of the earlier poem and some of its lines.

I have chosen to dwell on this moment in Coleridge's career because it presents in an unusually vivid and dramatic form the pattern of these years. On the one hand his belief in the 'one Life' of nature and in the possibilities of universal love was continuing to flourish, even in the face of the difficulties described in the Dejection Ode, on the other he was sympathetic to Wordsworth's insistence on the need to take a position of full responsibility in society; indeed, he went further, to work out a full religious position based on the supremacy of Reason and Will. (Ironically, the 'Hymn before Sunrise', which is in one sense a good example of Coleridge moving towards Wordsworth's sense of the actual, was censured by Wordsworth as a specimen of the 'Mock Sublime' – *CL*, IV, 974.) Throughout the rest of that decade he would be trying to accommodate the Wordsworthian position within the terms of a larger philosophy, reconcilable with the Christian tradition. And one of the ideas which would sustain him in this would be the belief that his love for Sara Hutchinson was of a nobler kind than that involved in his own marriage, bringing into play elements of his own being which were closer to religious experience than to the everyday world.

In the earlier events Coleridge had been impressed by a sense of Sara Hutchinson's permanent being, caught within the lineaments of her everyday self. Superficially she was a pleasant and reasonably intelligent person, but from time to time there was a moment of irradiation from within that revealed a further depth. A poem transcribed in his Notebooks (cf. *CN*, II, 2441) runs,

> All Look or Likeness caught from Earth,
> All accident of Kin or Birth,
> Had pass'd Away; there seem'd no Trace
> Of Aught upon her brighten'd Face
> Uprais'd beneath the rifted Stone
> Save of one spirit, all her own /
> She, she herself, and only she,
> Shone in her body visibly.

Similar intuitions of inner being provide a theme of his 'Letter to Sara Hutchinson'. Even in that poem, however, he acknowledged a darker strain and in the end had to admit that a satisfactory set of relationships had not emerged. The love of Sara's inner being had not proved to be the basis for a fully satisfying and permanent love between them; and Wordsworth, who had seemed to accept the validity of what Coleridge was doing, had himself ended by expressing disillusionment.

Yet in the despair that followed Sara's withdrawal and the quarrel with Wordsworth, Coleridge continued to explore the implications of what he had come to believe about the nature of human personality – his sense of a permanent being beneath the manifestations of personality. This sense was now transferred into his religious thought. Some years later he wrote, 'To feel the full force of Christian Religion, it is necessary, for many tempers, that they should first be made to feel, experimentally, the hollowness of human friendship, the presumptuous emptiness of human hopes' (*CL*, IV, 893). Consideration of Coleridge's religious thought is likely to lead one first to *Aids to Reflection* (1825). Initially, however, the link between this volume and his early thought may not appear very obvious. Those who come to *Aids* directly from the ferment of thinking and experiment in Coleridge's notebooks, letters and writings up to 1805 may, in fact, find it a rather disappointing book. What, they may ask, has happened to the inquiring spirit that was producing speculation after speculation in the early writings – 'throwing out in profusion', as Wordsworth put it in a letter to R. P. Graves, 'grand central truths from which might be evolved the most comprehensive systems'?[7] Indeed, the most provocative ideas in *Aids* are often tucked away in long footnotes, and even there they tend to be hedged around by a touch of mystery – a hint of truths reserved for the truly learned and for separate presentation.

In that sense, *Aids* comes as a disappointment; yet we must also acknowledge another fact: its effectiveness in its own century (with twelve editions in fifty years). For some writers in the generation after it was published, in fact, it held an almost talismanic status. Thomas Arnold listed it as one of the few works in English capable of greatly improving the mind.[8] John Sterling wrote 'I have read the *Aids to Reflection* again and again, with ever new advantage' and one of his friends described it as a book to which many 'owe even their own selves'; Julius Hare made it central to his characterization of Coleridge as 'the true sovereign of modern English thought'.[9] Maurice, describing his 'deep and solemn obligations', commented on the number of 'simplest, most childlike men and women' whom he had heard express their gratitude after having read it.[10] F. J. A. Hort described it as a book to read again and again.[11] As late as 1904 Dr Wace, then Dean of Canterbury, quoted from it in an address to the Church Congress at Liverpool as a book he would like to see more read;[12] in the following year (perhaps as a result) yet another reprint appeared. But a decline in popularity was now in motion; in America, where it had been even more influential and remained a university textbook for many years, the book suffered a similar fate.

It is not difficult to suggest reasons for that early success, or for that later decline. Coleridge's argument in the book rests upon two suppositions: the need to approach Christianity with an open and inquiring mind and the need to accept man's corruption and his need for a redeemer. Anyone who shared this attitude and this belief, even vestigially, was likely to find Coleridge's arguments persuasive, but the assault on such moral presuppositions that gathered momentum following the rise of psychoanalytic thinking made that belief more problematic than it had been. Similarly with one of the central running themes of the book, epitomised in the biblical text 'if any man shall do his will, he shall know of the doctrine, whether it be of God' (John 7:17). This reaches its climax in the celebrated dicta, '*Evidences* of Christianity! I am weary of the Word. Make a man feel the *want* of it; rouse him, if you can, to the self-knowledge of his *need* of it; and you may safely trust it to its own Evidence' and 'Christianity is not a Theory, or a Speculation; but a *Life*. Not a *Philosophy* of Life, but a Life and a living Process . . . TRY IT.'[13] To Victorians who were beset by incursions of doubt the course that Coleridge offered was attractive – and also in many cases effective, for Coleridge was perceptive enough to know that commitment to a cause could often in fact bring with it conviction. Even in the nineteenth century, however, there were some who hesitated. Arthur Hugh Clough, who had been present at a discussion in Oxford when *Aids to Reflection* was the subject,[14] was much influenced by Coleridge, as one might expect from a pupil of Thomas Arnold; yet he also wrote in a letter in 1841,

I should like much to have heard Carlyle's complaints against Coleridge. I keep wavering between admiration of his exceedingly great perceptive and analytic power and other wonderful Points and inclination to turn away altogether from a man who has so great a lack of all reality and actuality.[15]

It may be that he had Coleridge's arguments in mind (as well as Carlyle's) when he wrote in 'Amours de Voyage',

Action will furnish belief: but will that belief be the true one? –

as also

> . . . and action
> Is a most terrible thing; I tremble for something factitious.[16]

Could one, in the end, trust what was revealed in the act of believing?

The major Victorian response to Coleridge, however, was to the spirit that was felt moving in his writings. It was that above all which John Tulloch dwelt on when he gave an account of Coleridge in 1855, as part of his survey of early nineteenth-century religious thought. He praised its sense of religion as a living body of thought; he also wrote, 'It is a book which none but a thinker on Divine things will ever like. It is such a book as all such thinkers have prized.'[17]

This is an appraisal Coleridge himself would, perhaps, have found disappointing. It was his express intention to interest those who did not normally 'think on Divine things' but were willing to come to Christianity with an open mind. And he hoped to do so by leading his reader from one way of thinking to another. His very title, *Aids to Reflection*, gives a clue to the process. The word 'reflection' is, at one level, commonplace in eighteenth-century thought. Used by Locke to indicate some of the inner workings of the mind, it also indicates the faculty which is thought to raise human beings above the animals. To have a mind 'strengthened by habits of reflection' was a common ideal of the time.[18] Yet the word meant more than that to Coleridge – as one may see from the recurrence of images involving reflections, both in his poetry and elsewhere. For Coleridge, moreover, reflection is not just a mirror-like response to the external world but an opening of the mind to light-giving influences which are already there in its depths. The point is made indeed early in *Aids* concerning the human soul:

> Nothing is wanted but the eye, which is the light of this house, the light which is the eye of this soul. This *seeing* light, this *enlightening* eye, is Reflection. It is more, indeed, than is ordinarily meant by that word; but it is what a *Christian* ought to mean by it, and to know too, whence it first came, and still continues to come – of what light even this light is *but* a reflection. This, too is THOUGHT.[19]

Throughout *Aids* Coleridge pursues a double path; trying to convince through sweet reasonableness yet also assuming that a right use of the reason will result in an illumination from within. He invites his readers to use their intelligence; he argues that faith cannot ultimately contain anything that is contrary to reason; yet in the end he is bound to fall back on the position that truth will be found to provide its own evidence, if it is once believed in.

> I assume a something, the proof of which no man can *give* to another, yet every man can *find* for himself. If any man assert, that he *can* not find it, I am *bound* to disbelieve him! I cannot do otherwise without unsettling the very foundations of my own moral Nature.[20]

In such a situation Reason and Will become paramount. We may use our reason to say that some of the more extravagant excesses of Calvinism cannot be the ultimate truth; yet in some sense we must still adopt a doctrine of divine election, since the ultimate initiative has to be left with God. If various of the doctrines of the atonement are repugnant to our own moral sense, we may reject them as proper accounts of what happens in redemption; yet we cannot reject the fact itself of redemption and man's need for it.

Such a position, while acceptable to those who were already disposed to agree with Coleridge, was less likely to convince those who did not share his basic premises; and indeed there comes a point in *Aids* when, having just set out his own form of the doctrine of redemption, he passes into a teasing and gnomic statement which suggests that his theology rests on further forces than he is willing to bring into play at this moment:

> I will merely hint, to my more *learned* readers, and to the professional Students of Theology, that the origin of this error is to be sought for in the discussions of the Greek Fathers, and (at a later period) of the Schoolmen, on the obscure and *abysmal* subject of the Divine *A-seity*, and the distinction between the θέλημα and the βουλή, i.e. the absolute Will, as the universal *Ground* of *all* Being, and the Election and purpose of God in the Personal Idea, as the Father. And this View would have allowed me to express (what I believe to be) the true import and scriptural idea of Redemption in terms much more nearly resembling those used ordinarily by the Calvinistic Divines, and with a conciliative *show* of coincidence. But this motive was outweighed by the reflection, that I could not rationally have expected to be understood by those, to whom I most wish to be intelligible: et si non vis intelligi, cur vis legi?[21]

When Coleridge begins to deal in riddles and hints, it is well to be attentive, since he is often giving clues to another current in his mind which explains some part of what is happening in his present text. And so it is here. The word 'abysmal', italicised, takes the eye first. Stressed like that it looks like a joke, and no doubt Coleridge intended this;[22] yet in this context how can it really be? The eye travels on to the word 'A-seity' ('Unselfness') and on again to the distinction between the Absolute Will, the Ground of Being, and the Election of God in the personal Idea as the Father. Coleridge, it appears, is implying that God as a person proceeds out of an absolute deity which is by nature impersonal. And this sends one back to one of his most striking statements about God, in a letter of 1803 to Matthew Coates, an old Bristol friend:

> Believe me, I have never ceased to think of you with respect & a sort of yearning – you were the first man, from whom I heard that article of my Faith distinctly enunciated, which is the nearest to my Heart, the pure Fountain of all my moral & religious Feelings & Comforts – I mean the absolute Impersonality of the Deity. The Many would deem me an Atheist; alas! I know them to be Idolators.   (*CL*, II, 1022–3)

We are also reminded of a key text in Coleridge's accounts of his religious beliefs: the sentence in *Biographia Literaria* where he writes of his early doubts, 'For a very long time indeed I could not reconcile personality with infinity; and my head was with Spinoza, though my whole heart remained with Paul and John' (*BL*, I, 134). This may remind us of writings such as 'The Ancient Mariner' where infinity and personality are twin factors; it also takes us back to his collaboration with Wordsworth. Let us consider their usages of 'abyss'. The word does not often occur in Coleridge's poetry,[23] but it is an important one for Wordsworth and tends to occur at moments of considerable significance. We find him writing of clever philosophers for example as being devoted to thought that reflects

> To proud Self-love her own intelligence;
> That one poor, finite object, in the abyss
> Of infinite Being, twinkling restlessly . . .
> (*The Excursion*, IV. 992–4)

And in the two central incidents of *The Prelude*, the crossing of the Alps and the ascent of Snowdon, it occurs again crucially (though not, interestingly, in 1805 but in 1850): 'Imagination. . . . That awful Power rose from the mind's abyss / Like an unfathered vapour . . .' (VI. 592–5). Again, the moon seen shining over Snowdon is seen as

> the emblem of a mind
> That feeds upon infinity, that broods
> Over the dark abyss, intent to hear
> Its voices issuing forth to silent light
> In one continuous stream . . .
> (XIV. 70–4)

This is reinforced, again in 1850, by the description of the fissure in the clouds as a 'fixed, abysmal, gloomy breathing-place' (XIV. 58).

The mystery of being is an abyss which human intelligence cannot comprehend. Wordsworth recalls how in his childhood he 'communed with all that I saw as something not apart from, but inherent in, my own immaterial nature' and how, going to school, he would clutch at a wall or a tree to 'recall myself from this abyss of idealism to the reality'.[24] One might think of such a state of mind as paradisal – particularly when one thinks of the Immortality Ode; yet for Wordsworth it is an 'abyss of idealism': it seems to threaten him with madness.

There is also, however, a lurking sense that at the heart of the abyss subsists the creative power itself, impersonal, unknowable. Imagination comes forth as 'an unfathered vapour'. Just as the cloudy mountains and caverns of Abyssinia hide the fountains of the Nile, so is it with the mystery of being in humans and in the universe alike. And, although the general speculation here may sound very idiosyncratic, it has a respectable ancestry. In his *Exposition of the XXXIX Articles of the Church of England*, published in 1710, William Beveridge for instance writes of the Living God as 'not only the Abyss of Life in Himself, but the Fountain of Life to Us' (p. 2).

This sense that ultimate Being, whether in the human unconsciousness or in the universe generally, is an incomprehensible abyss which is yet the source of all that is fountainous in human nature and in the world seems to be central for Coleridge; yet he hardly knew how to express it or to work it out. He could affirm it over and over again, as in making a distinction between τὸ Θεῖον and ὁ Θεός, the divine and God the father – or, in human beings, between 'personëity' and 'personality'. Commenting on the phrase in Genesis, 'darkness was upon the face of the deep', he interprets the deep as 'the byssus abyssus, the deepless Depth'. In his annotations to Boehme he writes,

> In all Living there is ever an aliquid *sup*positum (a something placed under) which can never (be) lifted up into the intelligible – it is the Darkness that is the Bearer of all Light. But it is peculiar to God that he hath the ground of *his* Existence within himself

and

> I AM in that I AM, is God's self-affirmation, and (that) God verily is, is all we can affirm of him; (that) to which no addition can be made, when we speak of *the total God*.[25]

Coleridge's own ambiguous attitude to such questions, his tendency to relegate them to footnotes or notebooks, or promise further elucidation in some future work, is partly owing, no doubt, to the difficulty which he faced as soon as he tried to discuss them in a way which would be acceptable to Christian thinkers. The idea of the impersonality of God was one which, if expounded in anything but negative terms, could all too easily be taken as pantheism. But this same sense of further mystery made him particularly fascinating to the young men of the time. His advocacy of an impersonal spirituality probably had its part to play in the rise of the Oxford Movement, for instance. Individual writers as diverse as John Henry Newman and Mark Pattison could take what they valued from Coleridge and move on to take up positions of their own.[26] Others who are thought of as particularly Coleridgean, such as John Sterling, F. D. Maurice and Charles Kingsley, either met Coleridge personally or were close to people who had known him.[27] Even if they were sometimes disturbed by a sense of something a little specious in Coleridge, with his constant displays of learning, they retained a sense that after all this man had something important about him, that there was an ineluctable genuineness beneath even his apparent prevarications.

That sense would have been clarified for them, perhaps, if they had been able to know the full story of Coleridge's career, which has really become available only in recent years, with the publication of notebooks, letters and other manuscripts. *Aids to Reflection*, for example, contains extensive quotation from Robert Leighton, who might seem an unlikely choice as the presiding figure in such a work; yet its underlying themes become a good deal clearer when one grasps his full significance for Coleridge. He was not a writer who had been chosen at random but one who had actively come to his rescue some years before.

At the end of 1813 he had suffered a week of severe illness, in which (to quote his own account) 'tho' driven up and down for seven dreadful Days by restless Pain, like a Leopard in a Den, yet the anguish & remorse of Mind was worse than the pain of the whole Body. – O I have had a new world opened to me, in the infinity of my own Spirit!' (*CL*, III, 463–4). To another correspondent he described that new world in greater detail:

You have no conception of what my sufferings have been, forced to struggle and struggle in order not to desire a death for which I am not prepared. – I have scarcely known what sleep is, but like a leopard in its den have been drawn up and down the room by extreme pain, and restlessness, worse than pain itself.

O how I have prayed even to loud agony only to be able to pray! O how I have felt the impossibility of any real *good will* not born anew from the Word and the Spirit! O I have seen far, far deeper and clearer than I ever saw before the ground of pernicious errors! O I have seen, I have felt that the worst offences are those against our own souls! That our souls are infinite in depth, and therefore our sins are infinite, and redeemable only by an infinitely higher infinity; that of the Love of God in Christ Jesus. I have called my soul infinite, but O infinite in the depth of darkness, an infinite craving, an infinite capacity of pain and weakness, and excellent only as being passively capacious of the light from above. Should I recover I will – no – no may God grant me power to struggle to become *not another* but a *better man* – O that I had been a partaker with you of the discourse of Mr Robt Hall! But it pleased the Redeemer to appoint for me a sterner, fearfuller, and even more eloquent preacher, if to be impressive is to be eloquent. O God save me – save me from myself. . . .   (*CL*, III, 463)

The crisis had persisted throughout the spring of 1814, when Coleridge visited Bristol and was stung to respond to a letter from Joseph Cottle, who had just discovered the extent of Coleridge's drug addiction and urged him to rouse himself. Coleridge replied that this was like asking a man paralysed in both arms to rub them briskly together. Cottle replied immediately urging him to pray, upon which he wrote (*CL*, III, 478),

O I do pray inwardly to be able to *pray*; but indeed to pray, to pray with the faith to which Blessing is promised, this is the reward of Faith, this is the Gift of God to the Elect. O if to feel how infinitely worthless I am, how poor a wretch, with just free will enough to be deserving of wrath, & of my own contempt, & of none to merit a moment's peace, can make a part of a Christian's creed; so far I am a Christian – –

In another letter to Cottle at this time, however, he discussed the question of prayer in a less agonised manner, declaring that

Christians expected 'no outward or sensible Miracles' from Prayer; 'it's effects and it's fruitions are spiritual, and accompanied (to use the words of that true *Divine*, Archbishop Leighton) "not by Reasons and Arguments; but by an inexpressible Kind of Evidence, which only they know who have it"' (*CL*, III, 478–9).[28] In the remainder of the letter he described further the wretchedness of his own condition and his desire to have himself put under some kind of permanent supervision.

The mention of Leighton in that letter indicates the extent to which his writings were assisting Coleridge's fight for spiritual survival at this time. In the same month he wrote in the copy of Leighton's writings that a Mr Elwyn had lent him,

> Surely if ever Work not in the sacred Canon might suggest a belief of inspiration, of something more than human, this it is. When Mr E[lwyn] made this assertion, I took it as an hyperbole of affection, but now I subscribe to it seriously & bless the Hour that introduced me to the knowledge of the evangelical apostolic Archbishop Leighton.[29]

In later notes he was to develop an image of Leighton's commentary on the first epistle of Peter as a true reverberation from the inspiration of the gospels – 'Next to the inspired Scriptures, yea, and as the *vibration* of that once struck hour remaining on the Air . . . .' (*CN*, IV, 4867, cf. *CL*, V, 198). If this sense of a timeless truth speaking to him was comforting it was also alarming. When Leighton writes, 'If any one's Head or tongue should grow apace, and all the rest stand at a stay, it would certainly make him a Monster', Coleridge recognises the picture guiltily and writes down repeated cries for mercy. When Leighton writes of a sick man that 'the kindness and Love of God is then as seasonable and refreshing to him, as in Health, and possibly more', he writes in the margin, 'To the regenerate; but to the conscious Sinner a Source of Terrors insupportable' – and then, perhaps aware that he has just written a capital *S* and a capital *T* he continues, 'S. T. C. i.e. Sinful, Tormented Culprit'. Yet he is also sustained by Leighton's assurances concerning the grace of God. On a passage concluding, 'though I saw, as it were, his Hand lifted up to destroy me, yet from that same Hand would I expect Salvation', he writes, 'Bless God O my soul! for this sweet and strong Comforter. The Honey in the Lion.' On the sentence,

' . . . such an Assent as this, is the peculiar Work of the Spirit of God, and is certainly saving Faith', he comments, 'Lord I believe! help thou my unbelief. My natural reason acquiesces. I believe enough to *fear* – & grant me the Belief that brings sweet Hope.'[30]

The help that he had received from Leighton was to be remembered, and to lead to the further work a few years later which led to the production of *Aids*. At the back of his mind there was no doubt a hope that what had supported him so powerfully might also work on others. He warmed particularly to Leighton's blending of warnings and assurances with a strong imaginative sense that linked with his own. Above all he admired the *chastity* of Leighton's imagination:

> a *subduedness*, a self-checking Timidity, in his Colouring, a sobering silvery-grey Tone over all . . . by this sacrifice of particular effects giving an increased permanence to the impression of the Whole, and wonderfully facilitating its soft and quiet *Illapse* into the very recesses of our Conviction.   (*CL*, V, 199).

(He seems also to have felt that such writing sprang from the impersonal element of the author's nature, his personeity rather than personality. This was a feature equally of his great admiration for Luther, whose doctrine of justification by faith relied likewise not on a self-conscious personal response, but on a more impersonal acceptance within the depths of one's being).

At this moment, when Coleridge responds gratefully to the presence of a calm and mediating spirit that seems to acknowledge the various currents of his own agitated mind and yet to offer a means of reconciliation, we may be reminded of a later occasion when a literary figure turned to the seventeenth century with a similar sense of relief and gratitude. The gesture is surprisingly close, in fact, to one which was made by T. S. Eliot when he was moving out of his own spiritual crisis a century later. Torn by the contradictions of his own thought and dogged by the pain of an unhappy marriage which yet involved him in a deep sense of his own responsibility, Eliot too was to look for a lifeline and to find it in the writings of an earlier English divine – Lancelot Andrews, born half a century before Leighton.[31] As with Coleridge, such a gesture comes as a surprise and a disappointment to many readers after the restless and brilliant work of Eliot's early years. The early Eliot had been writing in a way which started new paths in the mind and communicated to the reader a vivid sense of intellectual activity. After Eliot's conversion his writing would always be more precisely controlled: a work more clearly of the sceptical imagination which would win the reader's respect, but in a less exciting way.

It is much the same with Coleridge. The intellectual activity of the years up to 1805 spills rapidly into notebooks and letters; in later years it tends rather to be siphoned off into footnotes and appendixes.

Yet in each case a further self-recognition is at work. Eliot and Coleridge alike found it necessary to accept the presence of guilt; sin and damnation were too important to be regarded simply as aspects of another phenomenon. Each, likewise, saw the problem of persisting as a liberal critic in isolation from the actual society surrounding him; maintaining in addition that that problem could not be resolved by commitment to some large ideal, some universal brotherhood beyond all existing institutions, but that it called for alignment with a particular body which had arisen within a particular national culture. Both, following this path of reasoning, found themselves embracing the Anglican faith – and more particularly that faith as it had flourished and been expressed in the seventeenth century: Eliot from outside it, Coleridge from his own immediate family past.

It is this common recognition which sets Coleridge and Eliot alike apart from the thinking of Schleiermacher (if we may pause for a moment to consider the other great figure honoured in this volume). Coleridge himself made very few references to his contemporary, though he annotated his works on St Luke and Timothy. In a note on Heinrich[32] he referred to 'the terribly pietistic cant of the Schliermacher School',[33] but it is not clear how far he would have extended this censure to Schleiermacher himself. One might have expected a more sympathetic attitude on Coleridge's part. Both men came under the influence of Moravianism: Schleiermacher directly and thoroughly in his upbringing, Coleridge through his discovery of and enthusiasm for Jacob Boehme.[34]

There are other resemblances between the two men. Schleiermacher's chief contribution, like Coleridge's, was seen to have

lain in the general direction of his teaching. He encouraged all
that was growing and budding in his time and castigated the
commercial spirit which he thought to be dominant in England.
His great contribution, however, lay in his ability to speak to
students who were in a state of doubt and looking for new ideas
with which to confront the new age.

Coleridge as a young man might well have warmed to
Schleiermacher, who had written to his father about 1787,

> I canot believe that He who only called Himself the Son of
> Man was the everlasting, true God. I cannot believe that His
> death was a substitutionary propitiation, because he himself
> has never expressly said so, and because I cannot believe that
> it was necessary. For God who manifestly has not created
> man for perfection but only to strive after perfection, cannot
> possibly will to punish them because they have not become
> perfect.[35]

These were doctrines which Coleridge, likewise, found it hard to
accept. Yet he came to believe firmly that the doctrine of
redemption, however defined, corresponded to human need, so
that in later life he might well have concurred with Karl Barth,
who wrote in *The Word of God and the Word of Man*,

> With all due respect to the genius shown in his work, I can *not*
> consider Schleiermacher a good teacher in the realm of the-
> ology because, so far as I can see, he is disastrously dim-sighted
> in regard to the fact that man as man is not only in *need* but
> beyond all hope of saving himself; that the whole of so-called
> religion, and not least the Christian religion, *shares* in this
> need; and that one can *not* speak of God simply by speaking of
> man in a loud voice.[36]

Coleridge, likewise, had come to believe that Christianity could
not remain true to itself without these doctrines; indeed, in *Aids
to Reflection* he attacked those who believed that one could deny or
renounce such doctrines as the corruption of man's will, the
responsibility of man in a religious sense, the divinity of Christ,
sin and redemption through the merits of Christ, grace and so on
without making any breach or rent in the essentials of Christian

faith; and who could agree with Dr Paley that 'the Rent has not reached the foundation'.[37]

For Coleridge the rent *had* reached the foundation when such beliefs were denied; yet, as was suggested earlier, the unity of Reason and Will in the soul by which he tried to preserve his own attitude involved imposing limits to the free play of his own imagination which set up a different division in his nature – a division which was equally threatening at times. The sense of the impersonality of the divine nature in its essence seems to have provided him with one of the mediating concepts in his attempt to reconcile his sense of sin with the surviving power of his own creative experience.

We return to Coleridge on Scafell in 1802, where, in the affirmation quoted at the outset, he exalted Reason and Will at the expense of the powers which he knew best in his dream-life, and which produced fears and pleasures by turns. The pressures of society and the logic of his own position forced him readily enough into that position, yet we feel that when he was most faithful to them it was at the expense of being unfaithful to himself. The fact that he could make such a calm affirmation in a position which, considered imaginatively, was both fearful and dizzying, was welcome, but not totally satisfying.

And what of the solution which Coleridge found on that occasion? We left him perilously situated, and some readers may have been wondering how he could possibly have escaped from his alarming position. His account goes on to record how as he looked down he could see some stones which had fallen on to the ledge far beneath him, making it even more dangerous to try and drop to it, and which he realised had been piled there by a shepherd trying vainly to reach a sheep that had become cragfast like himself, and whose body he had just passed. But then he saw something a little less alarming:

As I was looking at these I glanced my eye to my left, & observed that the Rock was rent from top to bottom – I measured the breadth of the Rent, and found that there was no danger of my being *wedged* in / so I put my Knap-sack round to my side, & slipped down as between two walls, without any danger or difficulty – the next Drop brought me down on the Ridge called the How / I hunted out my Besom

Stick, which I had flung before me when I first came to the Rocks – and wisely gave over all thoughts of ascending Doe-Crag. (*CL*, II, 842–3)

That escape of Coleridge's, descending heedlessly into an apparently impossible position and then finding a way out by discovering a space where he *could* fit and manipulate himself has often struck me as an apposite emblem for much of his later course through life, caught between the contradictory demands of two visions of the world, both of which he believed in profoundly, yet which he could not satisfactorily reconcile. He seeks out ways that *are* open to him: arguing his way through this position and that and offering aids to those who may be in a similar predicament.

T. S. Eliot made his way through life more successfully, since he was able to accept and organise his contradictions more consciously. After a dinner in the 1930s where he had found himself arguing with a young Marxist, he commented to his host on the conviction he had shown: 'They seem so certain of what they believe; my own beliefs are held with a scepticism which I never even hope to be quite rid of.'[38] Coleridge could not quite have accepted such a division in his intellectual life: he was looking for a more direct conviction. Yet he resembled Eliot in recognising a level at which belief could not readily be communicated from one human being to another, and like Eliot he recognised that some of the problems posed by the attempt to create a personal religion might be solved by accepting the possibility and desirability of a more impersonal relationship to God.

Yet to do so – to reconcile personality with infinity – was always to manoeuvre his way in a difficult place: he must continue to look for the positions in which the positives supported him best.

Carlyle, as is well known, was disappointed to meet Coleridge and find an aging, rather apologetic man who seemed far from the intellectual leader that he was looking for.[39] Carlyle, however, saw him only once or twice, and then at a difficult time of his life (the time, incidentally, when he was trying to pull *Aids to Reflection* into a unified whole). F. D. Maurice, who knew him over a longer period, remarked more perceptively, 'I rejoice to think that those who have most profited by what he has taught them, do not and cannot form a school'.[40] There are of course writers in the nineteenth century whom we think of as Coleridgeans – including Maurice himself – but we find ourselves using the term loosely. There is indeed no one Coleridgean school. Coleridge's value as a man was more often to stimulate writers such as Lamb, Hazlitt and De Quincey, or thinkers of the next generation, into finding their own identities as artists or thinkers.[41]

In the twentieth century Coleridge has been rediscovered as a man of extraordinary intelligence whose investigations can still provide a fertile ground for new ideas and speculations.[42] But Coleridge was not, and never set out to be, just a thinker of seminal thoughts. Everything that he did was done with the ultimate aim of solving the riddle of the universe and the puzzle of man's role within that universe, so that there was always a subtle weighting even to the lightest of his *aperçus*. No one has ever adopted Coleridge's solution in all its details, since no one has gone through life by the same tortuous way; but as the years pass we can see the importance of the later windings as examples of the now familiar problem which arises when an individual tries to keep faith with more truths than he or she can quite cope with.

In the nineteenth century the Romanticism of the individual made such a stance difficult to accept or admire. The call was for heroes, for single-minded leaders who would take mankind forward in the midst of current difficulties. In the twentieth century we have become more suspicious of those who propose simple solutions – if only because they usually end up leading their followers into violent battles of one kind or another. We have learned that human beings need to find means of plotting a way through the contradictions of their existence – and that the best they can hope for is to do so at once inventively and with a sense of their own human dependence and need. The figure of the later Coleridge, caught continually between creativity and fear to a degree that few have matched, yet still continuing to move on, becomes increasingly fascinating.

NOTES

1. See *Coleridge's Verse. A Selection*, ed. William Empson and David Pirie (London, 1972) p. 18.

2. William Hazlitt, *Complete Works*, ed. P. P. Howe (London, 1930–3) XVII, 113–14, 121.

3. *BL*, I, 99.

4. *CN*, I, 1717 (cf. 1710).

5. The borrowings are listed in George Whalley, 'Samuel Taylor Coleridge: Library Cormorant', unpublished PhD thesis (London, 1950) appendix B.

6. For an earlier, more orthodox use of this phrase see the 1796 version of 'Religious Musings', ll.l–8 (*Poems*, ed. John Beer (London, 1963) p. 64), following Milton's 'The Passion', stanza VI.

7. Wordsworth, *Prose Works*, ed. A. B. Grosart (London, 1876) III, 441.

8. A. P. Stanley, *Life and Correspondence of Thomas Arnold* (New York, 1895) II, 174. This and a number of the following references are in C. R. Sanders, *Coleridge and the Broad Church Movement* (Durham, NC, 1942).

9. See Julius Hare, 'Sketch of the Author's Life', prefixed to John Sterling, *Essays and Tales* (London, 1848) I, xlvi, xiv–xv.

10. Dedication to F. D. Maurice, *The Kingdom of Christ*, 3rd edn, 2 vols (London, 1883) I, xix.

11. A. F. Hort, *Life and Letters of F. J. A. Hort*, 2 vols (London and New York, 1896) II, 329.

12. Report in the *Guardian*, 7 Oct 1904, quoted in Lucy Watson, *Coleridge at Highgate* (London and New York, 1925) p. 99.

13. *Aids to Reflection*, 4th edn (London, 1825) pp. 397, 195.

14. Katharine Chorley, *Arthur Hugh Clough: The Uncommitted Mind* (Oxford, 1962) p. 60.

15. *Correspondence of Arthur Hugh Clough*, ed. F. L. Mulhauser (Oxford, 1957) I, 106.

16. 'Amours de Voyage', V, ii; II, xi; *Poems* (London, 1891) pp. 308, 289.

17. John Tulloch, *Movements of Religious Thought in Britain during the Nineteenth Century* (London, 1885) p. 9.

18. Cf. Coleridge's praise of Mary Evans in precisely these words in 1793: *CL*, I, 51.

19. *Aids to Reflection*, p. 5.

20. Ibid., p. 133.

21. Ibid., p. 328.

22. The first usage in English recorded by *The Oxford English Dictionary* is from Coleridge's *Biographia Literaria* (1817) and in a jocular setting: 'O! how I felt the anti-climax, the abysmal bathos of that *fourpence!*' (*BL* I, 116).

23. Apart from several usages in his translation of Schiller's *Wallenstein*, 'abyss' and 'abysm' occur only in 'The Destiny of Nations' (lines 109 and 284) and 'Ne Plus Ultra'.

24. See the Fenwick note to the Immortality Ode: William Words-worth, *Poetical Works*, ed. Ernest de Selincourt and Helen Darbi-shire, 5 vols (Oxford, 1947) IV, 463.

25. Coleridge, *Collected Works*, XII: *Marginalia*, ed. George Whalley, I (Princeton, NJ, 1980) 585, 618 (cf. 636).

26. See, e.g., Newman, *Apologia Pro Vita Sua*, ed. M. J. Svaglic (Oxford, 1967) p. 94, and note, pp. 525–6; Mark Pattison, *Memoirs*, ed. Mrs Pattison (London, 1885) pp. 164–7.

27. Maurice knew Sterling; Kingsley knew Maurice and had attended a school run by Coleridge's son Derwent.

28. Cf. Robert Leighton, *Expository Works* (Edinburgh, 1748) I, 83.

29. Flyleaf comment in a copy of the above (1748) edition, to be published in *Marginalia*, op.cit., III (forthcoming).

30. Ibid., I, 213, 219, 75, 82.

31. T. S. Eliot, 'Lancelot Andrews' (1926), repr. in *Selected Essays*, 3rd edn (London, 1932) pp. 341–53.

32. His annotations to these works, which are in the British Library, will be printed in *The Collected Works: Marginalia*.

33. Note to J. C. Heinroth, *Lehrbuch der Anthropologie* (Leipzig, 1822) title-page: *Marginalia*, op.cit., II, 999.

34. See my essay 'Ice and Spring: Coleridge's Imaginative Education' in *Coleridge's Variety*, ed. John Beer (London, 1974) pp. 58–66, 78–80. When the young Coleridge was charged with being a Jacobin, his brother James retorted, 'No! Samuel is no Jacobin; he is a hot-headed Moravian' – a defence which Coleridge approved: see his *Table Talk* for 23 July 1832.

35. J. A. Chapman, *Introduction to Schleiermacher* (London, 1932) p. 21, citing W. Dilthey, *Das Leben Schleiermachers* (Berlin, 1870) I, 31.

36. Karl Barth, *The Word of God and the Word of Man*, tr. D. Horton (London, 1928) pp. 195–7, cited in Chapman, *Introduction to Schleiermacher*, pp. 15–16.

37. *Aids to Reflection* (London, 1825) p. 339.

38. Hugh Sykes Davies, 'Mistah Kurtz: He Dead', *Eagle*, LX (May 1965) 139.

39. See his letter of 24 June 1824, *Collected Letters of Thomas and Jane Welsh Carlyle*, ed. C. R. Sanders and K. Fielding (Durham, NC, 1976–   ) III, 90–1.

40. Dedication to Maurice, *The Kingdom of Christ*, p. 6. Much the same, interestingly, was said of Schleiermacher, in spite of the so-called 'Schleiermacher school': see J. A. Chapman, op.cit., p. 28.

41. See John Beer, *Coleridge's Poetic Intelligence* (London, 1977) pp. 265–78.

42. See especially I. A. Richards, Introduction to *The Portable Coleridge* (New York, 1950) pp. 1–55, and Kathleen Coburn, *Inquiring Spirit* (London, 1951).

4 Inside without Outside: Coleridge, the Form of the One, and God

JAMES S. CUTSINGER

The word 'aesthetic' is capable of expressing at least two meanings: a basic, even etymological, sense, where perception or *aisthēsis* is the focus; and a broader, though more common, meaning, in which attention is directed through perception to a certain form or pattern, as in music or art. Any sensitive consideration of the relationship between Romanticism and religion in the thought of Samuel Taylor Coleridge must be faithful to both these meanings.[1] This essay intends to stress that double significance by examining, not the meanings individually, but the unity between them, between perception and form. More precisely, I aim to propose the following thesis: that, for Coleridge, romantic religion can best be served only when the second reference of 'aesthetic' is allowed to permeate and transform the first; or, in the terms supplied by his *Biographia Literaria*, only when the 'secondary imagination' of the artist or poet begins to alter and enhance the 'primary imagination' of human perception as a whole.[2] Before turning to this thesis, however, it is important initially to be reminded of three essential facts: Coleridge's extraordinary attentiveness, his special attentiveness to attention itself, and his attentive quest for unity.

I

Above everything – above all other interpretative insights – it should be said first that Coleridge *saw*. In a way that few people have ever seen anything, he seems to have seen everything. He inspected. He contemplated. He meditated – on all that his perception encountered. 'I find by an accurate calculation', he declares characteristically in an early notebook, one of the myriad memorandum books he always kept for recording his perceptions, 'that on each of my fingers there is a yearly growth of nail amounting to 2½ inches', and there follows a detailed record of his measurements of the 'total of Nail' in both length and breadth (*CN*, II, 2522). How many people have made this calculation, or been scratched by a cat in a dark room in an effort to determine whether the sparks of static electricity produced in petting the animal could be refracted by a prism (*CL*, II, 713–14). Coleridge had!

This unceasing attentiveness, exercised regardless of subject and constantly demanded of his interlocutors and readers, illumined much more than the world around him, however; it cast light upon itself. Coleridge's discerning eye was endeavouring always to direct its glance reflexively, as he attended to the act of knowing in the act *per se*. 'There is one art', he wrote, 'of which every man should be master, the art of reflection', and of this art he seems indisputably a master of masters.[3] Students of his thought know well the frequency and acuity of his surprising, but always telling, psychological – even psychographical – observations. The following, for example, comes again from one of the notebooks, his usual place for depositing the more intimate or idiosyncratic, sometimes heretical, of his ideas:

> I feel that there is a mystery in the sudden by-act-of-will unaided, nay, more than that, frustrated, recollection of a Name. I was trying to recollect the name of a Bristol Friend. . . . I began with the Letters of the Alphabet – A B C &c. – and I know not why, felt convinced that it began with H. I ran thro' all the vowels, a e i o u y, and with all the consonants to each – Hab, Heb, Hib, Hob, Hub and so on – in vain. I then began other Letters – all in vain. Three minutes afterwards, having completely given it up, the name, Daniel, at once stared up, perfectly insulated, without any the dimmest antecedent connection, as far as my consciousness extended.

To this account, so amusing because so familiar to us all, Coleridge then appends, however, in a manner, one hazards, not so familiar, a deeply reasoned excursus concerning the difference between 'Mind' and 'Consciousness', which culminates in a theory about a kind of thought 'not assisted by any association, but the very contrary – by the suspension and *sedation* of all associations'.[4] Inquiry into the processes of attending guided the Coleridgean philosophy from start to finish.

In this respect, in his interest in mental acts, Coleridge was, of course, a typical Romantic. Like many others of his day, he was deeply disturbed by the restricting forces of custom and habit, 'the film of familiarity and selfish solicitude',[5] and he was pledged to the prospect of transcending such restrictions by the power of the imagination. 'From my very childhood', he explains in a letter to a friend, 'I have been accustomed to *abstract* and as it were unrealize whatever of more than common interest my eyes dwelt on; and then by a sort of transfusion and transmission of my consciousness to identify myself with the Object' (*CL*, IV, 974–5). By unrealising the things around him and by aiming thus 'so to represent familiar objects as to awaken the minds of others to a like freshness of sensation concerning them',[6] Coleridge made certain to lose no opportunity in the exercise of his knowing, in the activity of thought and power of mind which Kant had forced him to respect. He intended, moreover, as far as it lay within his power, to spur his correspondents and conversation-partners into the same 'unrealisation'. Coleridge believed he had seen the world anew, and he wished for others to share his vision through the development of their own powers of reflection. 'You are going', he warned his reader, 'not indeed in search of the New World, like Columbus and his adventurers, nor yet an other world, that is to come, but in search of the other world that *now* is, and ever has been tho' undreamt of by the Many, and by the greater part even of the Few'.[7]

The 'other world that *now* is' was above all, for Coleridge, a world of unity. Here again he was paradigmatic of his time. With fellow Romantics, he could rest content only with a vision where everything was related: subject and object, spirit and nature, all united in what M. H. Abrams has called 'a metaphysics of integration'.[8] Robert Penn Warren has said that imagination restructures experience in the interest of a fresh experience of structure.[9] For Coleridge, the reverse was true. In his case a fresh experience of structure – of form, organisation, and relationship – was in the interest of that restructuring and transforming of experience which concerned him so profoundly. If only one could see with greater penetration into the meaning of relationship, into unity, he believed, one might find the power to revision a world grown stale and lifeless. 'What did he talk about?' Donald Stauffer answers his own question: 'Everything. Yet essentially his one never-entirely-forgotten subject was relationship – relating parts, or fusing disparates, within a single reality'.[10] A fascination with geometry and the language of shapes, a transcendental philosopher's interest in the unity of knower and known, and an alchemist's insight into the unity of soul and universe – in each of these respects, Coleridge disclosed his love of oneness and wholeness.

Coleridge was attempting not simply to alter his perceptions, to 'unrealise' his sensations, but to alter them in a particular way and after a special pattern; in virtually every syllable he wrote, he aimed to conform human perception to the form of unity and to pass thus from a mere seeing, the 'despotism of the eye'[11] – that is, a strictly empirical perception of discrete objects and events – to an experience deeper than surfaces and deeper, therefore, than collections and aggregations. For Coleridge, perception was never to remain physical or sensational alone. Or, if it did, it was certainly never to claim for itself contact with the really real, 'the indwelling and living ground of all things'.[12] In this regard, his Platonism, always present, is clearly prominent. The noetic or supersensible character of the Coleridgean 'perception' and the pre-material or spiritual character of the world which he wished to disclose must be clearly reaffirmed. 'It is peculiar to [my] philosophy', he wrote,

> to consider matter as a Product – coagulum spiritûs, the pause by interpenetration of opposite energies. While I hold no matter as *real* otherwise than as the copula of these energies, consequently no matter without Spirit, I teach on the other hand a real existence of a spiritual world without a material. (*CL*, IV, 775)

For Coleridge, the consideration – of matter as a product – was always propaedeutic to the teaching – of spirit without matter, of the inside without outside to which the title of this essay points.

Progress has so far been made on common and well-established ground. It is important now, however, to add to the initial observations a further essential point. Lest one fall prey to an empty platitude, it is necessary to add that the Coleridgean 'One' was most specific. Indeed, there is a crucial sense in which his entire philosophy was, rather than a search for unity simply, an investigation and judgement of kinds of unity and a perfecting of the truest and deepest oneness possible. 'I am sure', he declared, 'that two very different meanings if not more lurk in the word, *one*' (*CN*, II, 2332). Coleridge's interpreter would be mistaken, therefore, not to pursue the matter more carefully. It is easy, of course, simply to invoke the idea of unity, to intone solemnly the almost incantational formulas with which it has been expressed, and to superintend their application to the Coleridgean poetics, theology, epistemology and metaphysics, without ever asking the question, which Coleridge was always addressing to himself, 'Is the unity thus expressed *true* unity?' Such a method neglects, however, if it does not in fact obscure, the very centre of Coleridge's purported vision, a centre he hoped to demonstrate in all his sundry distinctions of understanding from reason, fancy from imagination, allegory from symbol, and Aristotle from Plato.

Perhaps the most important thing to realise about Coleridge's interest in unity is the intensity with which it excluded any fundamental concern for the elements united. This is not intended to suggest what would be false, that unity somehow consumed or annihilated individuality in his thought. The opposite is the truth. A correct idea of unity, he believed, must preserve the multiplicity and diversity of all things and, accordingly, the integrity of each thing. Even so, he seems not to have been especially interested in the particular character or nature of any given element *qua* element, as an intrinsically valuable object of concern. It was always the *fact* of particularity, the *fact* of individuality, the *fact* of difference among things that Coleridge found so compelling, and not the particular, individual thing itself.

Again, this is not to say that his omnivorous attention never attended to a given thing itself. But when it did – when he looked at an apple, let us say, or took the cat mentioned earlier into a dark room – he was looking for the fact of distinction-in-unity, and not for differences alone. The special qualities of an apple, such as its chemical composition, which might be used to assess its unlikeness to an orange, occupied Coleridge's attention, not because they were evidence of how apples and oranges differ, but because (what he called in this case) 'the fact of introsusception in chemical combinations' (*CN*, III, 3883) could reveal to him, at a new level, the very nature of his constant theme: relationship, distinction-in-unity, the one beneath the many. An apple thus examined became for him a new unity, not an element in another, previous unity called 'fruit'. It became what he referred to on at least one occasion as a 'protophaenomon, – that is, an object of perception capable of stirring the imagination and altering human perception as a whole. Such protophaenoma, which included objects as diverse as the parts of speech and electromagnetism, were an essential part of Coleridge's maieutic method, with which he intended to awaken those who were searching always for differences, but who were oblivious to true unity. It is such people as these whom he seems to have had in mind in writing,

> The naturalist, who cannot or will not see, that one fact is often worth a thousand, as including them all in itself, and that it first *makes* all the others *facts*; who has not the head to comprehend, the soul to reverence, a *central* experiment or observation (what the Greeks would perhaps have called a *protophaenomon*); will never receive an auspicious answer from the oracle of nature.[13]

For Coleridge the hierophant, on the other hand, an apple or a cat *was* auspicious, for it could become a world, a microcosm, transparent to the very meaning of relationship, like the larger universe of which it was both a part and emblem. Coleridge was interested in everything; the interpreter must not forget that. But the interest was directed into things, not at them; it carried him, not among the objects of his perception, or between them, but through them and down a corridor of imagination like that of images produced in adjacent mirrors. 'My thoughts', he once lamented, 'are like Surinam Toads – as they crawl on, little Toads vegetate out from back & side, grow quickly, & draw off the attention from the mother Toad'. (*CL*, III, 94–5). It is easy, therefore, to begin to think that the unity he speaks of is merely a kaleidoscopic composite of his million illustrations, for, true to the measure of his own estimate, Coleridge's pluriform interests do provoke the reader's wonder. One has his warning, however, that the children come second to their mother: there remains a prior thesis and deeper unity, the perception of which must bypass all elemental differences.

II

Such a warning having been securely recorded, it is appropriate to begin following a less apophatic, more direct line of thought. For, though his works are filled with repeated caution, Coleridge was certain that much of a positive nature could be expressed, and understood, concerning his transformed sense of 'One'. His language was always polyvalent, as he mixed vocabularies as disparate as those of psychology and geology, philology and chemistry. But it was never amorphous. There appears throughout a definite form or shape, accentuated and clarified by his consistent use, among other devices, of geometrical or spatial allusions, analogies and 'protophaenoma'. Through these allusions, the present writer has felt his closest to the Coleridgean sense of form, and it is toward such terminology that this discussion will begin to turn. In this way, it should prove possible not only to illumine Coleridge's idea of unity, but to approach also his understanding of God and divine revelation. For 'there is in Form . . . ', he tells us, 'something which is not elementary but divine. The contemplation of Form is astonishing to Man and has a kind of Trouble or Impulse accompanying it, which exalts his Soul to God (*CN*, II, 2223). 'The *idea* of the Supreme Being', he writes, 'appeared to me to be as necessarily implied in all particular modes of being as the idea of infinite space in all the geometrical figures by which space is limited.'[14] The reader who remembers that the Coleridgean idea, like its Platonic predecessor, is never regulative only, but always constitutive, will recognise that these implications are more than logical and their proportionality more than accidental.

Coleridge's constant philosophical opponents during his middle and later adult life were materialism and sensationalism. Students of his work know the many changes that he rang on epithets describing such enemies. These were the philosophies, he declared, of the 'imbruted sensualist',[15] of the 'finger philos-

ophers' – that is, 'the men of "sound common sense" . . . those
snails in intellect who wear their eyes at the tips of their feelers,
and cannot even see unless they at the same time touch'.[16] In
every instance, his dissatisfaction with such systems issued from
his approach to unity; for, no matter how hard they might try, he
believed, no materialists or sensationalists could ever discover,
or provide, a true and abiding 'One'. Whatever else matter
might be, it was to be conceived as composed ultimately of
discrete impenetrables, 'indivisible and yet space-comprehend-
ing minims' (*CL*, IV, 758). And, whatever else sensation might
be, it was destined to stop short at surface, a matter of exteriors
and never substance. Therefore, neither of these related philosophies could suffice, he thought, in the expression of unity, but
only of division and superficial differences, for each of them
'knows only of distance and nearness, composition (or rather
juxtaposition) and decomposition, in short the relations of unpro-
ductive particles to each other'.[17]

It was largely in order to resist the effects of such antagonists
that Coleridge, in conscious imitation of Pythagoras and Plato,
conceived a 'geometric discipline . . . as the first προπαιδευτι-
κόν of the mind'.[18] One finds throughout his writings a fascination with pentads and heptads, for example, figures with which
he hoped to communicate the form of oneness in diverse topics,
from the relationship among the primary colours to that among
the acts of mind. 'There is throughout all nature', he wrote, 'an
aptitude implanted that all things may be related to each and to
all',[19] and his imaginative application of geometric figures to the
organisation of his thoughts seems to have been intended to
assist in making this aptitude clear.

And, yet, plane figures could have but a limited use. Every
such figure exists by virtue of a fixed division between the
included and the excluded, its inside and outside, however much
their several sides may cohere in a kind of unity. Therefore, their
kind of unity was not completely adequate to the Coleridgean
perception of 'One'. It is for this reason, perhaps, that Coleridge
can be overheard, especially in his notebooks, repeatedly despairing of the possibility of ever expressing, or even conceiving
fully, a unity of form beyond division. 'I would make a pilgrim-
age to the Deserts of Arabia', he confides, 'to find the man who
could make [me] understand how the *one can be many*! Eternal
universal mystery! . . . It is the co presence of Feeling and Life,

limitless by their very essence, with Form, by its very essence
limited – determinate – definite' (*CN*, I, 1561).

Although he despairs, Coleridge seems also to have discovered
here a certain clue. He realised that the supersensible perception
of true unity could exist only through the union of seeming
opposites, a union of the definite with the indefinite, the Pythagorean and Platonic 'limit' with 'the unlimited' – or, in Romantic dress, of form with feeling. It was necessary, therefore, to find
a means of expression, a 'protophaenomon', which would respect these twin components. He required a form which would
conform to the fluidity and movement of experience while still
providing that movement with a centre of gravity or central
unity. Clearly, such a form could not exist in pictured figures
alone, even pentads, lest feeling fall victim yet again to the
despotism of passive physical sensation. Nevertheless, as long as
the danger was recognised, geometry could still perhaps be used;
a language of space might still convey his point. Whether Coleridge actually travelled so directly this path of thinking, from the
Deserts of Arabia to an interest in space and spatial relationships, cannot, of course, be conclusively established. To suppose
that he might have, however, goes far toward explaining his
fascination, among other geometrical analogies, with the idea of
depth, both as a spatial symbol, though not – he emphasised –
as an attribute of space, and as a medium for experiencing God.
As has been indicated already, it is the latter possibility with
which this essay is especially concerned.

Readers of the *Biographia Literaria* are familiar with Coleridge's
'depth' in the expression of his debt to Wordsworth, in whose
poetry, he tells us, he had first discovered a double depth in the
'union of deep feeling with profound thought'.[20] Such language
might be taken lightly were it not for several indications, in
letters and notebooks alike, that deepness was for Coleridge no
superficial notion, but an idea of great precision. Thus, he once
requested of a perhaps bewildered correspondent that he 'conceive an *inside* or depth, by compulsory abstraction, *without*,
because *prior* to, an *outside*' (*CL*, IV, 1077). And thus, too,
Coleridge framed a kind of definition, distinguishing the form of
his own noetic perception from the errors of materialism:

The sole definition of matter is that which fills space – now it
is with length, breadth, and length relative to Breadth that

space is filled. In other words, Space has relation only to the *outside*. Depth therefore must be that *by* not *with* which Space is filled. . . . Depth therefore cannot be an attribute of matter.[21]

Careful study of passages such as these suggests that Coleridge aimed to employ the idea of depth for a very specific purpose; his injunction concerning 'compulsory abstraction' cannot help but remind us of his own childhood 'unrealisation', nor, it seems, would we be mistaken in connecting such abstraction with that supersensible mode of consciousness which had led him to his foundational perception of 'matter as a Product'. It seems clear as well that the use of 'depth' was in a sense quite different from the usual. Coleridge's depth was not that of a well, for it was not to be thought of as in any way a constituent or function of matter. On the other hand, depth was to him more than a banal metaphor or regulative idea; it was something distinct, distinctly prior – one could almost say 'creative' – '*by* not *with* which Space is filled'. And it pointed, he seems convinced, to a form of unity uncompromised by the edges, divisions and juxtapositions of physical objects or their representations in fancy. In order to begin sharing his perception, one must apparently imagine the 'appearance', to use the uselessness of such language, of a third dimension, beyond both length and breadth, but in the absence of the actual, concrete existence or pictorial representation of that dimension, which he calls here 'length relative to Breadth'. The shift of perceptual focus which takes place in looking at the two-dimensional depiction of a transparent cube, as the eye sees alternately the same figure in two perspectives, and with two differently directed, imaginatively constructed 'depths', may be a serviceable analogy to Coleridge's thought. For here there is certainly a depth uncontained by any material surfaces and disclosed, as he would surely have preferred, only by the mental act of seeking it, a 'depth *without*, because *prior* to, an *outside*'.

However such geometrical and spatial communications are to be interpreted, two facts are certain: first, that Coleridge intended by their means to freshen perception by pointing toward unity; and, second, that such maieutic exercises, like the quest for unity itself, were aimed toward nothing less than the knowledge of God. 'It is the duty and the privilege of the theologian', Coleridge asserted, 'to demonstrate that *space* is the ideal organ by which the soul of man perceives the *omnipresence* of the Supreme Reality, as distinct from the works, which in him move, and live, and have their being.'[22] If only he could somehow create a spatial language for expressing the abiding, inward unity of things, more intimate than exteriors allow, then, Coleridge felt, he would have put the soul in touch with God. Of course, 'that both time and space are mere abstractions I am well aware,' he confessed, 'but I know with equal certainty that what is *expressed* by them . . . is the highest reality, and the root of all power'.[23] If form, as he said above, 'exalts Man's soul to God', it does so by rendering itself transparent, spatial figures having become open to an influx of meaning from a source unencumbered by material exclusions.[24]

In addition to its many other, and lesser, sins, Coleridge believed, 'the mechanical system of philosophy . . . has needlessly infected our theological opinions'.[25] As we have seen, this system, with all of its attendant errors – psychological, metaphysical, epistemological – was what Coleridge had hoped to defeat in his drive toward unity. It must now be said specifically that, to him, the most dangerous of the effects of mechanism were decidedly theological. 'For a man who affirms boldly that what the senses have not given to his mind . . . *that* he will regard as nothing but words . . . cannot pretend to believe in God.'[26] 'The existence of an infinite spirit, of an intelligent and holy will, must on this system be mere articulated motions of the air.'[27] More precisely, the theological infection of materialistic philosophy seemed to him twofold, displaying itself in opposite, yet related, symptoms, opposed to one another but equally mistaken, because of equal deviations from true unity:

> With the exception of those who have strictly followed the Scriptures . . . I know none who has avoided one or the other of two evils – the one making the world have the same relation to God as a watch has to a watchmaker . . . and rendering the omnipresence of the great Being . . . a mere word of honor . . . – or the opposite error of carrying the omnipresence into a condition of nature-with-God, and involving . . . fearful consequences.[28]

Coleridge was, in short, in passages such as this at least, announcing himself opposed not only to deism – the bane of all

Romantics – but also, and as much, to pantheism, in spite of his own sometimes unguarded tendencies in that direction. Each of these opposite theologies he considered an error of extremity or imbalance, for each departed from a middle, and more Christian, way, the 'Theism of Saint Paul and Christianity', which was the unity, he thought, of three apparently conflicting elements: 'Spinosism', 'a mere *anima Mundi*', and 'mechanical Theism' or deism – that is, he explains, of 'Εν καὶ Πάντα ('one and all'), 'Εν δ' 'Απάντων ('one through all'), and 'Εν τε πρὸ πάντων ('one before all').[29] It is no part of this essay to do more than simply indicate, without analysis, the extraordinary measure of attentiveness that would be required were the interpreter to consider fully what a Christian theism of this Coleridgean kind might be. I would observe only that any region of being or meaning able to serve simultaneously as the antecedent unity or unifying source of all three of these distinct relationships, of *and*, *of* and *before*, would certainly be, as Coleridge claimed, utterly beyond the reach of empirical discernment.

For now, the most important point to be grasped is that deism and pantheism both, according to Coleridge, were symptomatic of false or inadequate unity. They were the theological results, to be precise, of the false, materialistic assumption that the unity of the world is merely atomic and juxtapositional. By presuming that the universe should be consistent throughout with their impressions of material objects, that the world can maintain integrity only at its surface, as it were, and only either by including or excluding all else, the mechanical philosophers had closed their minds to the presence of a transcendent God. For the *presence* of *transcendence*, and its perception, entailed a form of unity more open and more fluid, like that expressed by 'depth', and thus a world as much permeated as upheld by the divine. 'All false Systems may be reduced into these two genera', Coleridge therefore wrote:

> the former assumes a θεός 'ἔξω τοῦ κόσμου [a God outside the world], the latter a θεός ἐν κόσμω [a God in (the) world]. In the one the World *limits* God, in the other it *comprehends* him. Now the falsehood of both my be *taught*, both directly by subversion of the premises, and indirectly by the absurdity . . . of the inevitable consequences.

And yet, in order truly to master, so as to overcome, the
falsehood of these false theologies, something more, he felt, was
needed. The Coleridge who spent his life attending, and attending to attention, seems to have been convinced that a new order
of attention was required. A person must acquire not just new
concepts, but a new perception or vision. It was for the sake of
this end, this vision, that Coleridge seems always to have framed
his requests, definitions and injunctions, and thus also that he
continued, and concluded, the preceding observations, 'But the
Truth of the Contrary must be *seen*' (*CL*, IV, 768).

What Coleridge hoped to help theologians see, in order that
they should see the '*Truth*', was unity – not an aggregate or
synthesis or fusion, however intricate, intimate or exhaustive,
but a unity of feeling with form, with a result unpicturable,
because immaterial, yet geometrically exact. For the perception
of the true 'One' and an adequate conception of God were for
him of a single piece. 'Hast thou ever raised thy mind to the
consideration of EXISTENCE?' asks Coleridge.

> In vain would we derive it from the organs of sense: for these
> supply only surfaces, undulations, phantoms! . . . It is absol-
> utely One. . . . The truths, which it manifests are such as it
> alone can manifest, and in all truth it manifests itself. By what
> name then canst thou call a truth so manifested? Is it not
> REVELATION? . . . And the manifesting power, the source,
> and the correlative of the idea thus manifested – is it not
> GOD?[30]

NOTES

1. In this essay, the definition of the word 'Coleridge' is for the most
   part not 'a man who was born in 1772, inflated metaphysical
   swim-bladders, became addicted to a drug, wrote much, talked
   more, and finally died in 1834'. Rather the term 'Coleridge'
   describes a line connecting all those points, composed and plagiar-
   ised by the previously mentioned man, which may prove therapeutic in curing a now nearly dead post-Kantian theology of its
   empiricistic sickness. Though I shall refer to Coleridge many times
   as 'he', and though I allude throughout to the ideas along the
   Coleridgean line as though my application of them were intended

by a historical person, the style is meant only to avoid a certain awkwardness. In no important sense is this essay, finally, about a man. Such disclaimers seem necessary in an age as dominated as ours by historicistic applications of the genetic fallacy.

2. Coleridge, *Collected Works*, VII: *Biographia Literaria*, ed. James Engell and W. Jackson Bate (Princeton, NJ, 1983) I, 304.

3. Coleridge, *Aids to Reflection*, ed. H. N. Coleridge (Port Washington, NY, 1971) p. 64.

4. *Inquiring Spirit: A Coleridge Reader*, ed. K. Coburn (New York, 1951) pp. 30–1.

5. *Biographia*, II, 7.

6. Coleridge, *Collected Works*, IV: *The Friend*, ed. Barbara E. Rooke (Princeton, NJ, 1969) I, 110.

7. *Coleridge on Logic and Learning*, ed. A. D. Snyder (New Haven, Conn., 1929) p. 1.

8. M. H. Abrams, *Natural Supernaturalism* (New York, 1971) p. 182.

9. Robert Penn Warren, 'Formula for a Poem', *Saturday Review of Literature*, 22 Mar 1958, p. 23. Referred to in Ray L. Hart, *Unfinished Man and the Imagination* (New York, 1968) p. 248.

10. *Selected Poetry and Prose of Coleridge*, ed. Donald A. Stauffer (New York, 1951) p. x.

11. *Biographia*, I, 107.

12. Ibid., p. 148.

13. *Friend*, I, 481.

14. *Biographia*, I, 200.

15. *Aids to Reflection*, p. 71.

16. 'Magnanimity', in Coleridge and Robert Southey, *Omniana* (London, 1812) section 129.

17. *The Statesman's Manual*, in Coleridge, *Collected Works*, VI: R. J. White (Princeton, NJ, 1972) p. 89.

18. *Biographia*, I, 107.

19. Coleridge, *The Philosophical Lectures*, ed. K. Coburn (New York, 1949) p. 326.

20. *Biographia*, I, 80.

21. Quoted by Owen Barfield in *What Coleridge Thought* (Middletown, Conn., 1971) p. 202, n. 14, from unpublished manuscript.

22. 'Formation of a More Comprehensive Theory of Life', *Selected Poetry and Prose of Coleridge*, p. 580.

23. Ibid., pp. 605–6.

24. Words such as 'omnipresence' in the earlier quotation naturally raise the disputed question of Coleridge's pantheism, which will be further alluded to below. See Thomas McFarland's masterful *Coleridge and the Pantheist Tradition* (Oxford, 1969) for a full discussion of the problem.

25. *Biographia*, II, 75n.
26. *Philosophical Lectures*, pp. 361–2.
27. *Biographia*, I, 120.
28. *Philosophical Lectures*, p. 330.
29. *Biographia*, I, 246n.
30. *Friend*, I, 514–16.

5 The Impact of Schleiermacher's Hermeneutics on Contemporary Interpretation Theory

WERNER G. JEANROND

I INTRODUCTION

Until recently Friedrich Schleiermacher's thoughts on hermeneutics were not so widely acknowledged as his famous works on
Religion, the theological curriculum and the Christian Faith.
One reason for this was the state of their publication. Apart from
his two addresses to the Prussian Academy of Science in Berlin,
which form a coherent text, Schleiermacher's reflections on
hermeneutics are available to us mainly in the form of notes from
lectures which he delivered at the University of Berlin. In the
context of his collected works we find only one manuscript on
hermeneutics, the so-called *Kompendienartige Darstellung* of 1819,
edited and further enriched through student notes by Friedrich
Lücke in 1838. Lücke's edition, however, has never been repub-
lished and is fairly inaccessible. But editorial circumstances are
not the only reason for the longlasting unpopularity of Schleiermacher's hermeneutical thoughts. A second reason can be seen
in the propaganda against Schleiermacher the hermeneut, recently reformulated by Hans-Georg Gadamer in all four editions
of his work *Wahrheit und Method* (*Truth and Method*).

In his sketch of the history of modern hermeneutics Gadamer
deals with Schleiermacher's contribution under the heading

'Fragwürdigkeit der romantischen Hermeneutik' (Questionable-
ness of Romantic hermeneutics).[1] Although Gadamer has much
praise for Schleiermacher's redefinition of hermeneutics as the
art of avoiding misunderstanding and for his claim for the
universality of hermeneutics, he castigates his principle of divination as hopelessly romantic. And, although Gadamer agrees
with Schleiermacher's battle against a preformulated authority
of texts which manipulates the act of reading itself, he blames
him for overlooking the historical dimension of understanding
and for pursuing only the limited interest of a theologian in
hermeneutics. Thus Schleiermacher figures – for Gadamer – as
a romantic theologian and as such provides us with only one
point of hermeneutical theory, provoking merely historiographic
considerations.

This evaluation of Schleiermacher's hermeneutics did not
change much even when Heinz Kimmerle in 1959 – following
Gadamer's own suggestion – edited a number of previously
inaccessible lecture manuscripts by Schleiermacher which provided the material for quite a different picture from that deline-
ated by Gadamer.[2] Gadamer's verdict, however, remained un-
changed. In his epilogue to *Wahrheit und Methode* he admits only
to having insufficiently emphasised Schleiermacher's dipolar
interpretation theory (grammatical and psychological interpretation) and to having overemphasised the psychological
dimension.[3] Schleiermacher remained a questionable Romantic
who might be praised for his practical knowledge of the human
heart but who has no major theoretical contribution to make to
contemporary hermeneutics.

Here I should like to reflect anew upon the impact of Schleiermacher's hermeneutics on contemporary interpretation theory,
for I do not agree with Gadamer's judgement. Yet I shall also be
careful not to promote Schleiermacher uncritically as the forgotten hero of hermeneutical thinking or as the only classic of
contemporary hermeneutics.

After a brief look at the present editorial state of the relevant
texts by Schleiermacher I shall consider the main aspects of his
interpretation theory. I should like to examine the history of the
effects of Schleiermacher's thoughts on contemporary interpretation theory. And, finally, I should like to assess his significance
for our present hermeneutical debates and to illustrate briefly
the limitations and potential of six aspects of Schleiermacher's

hermeneutics. Thus, this paper does not attempt to give a history of modern hermeneutics since Schleiermacher. Rather, it attempts to engage us in a dialogue with this great hermeneut.

II A NEW INTEREST IN SCHLEIERMACHER'S HERMENEUTICS

A first critical study of Schleiermacher's hermeneutical reflections was made possible by Heinz Kimmerle's work. Kimmerle's introduction emphasised the necessity of a new assessment of Schleiermacher's hermeneutics which would need to be freed to some extent from Wilhelm Dilthey's perspective, which had shaped so effectively Schleiermacher's hermeneutical image hitherto. Kimmerle could convincingly show that Schleiermacher's hermeneutical reflections went far beyond the scope of a mere psychological reconstruction, as Dilthey had granted; rather, a new assessment of Schleiermacher would need to underline also the grammatical dimension of the understanding of texts. Moreover, in Schleiermacher's hermeneutics we find a general philosophical perspective of the phenomenon of understanding which was unprecedented in the history of hermeneutics (*HK*, pp. 5, 14, 15). Understanding, for Schleiermacher, depends on two dimensions at once: the linguistic dimension, which he calls the 'grammatical' or the 'objective' side of the one process and the individual act of grasping the sense which he calls the 'psychological' or the 'subjective' side of the same act of understanding.

The critical study of Schleiermacher's hermeneutics was helped further in 1977 by Manfred Frank's publication of Schleiermacher's *Hermeneutik und Kritik* on the basis of Lücke's 1838 edition but now enriched by some related texts and by critical notes. In the same year, Frank published also his own study *Das individuelle Allgemeine: Textstrukturierung und interpretation nach Schleiermacher*. Frank intended with his new edition to correct Kimmerle's thesis of Schleiermacher's increasing shift towards the psychological dimension of interpretation,[4] and through his monograph he wanted to demonstrate the actuality of Schleiermacher's hermeneutics with its anticipation of some of the modern linguistic or even structuralist interpretation theories.

Although the historical–critical edition of Schleiermacher's

work is under way, it will be some time before we have a new and
more refined corpus of Schleiermacher's texts on hermeneutics.
Thus, for the moment we have to work with Kimmerle's and
Frank's editions. As we have already seen with regard to Gadamer, the old image of Schleiermacher as a Romantic subjec-
tivist is still widely cherished. It is this image which I should like
to question in order to come to a more critical picture of
Schleiermacher's hermeneutical thinking and to free us for a
more helpful dialogue with his ideas.

III   TOWARDS A CRITICAL THEORY OF
INTERPRETATION

Schleiermacher defines hermeneutics as the art of understanding
mainly written utterances by other people (*HK*, pp. 75, 78, 82).
Hermeneutics concerns all aspects of understanding and not
only those instances where understanding seems to be difficult.
All understanding presupposes language, for in language we
think and through language we communicate. There is no
understanding without communication, and therefore hermeneutics and rhetoric, however distinct, cannot be separated (*HK*,
pp. 38, 78). Language occurs always as a combination of general
patterns of convention (its grammatical or objective aspect) and
of individual performance (its technical or subjective aspect).
Schleiermacher calls this latter aspect also the 'psychological'
aspect of interpretation (*HK*, pp. 48ff., 77); yet the exact terminology remains unclear. Only in a note of 1833 do we learn that
'psychological' means more the development of thoughts from
the whole of the *Lebensmoment*, whereas 'technical' means more
the reduction to a certain thinking or *Darstellenwollen* from which
a series of thoughts arises. Otherwise the technical aspect is the
understanding of the mediation and the composition, the psychological aspect the understanding of ideas and subordinate
thoughts (*HK*, p. 163).

The two main aspects of interpretation, grammatical and
psychological, are perfectly equal in the act of interpretation.
Thus every act of interpretation has to deal with its text as a
network of individually applied general rules. So every text is an
individual universal (*ein individuelles Allgemeines*). The particularity of composition forms the style of the text. No grammatical
consideration can produce a concept of a particular style, for the

very conceptualisation of the individuality of a text would dissolve this individuality. Thus, Schleiermacher aims at approximation rather than at the total grasp of a text's sense (*HK*, p. 115). He rejects every attempt of so called special hermeneutics to regionalise these hermeneutical insights or to manipulate the act of interpretation through the imposition of supratextual authorities. He calls for a general hermeneutics and he tries to unfold its universal conditions.

Therefore Gadamer's accusation of a theological bias in Schleiermacher's hermeneutical reflection is absurd.[5] Of course, Schleiermacher's point of departure into hermeneutical reflection is his theological need to interpret texts; yet he always insists that the theological interpreter has no prerogative when he tries to understand texts.

Through their syntactical structure and semantic composition the various meanings in every text form the sense of the text. The task of the interpreter is therefore to reconstruct the given discourse 'historically and in a way of divination, objectively and subjectively'. The ultimate goal of the interpretative act is 'to understand the discourse first as well and then even better than its author' (*HK*, p. 83). This formulation of the aim of interpretation, on the one hand, and the term 'divination', on the other hand, have given rise to much confusion and apparently provided the stimulus for Gadamer and other reviewers of Schleiermacher's hermeneutics to box him under the rubric 'exclusively romantic'. Manfred Frank, however, in his investigation has devoted much space to correcting this false image.

Gadamer wrongly associates the term *Gefühl* or *Einfühlung* with divination. He writes,

> It is true that Schleiermacher saw ... individuality as a mystery that could never be quite grasped; but even this statement requires to be taken only in a relative way: the barrier that remains here for reason and understanding is not in every sense insuperable. It is to be overcome by feeling [*das Gefühl*], and immediate sympathetic and conatural understanding.[6]

Nowhere in his hermeneutical texts does Schleiermacher use the term *Gefühl* in this way, and nowhere does he call for a sympathetic congeniality. Rather he insists that the difference between the individuality of the text and the individual reader can only be minimised through efforts of approximation, but never sublated in Hegel's sense. So Frank states correctly that Schleiermacher's motto 'to understand an author better than he understood himself' has nothing to do with a positivistic arrogance to obtain a better competence, but it means for the interpreter to risk again and again a deeper grasp of sense in history.[7] The components of the text, its grammatical structure, remain the same, but their sense has to be appropriated anew in every act of reading.

Thus, Schleiermacher's term 'divination' describes the courageous risk of an always preliminary grasp of the text's sense. Understanding is a never-ending task and challenge. The process of understanding is, as we have seen already, a dipolar activity: grammatical and psychological at once. Therefore we cannot, as Gadamer does, split this integrated activity. The psychological dimension which culminates in the always-preliminary divination of the sense, and the grammatical dimension, the deciphering and grasping of the whole of the text, depend on each other. One can never exclude the grammatical aspects from the hermeneutical circle.

Schleiermacher circumscribes the *grammatical* dimension of *interpretation* in this way: the grammatical interpretation is 'the art of finding the particular sense of a certain discourse in the language and with the help of the language' (*HK*, p. 57). He urges us to construct what the author of a text and its reader have in common. Language lives by participation. Nobody has all of it, but rather we share it. Thus, we cannot isolate any given word or sentence and explicate its meaning. Rather we have to examine every part of the discourse in its context. Here we are to define the meaning of a 'speech act' (*HK*, p. 59; *HF*, p. 89)[8] on the basis of its particular usage and to define the hitherto unknown usage from that meaning. This procedure never yields perfection, because of the individuality of every speech act. However, we have to risk approximation, and here Schleiermacher talks about *das Gefühl* which attempts to grasp the total meaning, though always aware that it is only a preliminary construction (*HK*, p. 61).

According to Schleiermacher the basis of such an approximation must be the possible linguistic common ground between author and original reader. Lexica and various methods of linguistic comparison might assist the modern interpreter. One such means of comparison is to seek parallel discourses of one author or of one time. For Schleiermacher the main task of grammatical interpretation, however, is to find out for every utterance the true usage which the author intended (*HK*, p. 64).

The *psychological interpretation* seeks to grasp the whole or the unity of the work. Schleiermacher considers its theme as the principle which had moved the author, and the character of its composition as the particular nature which reveals itself in the movement of the composition. Thus, the aim of the psychological interpretation is the complete understanding of the style. The general and the particular penetrate each other and their combination can be grasped only through divination.

After this brief description of Schleiermacher's approach to hermeneutics we have to ask if it is worthwhile to consider this approach today. Does it offer anything original to the present search for a critical theory of interpretation?

IV SCHLEIERMACHER'S CONTRIBUTION TO A CRITICAL THEORY OF INTERPRETATION

Gadamer's hermeneutical theory has provoked much criticism. His concept of the fusion of horizons, the horizon of the interpreter fusing with the horizon of the text, and his invitation to the interpreter to enter the tradition represented by the text have troubled many reviewers. Gadamer rejected any kind of methodological access to the truth of a text. Rather he insisted that the truth of a text appears in acts of conversation with the text where the reader submits himself completely to the text, and is played by the text.[9] Jürgen Habermas blames Gadamer for presupposing a state of innocence for the model of conversation and he warns that every given act of understanding might in fact prove to be yet another illusion. How do we know, he asks, that we really understand a text?[10] Paul Ricoeur asks Gadamer why a more methodological approach should endanger a deeper understanding of texts: Ricoeur proposes to learn from structuralist and formalist theories in order to approach texts in a two-dimensional way: our initial, naïve understanding needs to be validated by a thorough linguistic analysis of the text which leads to a second naïveté.[11] The combination of divination – that is, the initial naïveté – and of linguistic analysis in Ricoeur's thought reminds us immediately of Schleiermacher's dipolar hermeneutics. Therefore it seems worthwhile to examine Rocoeur's own discussion of Schleiermacher more closely.

Ricoeur welcomes Schleiermacher's contribution to hermeneutics for three reasons. First, he praises Schleiermacher's insistence that 'only the hermeneutics of sense is hermeneutics',[12] and, secondly, his conviction that the sense of a text can be grasped only by individual acts of interpretation which do justice to the structure of the text as well as to the projection of sense by the text. Thirdly, Ricoeur shows his appreciation of Schleiermacher's theory of style:

> He was one of the first to perceive that style is not a matter of ornamentation; it marks the union of thought and language, the union of the common and the singular in an author's project. The style displays a singularity inside the common resources of language, and, above all, in the style the formal aspect of the work's structure is joined to the psychological aspect of the author's intention.[13]

Ricoeur, however, criticises Schleiermacher's unclear distinction between technical and psychological interpretation, on the one hand, and the swimming boundaries between grammatical and psychological interpretation, on the other. And he regrets that Schleiermacher never distinguishes clearly between the two possible orientations of technical interpretation: 'towards the idea which governs the work or towards the author considered as a psychological being'. In an earlier article, Ricoeur had already argued in favour of his own orientation, towards the idea which governs the work.[14]

The text, and not its author, represents for Ricoeur the aim of interpretation. A written text gains a distance from the author's intention, from the original situation of discourse and from the original audience. Such a text, for Ricoeur, is a work which needs and deserves interpretation. Schleiermacher wanted to understand the text as well as, and even better than, its author did. Ricoeur wants to understand the text independently from its author; for him the text is a potential of sense on its own which provokes its readers.

Besides Gadamer and Ricoeur, Manfred Frank has dealt extensively with Schleiermacher's hermeneutics. In his attempt to save it from being either unjustly condemned or forgotten in contemporary hermeneutical discussion, Frank has claimed a certain originality which unfortunately went so far as to overlook Ricoeur's dialogue with Schleiermacher, so that Frank blames Ricoeur for not having engaged in such a dialogue.[15] Frank for his part sees in the return to Schleiermacher's hermeneutics a chance to overcome the present conflict between structuralist text analysis and *sinnverstehender Interpretation* (best translated as 'interpretation which seeks to understand the sense of a text').[16]

Such interpretation does not take seriously enough the grammatical dimension of interpretation and overestimates the power of the subject to form the final criterion of truth. Structuralist analysis, by contrast, in its methodological abstraction, does not enlighten the work of the sense – that is, all phenomena of style and symbols of an unregulated individuality. Schleiermacher's contribution to modern interpretation theory, then, lies in his oscillation between the universal rules or conventions of discourse and the individual creations of discourse and hence the alterations of language as a whole. No grammar can predict individuality. This is the limitation of all semiotic procedures. That is why Schleiermacher calls for 'divination' as our chance to grasp individuality. Therefore, interpretation remains an act. It demands that the interpreter engages in a productivity which keeps path with the productivity of the author.[17]

V THE IMPACT OF SCHLEIERMACHER'S HERMENEUTICS ON CONTEMPORARY INTERPRETATION THEORY

What then can we learn from Schleiermacher's hermeneutical reflections? I think the question is best answered by both an account of Schleiermacher's actual impact, and reflection upon his possible impact on the development of hermeneutical theory. We have corrected Gadamer's partially distorted view of Schleiermacher's hermeneutics and we have taken account of Ricoeur's and Frank's dialogues with Schleiermacher. Now I should like to consider Schleiermacher's possible impact on interpretation theory in a more systematic manner. Therefore I propose to reflect upon six topics in contemporary hermeneutics in terms of what Schleiermacher might still contribute and where his thought has been transcended by modern developments. These six topics are: (1) the problem of a theory of text; (2) the dialectic of text and reading; (3) the theory of style; (4) hermeneutics and criticism; (5) the aims of interpretation; and (6) the fact of pluralism in interpretation.

(1) The problem of a theory of text

Schleiermacher was one of the first modern thinkers to reflect upon the question, 'What is a text?' A closer look at many hermeneutical treatises teaches us that most of them talk about interpretation yet never define what it is that they actually set out to understand. We know too well how much exegesis and preaching in the Christian tradition have indulged in singling out words or passages from larger textual entities in order to prove what they had decided to communicate anyway. Modern versions of fundamentalist conviction still use the biblical texts as quarries for their own intricate purposes. Schleiermacher saw that problem clearly and warned on a more pragmatic note never to take verses out of their context and on a more theoretical note that one of the first hermeneutical principles is to take a text seriously as a text (*HK*, pp. 45ff.). He describes a 'text' as a structured composition in a particular style. The individual sense of a text can only be grasped through interpreting the whole through its parts and the parts through the whole. Schleiermacher also was already aware of the problem of the identity of a text, although he did not solve that problem.

When we take, for instance, the Prologue to John's Gospel as our text to be interpreted, we must be aware that we are in fact dealing with only a part of the larger unity that is the entire Gospel. Yet, when we take the Fourth Gospel as a whole, we are aware that it is only one part of a larger unity, that is the New Testament, or even the combined canon of Old and New Testaments. On the one hand, Schleiermacher favoured the largest possible unity as the framework of every interpretative effort, but, on the other, his theory of style favoured a more restricted definition of the boundaries of any given text. Here he remains undecided: shall we interpret the work governed by one idea, or shall we interpret the author – let us say, John – through all his different works?

On another level, text theory has gone far beyond Schleiermacher: he did not see the dynamic nature of a text. Although he calls for a distinction of main and subordinate thoughts in every text (*HK*, pp. 108ff.), he still treats texts as static entities. Here, the works of the Prague School of linguistics and recent scholarship in text linguistics have shown how every text unfolds itself as a dynamic process as soon as the reader allows it to become alive. This insight has also led to a more elaborate theory of reading.[18]

(2) The dialectic of text and reading

One really cannot deal with texts appropriately without considering the problems of reading them. Without reading, texts remain distributions of ink on paper. Through reading, however, they are allowed to unfold their *Gestalt* and their sense. Reading itself is a process motivated by the text's promises and by the reader's expectations. Yet what controls reading – the reader's genre and style of reading, or the genre and style of the text, or both, and in what relationship?

I should like to illustrate two options briefly by mentioning Wolfgang Iser's[19] and Stanley Fish's[20] theories of reading. Iser examines the act of reading in terms of the effects of the text; Fish analyses the act of reading in terms of the influences of the community of interpreters on the text. Iser sees the text as an objective unity displaying its particular character through specific procedures which help the reader to fulfil the text's demands. This kind of theory, however, would be rejected by Fish as yet another attempt to come to an objective text interpretation. Instead of such models of demonstration, Fish proposes persuasion as the basic model of text critique. He suggests that literature 'is the product of a way of reading, of a community agreement about what will count as literature, which leads the members of the community to pay a certain kind of attention and thereby to *create* literature'.[21] Fish's theory leads to a happy pluralism, the price of which is the identity loss of texts.

Both theories show important insights into the dialectic of text and reading. Yet both theories distort this dialectic. Schleiermacher's consideration of interpretation seem to me to be more accurate. Although he does not emphasise the process character of text and reading, he underlines the dialectical nature of the act of interpretation. Each such act has to reconstruct the text in terms of its individuality, which is achieved through its particular style, yet each such act lives also in the personal ability to divine a sense in the text. The balance between the linguistic identity of a text and the necessity for the reader to risk a personal, though linguistically responsible, reading seems to be more promising than the proposals of Fish or Iser.

(3) The theory of style

Ricoeur and Frank independently discovered the important contribution which Schleiermacher made towards a theory of style and through that theory to philosophy. Ricoeur reminds us of Aristotle's dictum 'that man contemplates universals, but produces individuals' and he praises Schleiermacher for his penetrating suggestion for the hermeneutical and philosophical development of Aritotle's insight.[22] Strangely enough, much modern scholarship in stylistics does not acknowledge Schleiermacher's great contribution. Gadamer, despite his own comments on style in his first appendix to *Truth and Method*, does not discuss Schleiermacher's notion of style. Here he sees 'style' purely as normative, so that, when he considers the question of whether one could use the concept of style in political history, he reaches this surprising conclusion: that an analysis of history under the perspective of style would miss the fact that something is taking place in history, something more than what can be clearly understood. It was Schleiermacher's merit to show how we as individuals produce actions and works which cannot be fully unpacked by concepts. This existence of individuality leads him to the development of his concept of style.

(4) Hermeneutics and criticism

Hermeneutik und Kritik and *Kritische Hermeneutik*, with their equivalents in other languages, are much favoured book titles today and not only in Germany. They suggest the need for criteria for a critical theory of understanding. 'Critical' can have many meanings. Schleiermacher too talked of the close relationship between *Hermeneutik* and *Kritik*. Under *Kritik*, however, he understood the need to assess the degree of authenticity of a text, that procedure which in biblical scholarship we name *Textkritik*.

Jürgen Habermas's insistence on the need for a depth hermeneutics whose aim is to examine possible systematic distortions of the situation of communication is in some way also known to Schleiermacher. He too did not fully trust the communicative power of language. Rather he was aware of the limits of understanding – unlike his idealist successors, who, like Gadamer, still believe in the dynamics of a language which speaks itself and produces truth if we only let it speak. Schleiermacher says in his lecture on dialectics in 1822, 'Even in language we find error and truth; even an incorrect thinking can become common knowledge, so that the thinking no longer coincides with what is thought (*HF*, p. 460). Schleiermacher deals with the concept of *Kritik* (criticism) in our modern sense of the term under the title 'dialectic'. He states in his marginal comments of 1828 that general hermeneutics are connected not only with *Kritik* (authenticity, *Textkritik*), but also with grammar. But, since all correct thinking aims at correct speaking, so *Hermeneutik*, *Kritik* and *Grammatik* are all linked also with dialectic. In a lecture of 1818 he defines dialectic 'as such an unpacking [*Auflösung*] of the thinking in language that a perfect communication occurs when one aims always at the highest perfection, the idea of knowledge' (*HF*, p. 411). But he adds in his 1822 lecture on dialectics that we can only approach the really known through a critical procedure which takes care to distinguish the individual and tries to understand it in its positive status and in its limitations.

The close connection between hermeneutics and dialectic in Schleiermacher's thought is not yet fully appreciated. Frank has pointed us to Schleiermacher's lectures on dialectic, and my own examination of these texts has convinced me that Schleiermacher was indeed much more aware of the need not only for *Textkritik* (critique of authenticity) but also for *Sachkritik* (critique of the text's sense) than most of our contemporary hermeneuts are.

(5) The aims of interpretation

Schleiermacher did not distinguish clearly between the aims of interpretation. Of course, in every given act of interpretation the interpreter should be clear what he aims at first: the interpretation of an author, a period or even the whole of history or creation. A post-Ricoeurian return to Schleiermacher might be fruitful here.

In his interpretation theory Ricoeur is concerned about written texts as works – that is, their potential of sense as actualised by the reader whose self is enlarged by the projection of a (new) world in the interpreted text. Yet, as the text points forward to its sense, so it also points backwards to its author and his world. However, every work contains a sense in itself which is disclosed in the act of reading.

Paul's letters, for instance, disclose as individual works a sense on their own; yet they also point back to Paul and to the life and problems of the Early Church and in Schleiermacher's terminology, to the style – that is, the individuality – of Paul and of the Early Church.

Therefore I propose to distinguish between various possible functions of reading: one function could be the *documentary* interest of a reader who wants to learn about writings in the Early Church; another function could be the *biographical* interest in finding out about the life of Paul through reading his texts; yet another function could be a *theological* interest in the experiences and reflections of Paul regarding God's salvific activity in Jesus Christ. Thus, it is important that we know exactly what we do in every given act of interpretation. We should always be aware that we never grasp the whole of a text's potential, since our perspectives limit us.

(6) The fact of pluralism in interpretation

A direct consequence of Schleiermacher's concepts of divination and style is the insight into the fact of pluralism in interpretation. No one interpreter can ever fully grasp the individuality of a work or of an author through his works. There remains always an insurmountable difference. Yet Schleiermacher's theory is not open to a throroughgoing pluralism. For his psychological interpretation is always controlled by the grammatical interpretation. The interpreter is not free to do with the text what he desires. Thus, Schleiermacher's pluralism is a limited pluralism, limited in so far as it takes the text seriously.

Schleiermacher writes at the end of his Academy Discourse of 1829 that the state of the hermeneutical discipline is still chaotic and that he hopes that hermeneutics will soon receive the *Gestalt* it deserves, together with a coherent set of rules (*HF*, p. 346). This task is certainly not yet achieved. Yet that we know something of what happens when we try to understand texts is in large part owing to Friedrich Schleiermacher's ideas and suggestions. One thing, however, he made ultimately clear to all hermeneuts: a total understanding cannot be achieved. Thus, even the skilled interpreter must be aware of his individuality, and so, necessarily, of his own limitations.

NOTES

1. Hans-Georg Gadamer, *Truth and Method*, trs. William Glen-Doepel (London, 1975) pp. 153–92.
2. Schleiermacher, *Hermeneutik*, ed. and intro. Heinz Kimmerle, 2nd edn (Heidelberg, 1974). All English translations in the present essay are my own, following this edition. References (prefixed *HK*) in text.
3. Hans-Georg Gadamer, *Wahrheit und Methode*, 4th edn (Tübingen, 1975) p. 528. This 'Nachwort' is unfortunately not included in the English translation.
4. Schleiermacher, *Hermeneutik und Kritik. Mit einem Anhang sprachphilosophischer Texte Schleiermachers* ed. and intro. Manfred Frank (Frankfurt am Main, 1977) pp. 60ff. Translations in the present essay are my own. Further references (prefixed *HF*) in text.
5. Gadamer, *Truth and Method*, p. 173.
6. Ibid., p. 168.
7. Cf. Manfred Frank, *Das individuelle Allgemeine: Textstrukturierung und interpretation nach Schleiermacher* (Frankfurt am Main, 1977) p. 361.
8. Schleiermacher was probably the first to use the term *Sprechakt*.
9. See Gadamer, *Truth and Method*, pp. 235–78.
10. Jürgen Habermas, 'Der Universalitätsanspruch der Hermeneutik', in *Hermeneutik und Ideologiekritik. Theorie Diskussion* (Frankfurt am Main, 1971) pp. 120–59.
11. Paul Ricoeur, *Hermeneutics and the Human Sciences: Essays on Language, Action and Interpretation*, ed. John B. Thompson (Cambridge and Paris, 1981) pp. 60ff., and *Interpretation Theory: Discourse and the Surplus of Meaning* (Fort Worth, Texas, 1976) pp. 71–95.
12. Paul Ricoeur, 'Schleiermacher's Hermeneutics', *Monist*, 60 (1977) 181–97 (quotation from p. 183).

13. Ibid. p. 188.
14. Paul Ricoeur, 'The Hermeneutical Function of Distanciation', *Philosophy Today*, 17 (1973) 129–41.
15. Frank, *Das individuelle Allgemeine*, p. 135. In his article 'Der Text und sein Stil: Schleiermachers Sprachtheorie', in *Das Sagbare und das Unsagbare: Studien zur neuesten französischen Hermeneutik und Texttheorie* (Frankfurt am Main, 1980) pp. 13–55, Frank still fails to acknowledge Ricoeur's reflections on Schleiermacher's theory of style.
16. See Frank, *Das individuelle Allgemeine*, pp. 247ff.
17. Ibid. p. 340.
18. See Werner G. Jeanrond, 'The Theological Understanding of Texts and Linguistic Explication', *Modern Theology*, 1 (1984) 55–66.
19. Wolfgang Iser, *Der Akt des Lesens: Theorie ästhetischer Wirking* (Munich, 1976).
20. Stanley Fish, *Is There a Text in This Class? The Authority of Interpretive Communities* (Cambridge, Mass., 1980).
21. Ibid., p. 97.
22. Ricoeur, 'The Hermeneutical Function of Distanciation' *Philosophy Today*, 17, p. 136.

6 Schleiermacher: True Interpreter

T. H. CURRAN

In June 1813 Friedrich Schleiermacher delivered a lecture to the Prussian Academy of Sciences on the problems which confound the interlingual translation of literary and philosophical texts.[1] While this may seem an unusual topic for the Dean of the Faculty of Theology at the University of Berlin to have chosen, Schleiermacher's analysis of the difficulties facing every serious translator represents a cornerstone of the modern German discussion of translation theory. Given the centrality of biblical translations to the realisation of Protestant piety, it may not seem so untoward for a Reformed theologian and pastor to grasp the nettle of the exchange of languages. In fact, Schleiermacher's treatise may be seen as standing in the same tradition as Dr Martin Luther's open letter on translation of 1530.

But, quite apart from this theoretical justification, Schleiermacher, shared with Luther a lifelong practical engagement with the work of a translator: he undertook and completed a translation of the works of Plato, an enterprise which in its own way is no less impressive than the Luther Bible. The enormity of the task is easily appreciated when we consider that Schleiermacher published the first volume of his Platonic dialogues in 1804, and that the last volume of these translations did not appear until twenty-four years later, in 1828. The success of the venture is apparent from the fact that these translations are still in print today.

There are three elements of Schleiermacher's treatise which deserve our special attention.

(1) Schleiermacher's lecture actually fixed a distinction in the German language between the activities of the interpreter (*Dolmetscher*) and the translator (*Übersetzer*), where the former is

understood to be the kind of linguistic enabler we should expect
to find at the United Nations or at international business confer-
ences. *Dolmetschen* (interpretation) presupposes a closely defined
community of interests, a ready access to the technical terms of
another language, and the reasonably tight 'fit' or correspondence of concepts and vocabulary which make international
trade and political or scientific agreements possible. We are all
talking about the same thing, so to speak.

As against this easy correspondence at an international level,
the *Übersetzer* (translator) has to cope with the essential incommensurability of our philosophical concepts, and the linguistic
distortions that occur when we try simply to replace one word by
another, rather than confine ourselves to reproducing the general 'sense' of an argument or literary passage. How often are we
told that a particular philosophical concept or a passage in
dialect or a sophisticated literary wordplay or figure of speech is
simply 'untranslatable'? The translator begins fully conscious of
the 'difference', the untranslatable residence which survives
every attempt at a faithful rendition of a literary or philosophical
text; by contrast the simultaneous 'interpreter' proceeds from
the confidence which the essential 'identity' of the subject matter
and compatibility of technical languages inspire.

(2) Faced with this final incommensurability of our conceptual worlds and the languages which give them life, the translator, Schleiermacher suggests, can proceed in one of two ways:
either he can leave his reader in peace and bring the author into
the 'thought world' of the 'target language', or, conversely, he
can demand that the reader make a greater effort to appropriate
the alien concepts, culture and language of the author – thus the
original author is left in peace, relatively speaking. The former
method (of leaving the reader comparatively secure) has had its
firm adherents – so that Dryden, for instance, could claim, 'I
have endeavoured to make Virgil speak such English as he
would himself have spoken, if he had been born in England, and
in this present age'.[2] Schleiermacher rejects as false historical
consciousness the translator's attempt to offer the reading public
the works of a classical author as he would have written them in
modern English or German – for such a 'translation' deprives
the author precisely of those characteristics which make him
classical *and not* modern, working in and with the languages of
antiquity *and not* French or German or English. Such translations

may be useful as exercises in cultural imperialism, the conquest of other tongues and concepts, but they are unlikely to stretch our imaginations in the interpretative work of appropriating the alien world view from which we have evolved – or may, indeed, never have known.

(3) Schleiermacher's lengthy sketch of the inherent difficulties of the work of translation ends with the remarkable assertion that translating is the particular vocation of a people whose land is in the 'heart of Europe'. Schleiermacher claims that through the massive toil of an army of translators, German culture has been enriched, in the same way as German soil has become more fertile and the German climate milder through the introduction of foreign vegetation. It was a particularly noble vision in the year 1813 (during the Napoleonic era), and it is of little less consequence in the new age of the European Community.

I would now like to comment on each of these three points from within the context of Schleiermacher's wider theological and 'ethical' thought.

(1) Some five years after his Academy lecture, Schleiermacher has occasion to use the word *Dolmetschung* in a famous letter to the philosopher Jacobi, dated 30 March 1818. There Schleiermacher argues that the Bible (i.e. the New Testament) is the original and originative interpretation (*Dolmetschung*) of Christian feeling or piety, and in view of this fact so foundational that those Scriptures can for ever only be better understood and developed. His use of the word *Dolmetschung* in this context gives some indication of the privileged status of those Scriptures: he must be implying the closeness of the 'fit' of that original experience of Jesus with its first articulation. As time goes on, the Christian documents will, of necessity, cease to have the immediacy of that first 'fit', the first *Dolmetschung*, and will become more and more the interpretations of 'translations' which go hand in hand with a developing Christianity.

It is interesting to note here that the success of Schleiermacher's greatest theological work, *The Christian Faith*, must be judged by the degree to which it remains a pure *Dolmetschung* of the actual Christian piety then to be discovered in the Protestant German believer. As the New Testament is thought to give an accurate account of the state of Christian religious feeling at its inception, so Schleiermacher's descriptive, dogmatic work is supposed to be 'logically ordered reflection upon the immediate utterances of the religious self-consciousness'.[3] That is to say, Schleiermacher's reformulation of the utterances of concrete Christian piety in the categories of dogmatic proposition intends to offer the Church a *description* of the actual piety of its believers without reference to speculative, philosophical ideas which are not grounded in Christian piety. Schleiermacher's *The Christian Faith* is emphatically not a speculative transformation of Christian doctrine according to some prevailing philosophical fashion, but a 'logically ordered' account of the Protestant piety then extant. Of course, in virtue of the demands of a coherent dogmatic system, Christian piety is 'translated' into a new language; but, because this system intends no material change to the *content* of its object (the religious feeling it describes), it may claim to be a *Dolmetschung* – an interpretation which does not allow any extraneous foreign elements to intervene.

In other manuscripts and lectures Schleiermacher gives solid theoretical support for this 'translation' of Christian piety into the categories of ordered, dogmatic reflection. In his hermeneutical writings, Schleiermacher refers to Christianity's power to formulate new conceptual language: the new concepts, he argues, arose from the distinctive Christian stimulation of the inner life.[4] In his lectures on Christian moral life, Schleiermacher talks of Christianity's introduction of a completely new form of the articulation of thoughts. It is almost as if he were arguing that Christian feeling is *sui ipsius interpres*, as if it were providing the Church with the concepts, categories and language according to which this piety can be objectively discussed.

And the Church responds in kind: Schleiermacher speaks of the 'institutions' which the Church establishes in order both to spread *and* secure the Christian understanding of the world and the language which expresses it. So the catechism performs at the level of the everyday what the discipline of theology is meant to establish on a higher plane.[5] Christian piety has then interpreted itself to the Christian believer from its inception, and the significance of *Dolmetschung* in this context is that it reminds us to interpret that selfsame Christian consciousness *without* the admixture of alien speculative and philosophical elements.

(2) Schleiermacher's two suggestions on how the author and the reader may be united, whether it be for the one or the other to make the primary shift in terms of language and culture, provides an interesting reflection on the problem of the so-called

'historical gap'. The famous distinction in biblical criticism between exegesis as establishing 'what the text meant then', and theology as establishing 'what the text means now' raises a similar set of questions. Following Schleiermacher's translation theory, we should be wary of any attempt to 'update' that original Christian witness, as if we were to imagine Jesus and his disciples commenting on present developments and problems in modern English or German! In this vein, Cardinal Newman actually offered a view of 'evolved doctrines' as

> evidently the new form, explanation, transformation, or carrying out of what in substance was held from the first, what the Apostles said, but have not recorded in writing, or would necessarily have said under our circumstances, of if they had been asked, or in view of certain uprisings of error . . . .[6]

For Schleiermacher, by way of contrast, there always remains a final incommensurability, a certain unrepeatable quality to anything profound necessarily first spoken within the borders of one particular language and the culture which nurtured it. This translator of Plato maintained that oriental and occidental languages could never become equivalent, and that there was not even much hope for classical Greek and modern German, since the latter had neither *nous* nor *logos*, but rather quite different concepts.[7]

For Schleiermacher there could never be alternative readings of Holy Scripture – what it meant and what it means – but only the deeper comprehension of that original *Dolmetschung* of Christian feeling within the ever-developing history of the Christian religion. From such a perspective the separating-out of original from contemporary meaning completely ignores the continuum which binds every Christian to the original bedrock of his Christian piety. The separation of past from present meaning is a pure abstraction, and in this separation the house of Christian faith would be built 'upon the sand'.

From Schleiermacher's preference for bringing the reader to the author – and not *vice versa* – we know that the deeper comprehension of the New Testament involves all the tools that the 'true interpreter' holds in his workshop: all his linguistic, philological and critical faculties must be fully engaged, even if all these put together cannot guarantee that perfect 'translation', that complete equivalence of language and concept, which must be every translator's goal. The point is – to use Eberhard Jüngel's neat formulation – on the one hand to understand biblical texts in an appropriate, timely way (*zeitgemäss*), and on the other hand to understand our own times in the light of sacred Scripture (*schriftgemäss*). This dialectical recognition that we do not '*first* understand the past and *then* proceed to understand the present', and that it is only in dialogue with our Christian past that we can attain a deeper appreciation of it and of ourselves, explains precisely why translation must be defined as a form of mediation. We do not stand in a simple relation of 'one-way dependence' with our past:[8] it enriches us, and we enrich it in turn.

So Schleiermacher argues that every member of a nation must *both* work within the parameters of his language *and* also bring out into the open what within the language would have remained only a potentiality without him. The individual and his language adorn each other with their unique treasures: 'The wisdom of every individual must be dissolved in this system of language. Everyone partakes of what is there, and everyone helps to bring to light what is not yet there but prefigured.'[9]

(3) In Schleiermacher's profound conviction that human languages are not commensurate and can never become equivalent, we have located one aspect of his opposition to the philosophical idealism of his contemporaries. Because philosophical concepts only see the light of day within the confines of a *particular*, concrete human language, the quest for a single (universal) philosophy must run aground. Yet, on the other hand, Schleiermacher sees with equal clarity that it is the essence of all thought to strive for the acquisition of unity; and it is just in this work of forging unity where there is division of language, culture and philosophical concept that the translator discovers the profundity of his calling.

Each new translation offers a kind of refuge for the alien, a shelter for the wayfarer. No great literary or philosophical text can find a permanent home in the way stations that we offer, yet even these tentative appropriations mean that it is no longer simply a stranger in our midst. Each new translation is a partial conquest by the human spirit of the divisions imposed upon us by space and time. Through our translations we may indeed 'redeem the time lost' and work towards the healing of the rupture within human community which must be our lot 'after

Babel'. With admirable succinctness Schleiermacher tells us, 'we cannot go back and must see it through'.

NOTES

1. Schleiermacher's lecture 'Über die verschiedenen Methoden des Übersetzens', in *Das Problem des Übersetzens*, ed. H. J. Storig, (Darmstadt, 1973) pp. 38–70. English trs. in André Lefevre, *Translating Literature: The German Tradition* (Assen, 1977) pp. 67–89.
2. Preface to Dryden's translation of Virgil, 1697.
3. Schleiermacher, *The Christian Faith*, tr. and ed. H. R. Mackintosh and J. S. Stewart (Edinburgh, 1928) § 16, Postscript.
4. Schleiermacher, *Hermeneutik*, ed. and intro. Heinz Kimmerle, 2nd edn (Heidelberg, 1974) p. 79.
5. Schleiermacher, *Sämtliche Werke*, I.xii: *Die christliche Sitte*, ed. L. Jonas, 2nd edn (Berlin, 1884) pp. 393, 400f.
6. John Henry Newman, *Certain Difficulties felt by Anglicans in Catholic Teaching Considered* (London, 1898) II, 314.
7. Schleiermacher, *Brouillon zur Ethik (1805/06)*, ed. H. -J. Birkner (Hamburg, 1981) p. 25.
8. For an important discussion of this question, see Nicholas Lash, 'What might martyrdom mean?' in *Suffering and Martyrdom in the New Testament*, ed. W. Horbury and B. McNeil (Cambridge, 1981) pp. 183–98, esp. pp. 187–8.
9. *Translating Literature: The German Tradition*, p. 86.

7   Romanticism and the *Sensus Numinis* in Schleiermacher

ROBERT F. STREETMAN

These words of Friedrich Daniel Ernst Schleiermacher (1768–1834) will surely be subjected to new assessments during the several events commemorating the 150th anniversary of his death: 'I, for my part, am a stranger to the life and thought of this present generation, I am a prophet–citizen of a later world, drawn thither by a vital imagination and strong faith; to it belong my every thought and deed.'[1]

This essay will illustrate the many ways in which this herald of an age to come was able to breathe new life into religion, through his rediscovery of the *sensus numinis*, during the Romantic period, and to utilise this revivified *sensus* as the basis for reintroducing religion to the thinking people of his age. I shall argue that taking seriously Karl Barth's statement that Schleiermacher 'wanted in all circumstances to be a modern man as well as a Christian theologian' will help to explain how he constantly extricated himself from potentially unholy alliances, while still appropriating something crucially important from the encounter with the various movements of his day.[2] The focus will be on the *sensus numinis* and on Schleiermacher's engagement with German Romanticism. And Romanticism, in turn, will be interpreted as an expression of the coincidence of opposing forces seeking creative reconciliation in a centre.

I   THE RESURGENCE OF THE *SENSUS NUMINIS*

The title of the present essay was suggested by an essay of Rudolf Otto entitled 'How Schleiermacher Rediscovered the *Sensus Numinis*'. In Otto's view, a survey of the history of Christianity revealed a continuing need for revitalisation through the stimulation of a creative genius in religious experience, who then became the catalyst for the renewal of the Church. Among such catalyst were Paul, Augustine, Francis of Assisi, Luther, the German Pietists (albeit in an abortive sense) and Schleiermacher. To Schleiermacher fell the task of completing a revivification that had only been discharged very inadequately by Pietism, 'as an endeavour to shake off the crippling shackles of lifeless orthodoxy and of a new scholasticism'.[3]

'The sense of the numinous' is the phrase which describes the power by which one apprehends the presence of the numinous dimension in any *religious* experience, regardless of how simple or complex that experience may be. In order for any experience to qualify as 'religious', that experience must contain a dimension of numinous depth. Now the term 'numinous' (coined by Otto as an alternative for 'the Holy') is 'the essentially religious element in religious experience, prior to, and apart from, any rational and moral overtones it [the Holy] may accrue, as it develops itself in experience and history'.[4] The *sensus numinis*, then, is the power by which the numinous dimension, the essential ingredient which is the foundation of religious experience, is apprehended. Thus, Otto was crediting Schleiermacher with revitalising religion and thereby bringing Christianity, with its head held high, into the modern age.

Schleiermacher never had access to the term 'numinous', since Otto did not coin it until several decades after Schleiermacher's death. The early Schleiermacher of the *Speeches* preferred to speak of religion as a 'sense and taste for the infinite', or in terms of 'feeling and intuition', while the later Schleiermacher of *The Christian Faith* spoke of 'the feeling of absolute dependence'. Terminological differences aside, however, Otto was undoubtedly correct in ascribing to him the role of catalyst for the renewal of Christianity. Yet it may be even more accurate (and certainly more faithful to Schleiermacher's thought) to recognise that the initial stimulus that triggered the catalytic reaction in him must have come from elsewhere – from the transcendent basis for numinous feeling. In other words, were this essay to have a subtitle, it would have to be 'How the *Sensus Numinis* Discovered Schleiermacher'. To careful readers of his early life it appears that the transcendent holy power which was apprehended through the *sensus numinis* had been plumbing the hearts of the German children of the last half-century of rationalism, in search of a suitable dwelling-place. On 21 November 1768, in a modest pastoral home in Breslau, the numinous finally discovered the sensitive heart that it had been seeking.

Account should here be taken of the deep experiential roots of the family which nurtured and nourished this young life. The paternal grandfather – the Reformed pastor Daniel Schleiermacher – had exhibited pietistic tendencies so intense that they swirled him into an extreme sectarian movement, and eventually caused him to be accused of dabbling in witchcraft and magical practices. In 1749 he fled to Holland to escape prison. His son Gottlieb was a case study in tension 'between the thought of the Enlightenment and orthodox preaching [which] gave his personality some contradictory traits'.[5] Over his entire lifetime, as a gifted intellectual, he devoured with relish the most crucial theological literature of the day. Letters to his son Friedrich continually recommended the works of Kant and other demanding thinkers to the young man. But, because of the problems of excess in the pietism of his father, Gottlieb suppressed the deep pietistic strains within himself, until, late in life, he encountered the Moravians. Although he held fast to his Reformed pastoral affiliation, he entrusted his children to the keeping of Moravian boarding-schools and one of their seminaries, all of which proved to be nearly perfect environments for developing and strengthening their pious feelings.

In later years, long after the tensions of the father had been reincarnated in the son, Friedrich could still say,

> Piety was the mother's womb, in whose sacred darkness my young life was nourished and was prepared for a world still sealed for it. In it my spirit breathed ere it had yet found its own place in knowledge and experience. It helped me as I began to sift the faith of my fathers and to cleanse thought and feeling from the rubbish of antiquity. When the God and the immortality of my childhood vanished from my doubting eyes it remained to me.[6]

He could acknowledge that the seed of piety had already begun to flourish at Gnadenfrei – the place of his first encounter with the Moravians.

Here it was that for the first time I awoke to consciousness of the relations of man to a higher world. . . . Here it was that that mystic tendency developed itself, which has been of so much importance to me, and has supported and carried me through all the storms of scepticism. Then it was only germinating, now it has attained its full development, and I may say, that after all that I have passed through, I have become a Herrnhutter again, only of a higher order.[7]

The tension between, on the one hand, a deep experiential faith rooted in the *sensus numinis* and, on the other, the honest doubt stemming from Enlightenment rationalism is evident in both of these quotations. But the most concise statement of Schleiermacher's doubts, some of which persisted for the rest of his life – and were only intensified by the stringency of Moravian censorship and surveillance – was given in a cataclysmic revelation of the eighteen-year-old to his father:

I cannot believe that he who named himself only the Son of Man was the eternal and true God; I cannot believe that his death was a substitutionary atonement, because he never expressly said so himself, and because I cannot believe it was necessary. God, who has evidently created humankind not for perfection but only for the striving after perfection, cannot possibly wish to punish persons eternally because they have not become perfect.[8]

After numerous painful struggles, gripped on the one side by the *sensus numinis* and on the other by an equally probing doubt, the young Schleiermacher grew to be a mature theologian, who refused to relax either pole of this tension. Rather he formulated and maintained positions which continually played one pole against the other as a check to extremes. After his Moravian period of school and seminary, and his rebellious entry to the Pietist University of Halle, which had also been moved deeply by the Enlightenment spirit, both sides of the tension had been developed to such a degree that they were present in strength in Schleiermacher throughout his life.

Karl Barth attempted to identify this tension in the young Schleiermacher, as he progressed toward maturity as a Christian

theologian, as between the cultural and the theological. In
Barth's view, 'He wanted in all circumstances to be a modern
man as well as a Christian theologian.' But it might be more
accurate to describe the two poles of the tension as the *sensus
numinis* and the critical rationalistic intelligence engendered by
the Enlightenment. Once we have corrected Barth's interpretation of the terms of the tension, however, the quotation serves us
well. For these polar impulses held each other in check. Paul
Tillich helps us to understand the process by which Schleiermacher coped with his theological inheritance:

> Friedrich Schleiermacher, the father of modern Protestant
> theology, was theologically educated within the framework of
> Protestant Orthodoxy. If you read his dogmatics, *The Christian
> Faith*, you will find that he never develops any thought without
> making reference to classical orthodoxy, and finally to the
> Enlightenment criticism of both, before he goes on to state his
> own solution.[9]

These three movements – Protestant scholasticism, Pietism and
the Enlightenment – are, then, the major components of Schleiermacher's religious heritage. It was the tensional dialectic of piety
and responsible doubt that guided him into the highly original
position which we celebrate today.

II   SCHLEIERMACHER AND ROMANTIC MOTIFS

In the decade before the beginning of the nineteenth century,
German Romanticism arose, and a great deal of its energy was
expended in overcoming some of the inadequacies that it saw in
the Enlightenment and in forging a new historical consciousness.
The young Schleiermacher occupied a formative position – both
in shaping and in being shaped by – the new Romantic spirit.
Indeed, during his first sojourn in Berlin (1796–1802), he was
an honoured member of the Romantic circle which convened in
the home of Henriette Herz, cultured wife of a prominent Berlin
physician. Within the circle, he gained the friendship of the
Schlegel brothers and Novalis, and made a few contributions to
the *Athenaeum*, which was the literary 'weapon in the struggle of
the youthful school against the defenders and upholders of the
old order and of rationalism'.[10]

This old order and rationalism was that of the Enlightenment, with its tendencies toward natural, rational and universal concepts of morality and religion. A spirit of tolerance had encouraged freedom of individual religious belief, yet the more dominant emphasis of the Enlightenment upon the orderliness of reason, and the resultant rational uniformity of the religious essence, was coercive of conformity. Conversely, Romanticism extolled individual creativity, the cultivation of the affective nature, and held in reverence the great periods of the past, such as the Middle Ages, in which cultural syntheses had been achieved.

Now these various traits were all synthesised, to one degree or another, in what Raymond Immerwahr, Paul Kluckhohn and others consider to have been the most 'salient characteristic' of German Romanticism: 'the striving to synthesize antinomies, to experience life in terms of polarities that are to be resolved in a higher unity'.[11] This conception of the coincidence of the finite and the infinite had roots as far back as Plato and Plotinus, yet in the form in which it was transmitted to the Romantics it was probably derived from Nicholas of Cusa (1401–64), of the late Middle Ages. Tillich explains this principle:

> His main principle was the *coincidentia oppositorum* (the coincidence of opposites), the coincidence of the finite and the infinite. In everything finite the infinite is present, namely, that power which is the creative unity of the universe as a whole. And in the same way the finite is in the infinite as a potentiality. In the world the divine is developed; in God the world is enveloped.[12]

In a memorable sentence from the *Speeches*, which were published anonymously and were addressed to the 'cultured' among the 'despisers' of religion, the young Schleiermacher wrote, 'Praxis is art; speculation is science; religion is sense and taste for the infinite.'[13] The last part of this quotation is already familiar to us. But now we are able to see a connection between the *sensus numinis* and the coincidence of opposites. In another passage he described religious contemplation *vis-à-vis* the coincidence of the infinite and the finite:

> The contemplation of pious men is only the immediate consciousness of the universal being of all finite things in and

through the eternal. To seek and to find this infinite and eternal factor in all that lives and moves, in all growth and change, in all action and passion, and to have and to know life only in immediate feeling – that is religion. Where this awareness is found, religion is satisfied; where this awareness is hidden, religion experiences frustration and anguish, emptiness and death. And so religion is, indeed, a life in the infinite nature of the whole, in the one and all, in God – a having and possessing of all in God and of God in all.[14]

Now the term 'infinite', as Schleiermacher made clear, was ascribed not 'to the supreme being as the world's originating cause but to the world itself'. The 'infinite', therefore, referred to the totality of the world as the *Naturzusammenhang*, or the coherence of nature. Nevertheless, he added that he left to the critics of this view 'the attempt to conceive of the world as a true "all" and "whole" without God'.[15] Later, in *The Christian Faith*, in his discussion of the divine causality, Schleiermacher examined the relation of God to the *Naturzusammenhang*, and the divine activity was presented as the transcendental conditioning-principle of all created reality. He further suggested that, so far as the religious subject is concerned, neither the world nor God can be imagined apart from one another, nor can they be confused nor equated with one another, since each is encountered by means of its peculiar form of the religious self-consciousness. Since the *Speeches* were written as an apologetic challenge to the intelligentsia of secular culture, Schleiermacher was eager to avoid the excessive use of theological jargon – even and especially the term 'God'. The term did, of course, occur; as Terrence Tice writes, 'When Schleiermacher uses the term "God" here he has prepared the way either by indicating a particular theological context or by serving it up as the term people normally employ for the supreme transcendental object.'[16] The focus of the phrase 'the infinite', therefore, was intentionally neutralised and was ascribed to the *Naturzusammenhang*.

This basic belief of Romanticism in the coincidence of the infinite and the finite held numerous other implications. When the Romantics extended this belief in an explicitly cosmological sense, they claimed to intuit the world as an organic and hierarchical unity:

Organic unity and totality, union and synthesis of component parts into a comprehensive whole having a firm and sure *centrum*: these new hypotheses give the romanticist his authoritative power. They demonstrate how finite man represented in himself the eternal and infinite in a form peculiar to none other than himself.[17]

The world was seen as a hierarchical organism, in which the highest order of being was humanity, since human nature is able to reflect, most faithfully, the infinite ground of everything finite. Within this hierarchical scheme, the State emerged as more than merely a means of political stability; it also was the principle of religio-cultural unity, or 'the unity of all cultural activities'. It should not be surprising, in the light of such an exalted concept of the State, to add that many adherents of Romanticism, including Schleiermacher, were nationalistically inclined.[18]

The words quoted above speak also of individual uniqueness. It is stated that the new hypotheses of Romanticism 'demonstrate how finite man represented in himself the eternal and infinite in a form peculiar to none other than himself'. Thus, the implications of the *coincidentia oppositorum* for the individual self must be brought into focus. One of the impelling motives of Romanticism was the yearning for harmony amid a matrix of antitheses – of finite and infinite, of time and eternity, and so on. Schleiermacher's later Christian writings made repeated reference to the several antithetical elements that were a part of this theological system – especially the pivotal antithesis of sin and grace. In this early period, each of the Romantics aspired to establish within himself a *centrum*, or locus, in which all antitheses were resolved and harmony was achieved. Nevertheless, in view of the aridity of much Enlightenment rationalism and because of the seriousness with which the Romantics viewed Kant's negative conclusions concerning the scope and limits of possible human knowledge, there was a widespread disillusionment with philosophy – and even more so with theology – so that some new medium had to be sought for the expression of the *coincidentia oppositorum*. At the base of this disillusionment was a concept of 'irony', which was particularly associated with the thought of Friedrich Schlegel. Here was the 'in spite of' element in Romanticism. In other words, the concept of irony meant for the Romantics 'that the infinite is superior to any finite concretion and drives beyond to another concretion'.[19] In spite of the inadequacy of the finite, the romantics felt driven to discover both their own individual uniqueness and the medium that would be most appropriate to its expression.

Individual creativity was appreciated and encouraged to the point of the recognition of genius and virtuosity, but what was especially significant was the *vocation* that now emerged for the Romantic, stemming from the disillusionment with philosophy and theology. A new medium of vocation was discovered in the area of culture that addressed most directly the affectional nature of man – the arts. Of special importance was poetry as an artistic medium:

> The conception that poetry is absolute reality, that it is equal to truth, not only pointed to a philosophic conviction beyond mere things, that beyond the phenomena of the empiric world lay the true world, but actually recognized in poetry a means of grasping the absolute. Here the infinite became finite; here the absolute became experience.[20]

The poet brought the absolute into experience, and, by virtue of his role as master of the medium of poetry, 'the artist becomes a mediator'.

As Schleiermacher charged in the opening chapter of the *Speeches*, it was a foregone conclusion to the 'cultured despisers' of religion that traditional religion had run its course. Thus no concept of religion then known could have hoped to be acceptable to the beautiful people of the mind, as a medium for their vocation. But, if conventional religion was at its lowest ebb, the arts were about to reach their crest. Could it be, then, Novalis and Friedrich Schlegel asked each other in letters, that a new religion might be developed through some medium of the arts? The challenge seemed irresistible. Schlegel would hope, through his 'universal poetry', to produce an aesthetic–esoteric religion of humanity and thereby would lift the human spirit, on the wings of art, above this world to the infinite.

Schleiermacher's primary vocation, however, was not to be the reinvigoration of conventional religion, nor the creation of a new religion through the arts, but rather to recover religious vitality through the rediscovery of the *sensus numinis*. Once he had experienced religion in its fullest and purest intensity, he was able to break away from traditional forms and concepts of religious expression – even such basic ones as 'God' and 'immortality'. In so far as these two terms were useful at all to the author of the *Speeches*, they were the products of the creative power of fantasy (*Phantasie* or *Fantasie*, sometimes translated as 'imagination') rather than the vestiges of the tradition that had weighed down the religious spirit with its 'dead letters'. As Blackwell has shown, the Romantics persuaded Schleiermacher to reconsider fantasy – which he had previously dismissed because he had equated it with the idea of the dominance of the youthful imagination over the rational side of life – as a means of enfleshing the experiences that had come to him through the *sensus numinis*. In Schlegel's words, 'Fantasy is the organ of men for the deity.'[21] Now fantasy, in this new understanding, came to be Schleiermacher's means of achieving theological *poiēsis*, not by producing poetic verse but by the power of fantasy to give rise to knowledge, through the power of association that it afforded for the experiences which were conveyed to him through the *sensus numinis*. Thus, it was through association that fantasy was able to *create* (poetise) a cohesive picture of the Whole, by giving form and shape to the data contributed by the *sensus numinis*.

While grateful to fellow Romantics for helping him to realise the positive possibilities of fantasy, Schleiermacher was ultimately unable to share their hope that the religion which they were attempting to create would lift humanity *above* the empirical world to union with the infinite. His was rather, in the apt phrase of Michael Ryan, a 'phenomenology of the finite spirit'.[22] True to his grounding in the phenomenal world of Kant's first *Critique*, Schleiermacher was convinced that any intimations of the infinite that lay within the limits of human perception must be mediated through the finite. Anything that promised more than this would be a chimera.

With this understanding in mind, Schleiermacher wrote, from inside the ranks of the Romantics (but never uncritically so), of the cultivation of individual creativity as a *way of devotion*. The element that he wanted to add was that the devotion ought to be *religious*. Nor did he have in mind an isolated individualism. As he made clear in his *Christmas Eve: Dialogue on the Incarnation*, he conceived of true individuality as stemming from a social and dialogical context. The truth emerged for him through dialogical encounter. Individuals, therefore, would be able to qualify and complement each other; the contribution of each individual carried infinite worth. Thus, in the words of Walzel,

> That which is individual is likewise infinite; it is the expression and reflection of infinity. Individuality in the highest sense, human individuality, springs from the union of the infinite and the finite. But in each individuality only those faculties are potential which determine the nature of humanity; hence each human being is a compendium of humanity itself. And when a man has found infinity within himself religion is achieved.[23]

As Schleiermacher addressed his fellow Romantics, his peculiar aim was to make clear that the way of devotion through individual creativity could indeed be devotion to *religion*, as the most faithful reflection of the ground of infinity, and not merely dedication to an ideal of art or culture (as admirable and as valuable as that may be, in itself).

One of the most striking expressions of the *coincidentia oppositorum* was the Romantic glorification of women and the exaltation of a creative androgynous tension in both sexes:

> the romantics rejected the notion that sexual difference defines individuality. Rather, they argued that as a person becomes an individual microcosm of reality, he or she becomes more and more androgynous. Someone who is only male or only female is not whole. To become whole, we must become both male and female, and to the extent that we do so we become more individual.[24]

It was obvious to the Romantics that their society was dominated by male values and that women were, for the most part, repressed, so that the dynamic of neither sex was able to make an imprint on the other. A part of the Romantic programme of reform, then, was an attempt to redress the balance. Woman, in her putative affinity for intuition, feeling and devotion to spiritual values, was perceived to be the model for the growth toward wholeness of her more coldly objective and rationalistically determined masculine counterpart.

Here was a polemical and rhetorical resort to the power of the feminine for the purpose of resurrecting and transfiguring the human spirit (male *and* female), which would have been a *skandalon* to the dry, Enlightenment rationalists. In championing the rights of women, the young Schleiermacher was doing as he was to do so many other times in his career. He was intentionally counteracting one imbalance – in this case, the rationalism of the Enlightenment – with an emphasis from the opposite direction which, by comparison with the predominant motifs of his day, could only be characterised as 'feminine'.

In Schleiermacher's case, the glorification of women was not merely the result of romantic idealisation but stemmed from several sources, one of which predated his entry into Romanticism. First of all, from his earliest days he had held some women in exceptionally high esteem, beginning with his admirable mother and an older sister, with whom he corresponded and counselled over a lifetime. On a later occasion he spoke of a young woman in whose home he had served as a tutor. This beautiful young woman, for whom he had held a secret love, died aged twenty-seven. Shortly after hearing this sad news he wrote, 'My sense for womanhood was first awakened in the Dohnas' domestic circle. The credit for this Friederike has carried with her into eternity. . . . Only through knowledge of the feminine mind and heart have I gained a knowledge of true human worth.'[25] Secondly, over his entire lifetime Schleiermacher shared his most important and original ideas with women. It should be noted that, of the four persons with whom he discussed the ideas leading to the writing of the *Speeches*, two were women (Henriette Herz and Dorothea Veit) associated with the Romantic circle (the other two being F. S. G. Sack, his ecclesiastical superior, and Friedrich Schlegel). Schleiermacher would surely have said that his esteem for women was based on cold, empirical observation of the gifted women he saw around him every day. The most famous woman in the Romantic circle was Henriette Herz, followed closely by Dorothea Veit and Rahel Levin. In addition to her other intellectual gifts, Henriette 'had command of eight languages and studied Sanskrit and Turkish'.[26] Such a woman was eminently worthy to be the intellectual partner of any man! It is only necessary to add that, in Schleiermacher's view, the intuitive nature of women made them virtually perfect vessels of the *sensus numinis*, and thus, ideal teachers of religious experience to men.

III RELIGION, RECEPTIVITY AND THE *SENSUS NUMINIS*

When Schleiermacher attempted to co-ordinate his thoughts concerning the nature of religion as an independent aspect of human experience, he reused three definitions, 'each having exactly the same weight'. First, religion is a 'sense and taste for the infinite'. Secondly, it is the means through which 'the universal being of all finite things in the infinite' grows and thrives within the believer. He pulled the two definitions together in the following way:

> Now sense may be the capacity either for perception [*Wahr-nehmungsvermögen*] or for receptiveness [*Empfindungsvermögen*]. In this spot it is the latter . . . . Whatever I perceive or receive, however, I must imagine [*einbilden*], and this imagining is what I call the life of the object within me. Now by the term 'infinite' I here mean not an indeterminate something but the infinitude of being in general. We cannot know this infinite immediately and in itself alone; we can know it only by finite means. In this way our inclination to posit a world and to inquire about it leads us from the individual details to the all, from the parts to the whole. Accordingly, the sense for the infinite is one and the same thing as the 'immediate life' of the finite within us as it is in the infinite.[27]

In the first expression, he suggested, 'add "taste" to "sense"'; in the second, 'make "the universal being of all finite things" explicit'. From the diverse strands of Schleiermacher's discussion of these two expressions, Tice offered a composite definition of religion:

> Religion is, from the viewpoint of one's imaginative reception of the infinite, what might be called 'sense and taste for the infinite'; or, from the viewpoint of what it is that one receives, 'the immediate life of the being of all finite things within us as it is in the infinite'.[28]

A third definition of religion, concerning 'the contemplation of pious men', has already been quoted. This 'contemplation' was, for Schleiermacher, a total openness of vision and spirit; for him it was, 'indeed, a life in the infinite nature of the whole, in the one and all, in God – a having and possessing of all in God and of God in all'.[29] He has here attempted to acknowledge a belief in God as the essential ground for the Universum, without importing into the God concept many of the traditional metaphysical and moral confusions that had undermined religion. At the end of the second speech, he redefined the concepts of God and immortality, in order to carry his new understanding of religion forward. He pointed out, among other things, that the *concept* of God was a result of the operations of God upon persons, in piety, and that immortality ought to be purified of the traditional interpretation, as the desire for individual survival beyond the grave, and recognised as the present reality that it is, as a person's grounding in the infinite.[30]

We can now consider the two terms which come the closest to a description of the essence of religion for Schleiermacher. They are *Anschauung* ('intuition', or, as Tice renders it, 'perspectivity') and *Gefühl* ('feeling'), and they were frequently conjoined in the second speech, on the essence of religion, in the original edition of 1799:

Finally, in order to fill out the general picture of religion I remind you that every perspective [*Anschauung*] is naturally bound together with some feeling [*Gefühl*]. Your organs mediate the connection between the object and yourselves. To reveal its existence to you that same influx of the object must arouse those organs in various ways and occasion a change in your inner consciousness. The resultant feeling, which you have probably often scarcely been aware of, can in some cases grow to such strength that you forget the object and even yourselves . . . .[31]

This experience can so completely dominate the self that it may, for the moment, impede the development of other emotional impressions. Yet his audience of cultured despisers would not, as Schleiermacher believed, simply attribute such force to the operation 'of external objects'.

You would agree, then, that that action within you lies far beyond the power of even the strongest feeling and must therefore have quite a different source within you. So it is with religion. . . . If you gain perspective on [the universe], then you must necessarily be gripped by various feelings. Except that in religion it is another and firmer relation between perspectivity and feeling which obtains, so that one's perspective is never so preponderant that feeling is virtually dissolved. . . . So it is that the special way in which the universe presents itself to you in your gaining of perspective makes up the distinctive character of your own individual religion, and likewise the strength of the corresponding feelings determines the degree of your religiosity.[32]

Anschauung and *Gefühl*, therefore, are bound together in an essential mutuality of operation:

Perspectivity without feeling is nothing and can have neither the right origination nor the right force. Feeling without perspectivity is also nothing. Both can only exist because and insofar as they are fundamentally one and undivided.[33]

When perspectivity and feeling mutually inform and qualify each other, religion emerges as a phenomenon of human experience.

Twenty years after the appearance of the *Speeches*, Schleiermacher produced his *magnum opus* of dogmatics, *The Christian Faith*. In that work, the initial problem was how the *sensus numinis* was to determine the method and content of theology in a distinctively Christian way. In his concept of religion, now defined as 'the consciousness of being absolutely dependent, or which is the same thing, of being in relation to God', Schleiermacher discovered 'the common element in all howsoever diverse expressions of piety, by which these are conjointly distinguished from all other feelings'.[34] The integrity of this form of consciousness, this 'modification of feeling or of immediate self-consciousness', was upheld in that it was said to be 'neither a Knowing nor a Doing', but is related to and also differentiated from both of these in a common ground that is not to be construed 'as a co-ordinate third or fourth entity'.[35] In discussing feeling, Schleiermacher explained that in the rhythm of life the subject consistently alternated between a receptivity and an activity – 'between an abiding-in-self [*Insichbleiben*] and a passing-beyond-self [*Aussich-heraustreten*]'.[36] Now, in contrast both to knowing (as epistemo-logical process) and to doing, feeling is a receptivity, and hence an abiding-in-self: thus 'the unity of these is not one of the two or three themselves. . . . The unity rather is the essence of the subject itself, which manifests itself in these severally distinct forms, and is, to give it a name, which in this particular connexion is permissible, their common foundation'. Within the experi-ence of self-consciousness, the self is always necessarily related to an 'Other' in 'reciprocity' – sometimes acting upon the latter in freedom, sometimes receiving the action of the other in depen-dence. But Schleiermacher regarded receptivity as always prior and 'primary', in order for the subject to take into itself direc-tional orientation and stimulation from the other. Moreover, an important distinction was to be maintained between the relation of the self to the other, as *reciprocity*, and the relation of the self to God, as *receptivity*.

For, by definition, the self's feeling of absolute dependence would have to preclude the consciousness of any incompleteness on the part of God, such that the self could either initiate or contribute anything that would add to the wellbeing of the Deity. Hence, in the feeling of absolute dependence, God is not to be *objectified* as the Other – neither as 'the world' nor as 'any single part' thereof, but is to be recognised as the '*Whence*' (*Woher*) of the subject – object relationship. This assertion meant that 'the *Whence* of our receptive and active existence, as implied in this self-consciousness, is to be designated by the word "God", and that this is for us the really original significa-tion of that word'.[37] The problem of the possible content of the word 'God' was at once posed, to which Schleiermacher replied that beyond its primary signification as 'that which is the co-determinant in this feeling and to which we trace our being in such a state',[38] the term can have no 'further content' which is not 'evolved out of this fundamental import assigned to it'.[39] Such a state of affairs threw dogmatics back into the one sphere in which Schleiermacher saw the possibility of a content: *Glaubens-lehre*, or faith's exposition of its own self-consciousness.

In *The Christian Faith*, 'receptivity' is Schleiermacher's term for the divinely created disposition toward feeling, or the *sensus numinis*, in Christian believers, and also, in its ultimate application, the basis for the conjunction of the divine and human natures in the Incarnation of the Redeemer. This concept, therefore, is of immeasurable help in explaining the basis, within human nature, for religious experience. As Schleiermacher saw it, receptivity was the vital 'link' between human nature prior to the Incarnation of the Redeemer and the basis for what happens in, through and after his appearance.

> we posit, on the one side, an initial divine activity which is supernatural, but at the same time a vital human receptivity [*eine lebendige menschliche Empfänglichkeit*] in virtue of which alone that supernatural can become a natural fact of history. This is the link which connects the corporate life before the appearance of the Redeemer with that which exists in the fellowship with the Redeemer, so as adequately to bring out the identity of human nature in both.[40]

As an expression of the divine good-pleasure, the implanting of the original disposition of receptivity was an *eternal* act. In the resultant evolution of the *sensus numinis*, through the cultivation of this receptivity, the religious propensity of the human race grew, until, as a *temporal* act of this ascending human nature, the Redeemer appeared in the person of Jesus of Nazareth. In the Redeemer, then, the 'supernatural [became the] natural'. The reason for the supernatural stimulus in the origin of the Redeemer was that he had to be freed from the initial corrupting influences of 'the corporate life of sinfulness', in which 'sin propagates itself naturally, so that an unhindered potency of the God-consciousness in Jesus cannot be understood simply as a product of that life'. But, once the Redeemer appeared, and founded his redemptive community, the new creation which was supernaturally initiated in him 'can become a natural fact of history'. The redemption which Christ achieved was 'supra rational' only in the sense that it was not 'explicable by means of the reason which dwells equally in all other men',[41] or else they also would have been able to bring about the redemption which Christ uniquely achieved. It was the same receptivity which then gave believers the power to appropriate this redemptive power and to propagate it in the Church, by preserving the impression of the sinless perfection of the Redeemer. This vital human receptivity, then, was the basis, in human nature, for authentic religious experience, as Schleiermacher understood it.

IV   IN BUT NOT OF ROMANTICISM

The question of Schleiermacher's relation to Romanticism must now be addressed. Explanations of this relation are numerous, and more often than not Schleiermacher has been caught between two extreme positions – that of the avid friends and that of the sometimes almost rabid foes of Romanticism. Friends of the Romantics might commend him for making a noble effort to be a part of this movement, but most of them would conclude that he did not go nearly far enough. Conversely, to the foes of the movement – most of whom were representatives of the traditional religion that the Romantics rejected and that Schleiermacher severely criticised – even the slightest resemblance of his thought to Romanticism, or reliance upon its language and concepts, was too much. Neither extreme properly elucidates Schleiermacher's position.

Statements of two critics are moderate and helpful assessments. For H. L. Friess, 'two salient facts' distinguished Schleiermacher from other Romantics:

> In the first place, he was a preacher by profession, whereas most of the others inclined to identify religion, especially the church, with the old order and its cultural limitations. In the second place, he had no marked literary gift, while the essential medium of the group's activity was literary.[42]

There is some truth in each of these judgements, although there must have been deeper roots in Schleiermacher than a sense of clerical vocation. A statement by M. Redeker is also helpful:

> In the encounter with his romantic friends he participated in their cultural world and used their language. But he ultimately did not succumb to the temptations of romantic fantasy and sentimentality, of their originality and sentimentality [*Empfindsamkeit*], because his decisive religious and theological conceptions were not rooted in romanticism . . . the novelty of

his piety and the systematic development of his ideas are discernible already prior to his Berlin period. . . . His systematic work in theology and philosophy soon led him beyond romanticism. Scholarship became for him much more than speculative play with ideas and concepts; it became the serious service on behalf of truth for the overcoming of fanaticism and empty scepticism.[43]

Redeker acknowledged that he had been strongly influenced by the opinion of Dilthey, who wrote, 'Like every genius he [Schleiermacher] was lonely in their midst and yet needed them. . . . He lived among them as a sober man among dreamers.'[44]

Although more helpful, these assessments are still too general. While making no pretence of exhausting the subject, I shall draw some conclusions which I hope will shed some more light on the relation. Perhaps there was a parallel of sorts between Schleiermacher's experience within, and his later alienation from, the Moravian community. Although circumstances forced him to sever his tie with the community, we have already noted his acknowledgement that piety had been his 'motherly womb', and that he later came to think of himself as 'a Herrnhutter again, only of a higher order'. His removal from the Romantic circle was neither as painful nor as complete as the severance from Moravian fellowship, yet it might be that the influence of Romanticism on the shaping of the substance of his system of Christian theology – particularly the utilisation of the pivotal *antithesis* of sin and grace and of the *coincidentia oppositorum* in his trinitarian doctrine of God – would warrant a description of him as a 'Berlin *Romantiker* again, only of a higher order'.

The factor which ultimately formed the difference, I suggest, was the very same conjunction of opposing forces that had been at work in him from the age of eleven – existential doubt apprehended through the *sensus numinis* and responsible doubt. We have seen that in his adult years 'he wanted in all circumstances to be a modern man as well as a Christian theologian'. These words express the form in which this dialectic grew in Schleiermacher's adult years. The two poles served as mutually conditioning factors, each restraining the other from pathological excess. Thus, critical intelligence restrained the *sensus numinis* from sweeping Schleiermacher into the same emotional vortex which had claimed his grandfather, while the *sensus numinis* pricked and quickened his rational side until he refused to settle for the arid solutions of scholasticism and the Enlightenment to the theological problems that troubled him in his day. It might be said, then, that on the basis of tensional dialectic he was 'fully in but never fully of Romanticism'.

In closing, here are some contrasts between Schleiermacher and the Romantics. First, he was unable fully to share the disdain tht the Romantics tended to feel toward religion. He could not agree that an entirely new religion needed to be created from the ground up. What was required was rather a recovery of the *sensus numinis* – the resuscitation of the spirit of religion which had almost been suffocated by the overlaying of the 'dead letter'. Second, the fluid and broadly inclusive Church community for which he pleaded in the *Speeches* and worked so energetically in later life was a far cry, indeed, from the Roman hierarchical bureaucracy to which Schlegel was eventually converted. Third, and closely connected to the second point, Schleiermacher was unable to ground religion on the authority of the past. The basis was that in feeling God is given to the subject 'in an original way'. Fourth, whereas the new religion to which Novalis and Schlegel had aspired was to have been aesthetic, esoteric and otherworldly, Schleiermacher's phenomenology of finite spirit utilised the *sensus numinis* to apprehend the infinite through the finite media of this world.

Schleiermacher's answers obviously cannot be the answers for the situation in which we live. Yet the questions which moved him the most are perennial ones, and his proposed solutions may still serve as a catalyst toward our own rediscovery of the *sensus numinis*, in the form that speaks most directly to us. If such should prove to be the case, then he truly will be aknowledged as 'a prophet–citizen of a later world'!

NOTES

1. H. L. Friess, Introduction to *Schleiermacher's Soliloquies*, tr. H. L. Friess (Chicago, 1957) p. 62.
2. K. Barth, *Protestant Thought: From Rousseau to Ritschl*, tr. B. Cozens, H. H. Hartwell and the editorial staff of the SCM Press (New York, 1959) p. 314.
3. R. Otto, *Religious Essays: A Supplement to 'The Idea of the Holy'*, tr. B. Lunn (Oxford, 1931) p. 68.

4. R. F. Streetman, 'Divination: Aesthetic and Religious Intimations of Otto's Numinous in English Language, Literature and Poetry', in *Papers of the Nineteenth-Century Theology Working Group: AAR 1982 Annual Meeting*, ed. M. C. Massey and G. Green (Berkeley, Calif., 1982) p. 94.

5. M. Redeker, *Schleiermacher: Life and Thought*, tr. J. Wallhausser (Philadelphia, 1973) p. 8.

6. Schleiermacher, *On Religion: Speeches to its Cultured Despisers*, tr. J. Oman (New York, 1958) p. 9.

7. Schleiermacher, *The Life of Schleiermacher as Unfolded in his Autobiography and Letters*, tr. F. Rowan, 2 vols, (London, 1860) I, 283f.

8. A. L. Blackwell, *Schleiermacher's Early Philosophy of Life: Determinism, Freedom, and Fantasy* (Chico, Calif. 1982) p. 7.

9. P. Tillich, *Perspectives on Nineteenth and Twentieth-Century Protestant Theology*, ed. C. E. Braaten (New York, 1967) pp. 11–12.

10. R. Otto, Introduction to Schleiermacher, *On Religion*, pp. xiv–xv.

11. R. Immerwahr, 'The Word *Romantisch* and its History', in *The Romantic Period in Germany: Essays by Members of the London University Institute of Germanic Studies*, ed. S. Prawer (New York, 1970) p. 34 and n. 1.

12. Tillich, *Perspectives*, p. 77.

13. *Friedrich Schleiermachers Reden über die Religion*, Kritische Ausgabe, ed. G. C. B. Pünjer (Brunswick, 1879) p. 49.

14. Schleiermacher, *On Religion: Addresses in Response to its Cultured Critics*, tr. T. N. Tice (Richmond, Va., 1969) p. 79.

15. Ibid., p. 159 n. 2.

16. Ibid., p. 22.

17. O. Walzel, *German Romanticism*, tr. A. E. Lussky (New York, 1932) p. 75.

18. See J. F. Dawson, *Friedrich Schleiermacher: The Birth of a Nationalist* (Austin, Texas, 1966); cf. Tillich, *Perspectives*, pp. 86f.

19. Ibid., p. 89; cf. Walzel, *German Romanticism*, pp. 41–6; and J. Forstman, *A Romantic Triangle: Schleiermacher and Early German Romanticism* (Missoula, Mont., 1977) chs. 1, 2.

20. Walzel, *German Romanticism*, pp. 28, 74.

21. F. Schlegel, *Anthenaeum*, in Forstman, *A Romantic Triangle*, p. 25; cf. Blackwell, *Schleiermacher's Early Philosophy of Life*, pp. 2.2–2.8.

22. J. D. Ryan, 'Response and Discussion', in *Schleiermacher as Contemporary*, ed. R. W. Funk (New York, 1970) pp. 211f.

23. Walzel, *German Romanticism*, p. 50.

24. *Women and Religion: A Feminist Sourcebook of Christian Thought*, ed. E. Clark and H. W. Richardson (New York, 1977) p. 174.

25. Blackwell, *Schleiermacher's Early Philosophy of Life*, quoted from the caption under the portrait of Gräfin Friederike Dohna, Figure G, after p. 148.

26. J. King, 'Schleiermacher's Catechism for Noble Women', *Hibbert Journal*, XXVI, no. 4 (July 1928) 710.
27. Schleiermacher, *On Religion*, tr. Tice, p. 158 n. 2.
28. Ibid., p. 159.
29. Ibid.
30. Ibid., pp. 147–9, 154–6.
31. Ibid., p. 355 n. 46; cf. Schleiermacher, *Reden über die Religion*, ed. Pünjer, pp. 69–70.
32. Schleiermacher, *On Religion*, tr. Tice, p. 355 n. 46.
33. Ibid., p. 356 n. 46.
34. Schleiermacher, *The Christian Faith*, tr. H. R. Mackintosh and J. S. Stewart (Edinburgh, 1928) no. 4, p. 12.
35. Ibid., no. 3, pp. 6, 8.
36. Ibid., p. 8.
37. Ibid., p. 16.
38. Ibid., p. 17.
39. Ibid.
40. Ibid., p. 365.
41. Ibid., p. 64.
42. Friess, Introduction to *Schleiermacher's Soliloquies*, pp. xxxviii–xxxix.
43. Redeker, *Schleiermacher: Life and Thought*, pp. 63f.
44. W. Dilthey, *Leben Schleiermachers*, I (Berlin, 1870) 260, 439; tr. and quoted in Redeker, *Schleiermacher: Life and Thought*, pp. 62f.

8 On Reading Nature as a Romantic

STEPHEN PRICKETT

I want to start with some quotations from the most popular poet of the Romantic era. I refer, of course, to John Keble, whose best-selling volume, *The Christian Year*, appeared in 1827 and was to sell an average of 10,000 copies a year for the next fifty years – a figure which makes even Byron's instant success pale by comparison. The theme is one common enough in Natural Theology over the preceding 500 years, but, as so often in the history of ideas, in its waning moments it was to attain in Keble's verse an explicitness rarely achieved before:

> There is a book who runs may read,
> Which heavenly truth imparts,
> And all the lore its scholars need,
> Pure eyes and Christian hearts.[1]

The 'book', of course, is the 'book of nature'. Earlier, in a more self-doubting mood he had confessed:

> Mine eye unworthy seems to read
> One page of Nature's beauteous book;
> It lies before me, fair outspread –
> I only cast a wishful look.[2]

Keble was not given to originality – indeed, solemnly advised his students against it – and in view of his reputation as a self-confessed Wordsworthian it would be easy to find in these, and other similar verses, direct echoes of Wordsworth. But in fact, of course, Wordsworth rarely, if ever, conflates 'nature'

126

with 'books' or 'language', preferring usually to contrast them.[3] Nor is Keble's Neoplatonism, with its detailed, almost medievally elaborated system of 'correspondences' particularly close to Wordsworth's theory of the imagination. Nevertheless Keble's image bears what might be called a 'family resemblance', in that it belongs to a whole cluster of such literary and linguistic metaphors of the period, describing the relationship between man and his environment in terms not of law, or even of harmony, but of *communication*. Metaphors from the music of the spheres or Newtonian mathematics were here replaced by those of publishing and even of speech.

Take, for instance, the following passage from a book by an American, Sampson Reed, published in 1826 – the year before *The Christian Year*:

> There is a language, not of words, but of things. When this language shall have been made apparent, that which is human will have answered its end; and being as it were resolved into its original elements, will lose itself in nature. The use of language is the expression of our feelings and desires – the manifestation of the mind. But everything which is, is full of the expression of that use for which it is designed, as of its own existence. If we did but understand its language, what could our words add to its meaning? It is because we are unwilling to hear, that we find it necessary to say so much; and we drown the voice of nature with the discordant jargon of ten thousand dialects. . . . Everything which surrounds us is full of the utterance of one word, completely expressive of its nature. This word is its name: for God, even now, could we but see it, is creating all things and giving a name to every work of his love, in its perfect adaptation to that for which it is designed.[4]

Though Reed was a Swedenborgian mystic, we should, even without his Wordsworthian title, *Observations of the Growth of the Mind*, have little difficulty in recognising the family resemblance to a sonnet by the Jesuit Gerard Manley Hopkins:

> Each mortal thing does one thing and the same:
> Deals out that being indoors each one dwells;
> Selves – goes itself; *myself* it speaks and spells,
> Crying *What I do is me: for that I came.*

For Reed, and even, it seems, for Hopkins, the analogy is scarcely a metaphor in the normal sense: language is, rather, perceived as an imperfect human surrogate for a system of communication divinely inherent in the natural order of things. Now, there is nothing particularly new about this 'imperfect surrogate' argument: it had been used with variations, religious or secular according to taste, by authorities as different in outlook as Augustine and Locke; what seems to be different about the Romantic use of this metaphor is the concept of *language* involved. Coleridge, as so often, is explicit where others are implicit.

> Even so it is in the language of man and of nature. The sound, *sun*, or the figures, S, U, N, are pure arbitrary modes of recalling the object, and for visual mere objects not only sufficient, but have infinite advantages from their very nothingness *per se*. But the language of nature is a subordinate *Logos*, that was in the beginning, and was with the thing it represented, and it was the thing represented.[5]

Here the alternative of natural religion to revelation as a source of religious insight is spelled out with a force unequalled since the medieval synthesis: 'nature' is nothing less than 'a subordinate *Logos*': the divine Word of God in creation, described in an echo of the opening words of John's Gospel.

We shall return to the *Logos*; what interests me here is not the divine language of nature, but the 'arbitrary' language of man as Coleridge describes it. Coleridge's theory of language seems to have been in a process of constant evolution and development throughout his life. We can nevertheless without much difficulty discern certain clearly defined stages in that development. From Hartley, Coleridge had inherited along with an empiricist theory of mind a corresponding theory of language. Words corresponded to 'things' – intially to material objects and their motions, but at greater levels of complexity and abstraction to thoughts – both alike mediated by little vibrations (or 'vibratiuncles') to the 'fibres of the brain' in the form of 'ideas', in the narrow empiricist sense of that word, as the basic building-blocks of thought.[6] Thus, though there may not necessarily be a one-for-one correspondence between 'words' and 'ideas', words are composed of 'ideas' in much the same way as complex molecules are composed of simpler atoms in modern chemical theory. On the precise details of this process Hartley is cautiously vague:

> And it happens in most Cases, that the decomplex [i.e. highly complex[7]] idea belonging to any sentence, is not compounded merely of the complex Ideas belonging to the Words of it; but that there are also many Variations, some Oppositions, and numberless Additions.[8]

Like most of his age,[9] Hartley is less interested in the nature of language than he is in its epistemological and psychological implications. As a result he tends to take the existence of language *per se* very much for granted. This is even more apparent when he comes to consider the relation of words to ideas – a relationship almost like that of bees to the flowers they pollinate:

> Since Words thus collect Ideas from various Quarters, unite them together, and transfer them both upon other Words, and upon foreign objects, it is evident, that the Use of Words adds much to the number and Complexness of our Ideas, and it is the principal means by which we make our intellectual and moral Improvements.[10]

What appealed to Coleridge about Hartley, of course, was not his empiricist framework but his claim to give a satisfactory and scientifically plausible account of the growth of the mind. Once that was no longer tenable, the accompanying empiricist assumptions about language were exposed. On 22 September 1800 we find Coleridge writing to Godwin,

> I wish you to write a book on the power of words, and the processes by which human feelings form affinities with them – in short, I wish you to *philosophize* Horn Tooke's System, and to solve the great Questions – whether there be reason to hold, that an action bearing all the *semblance* of pre-designing Consciousness may yet be simply organic, & whether a *series* of such actions are possible – and close on the heels of this question would follow the old 'Is Logic the *Essence* of Thinking?' in other words – Is *thinking* impossible without arbitrary signs? & – how far is the word 'arbitrary' a misnomer? Are

> not words etc parts & germinations of the Plant? And what is
> the Law of their Growth? – In something of this order I would
> endeavour to destroy the old antithesis of *Words & Things*,
> elevating, as it were, words into Things; & living Things too.
> All the nonsense of vibrations etc you would of course
> dismiss. (*CL*, I, 625–6)

As Coleridge's friends rapidly learned, the statement 'I wish you
to write a book on . . .' invariably meant that their correspondent was himself carried away by a new idea for a book. The
latter part of this passage is often quoted in isolation as evidence
for Coleridge's new-found organic conception of language and
his rejection of Hartley. What is omitted by so doing is the
opening reference to 'Horn [*sic*] Tooke's System'. Yet, taken as a
whole, what the passage suggests is that the rejection of the
Hartleian 'nonsense of vibrations' is in some way connected with
Coleridge's new-found enthusiasm for Horne Tooke – an impression reinforced by other favourable references to Tooke at
this time which contrast sharply with earlier disparaging remarks on his political activities (see, for instance, *CL*, I, 494 and
559–60).

The work of John Horne Tooke's that had so transformed
Coleridge's opinion of him was entitled *Epea Pteroenta*, or, more
colloquially, *The Diversions of Purley*. In it Tooke focuses on the
very problem of the relationship between words and thought
that we noticed in Hartley. In his *Essay Concerning Human Understanding* Locke had claimed that 'if we could trace them to their
sources, we should find, in all languages, the names which stand
for things that fall now under our senses to have had their first
rise from sensible Ideas'.[11] Tooke takes up Locke's challenge
simply by cutting the Gordian knot. Locke's *Essay*, he argues, is
not about human thought at all, but human *language*. 'In fact' –
a phrase which Tooke redefines by a masterpiece of tactical
definition to mean 'etymologically' – there *are* no abstract ideas
as Locke (and Hartley) had believed, because there are *no*
abstract terms. The 'real' meaning of a word is neither more or
less than its etymological root – which never changes. Thus, at a
stroke, the empiricist process by which complex and abstract
ideas are built up from the building-blocks of simple ones is
rendered unnecessary: we are left only with simple ideas, which

it is the task of etymology to expose, and so prevent our deception by what he called 'abbreviations'. Thus,

> CHANCE ('High Arbiter' as Milton calls him) and his twin-brother ACCIDENT, are merely the participles of *Escheoir*, *Cheor*, and *Cadere*. And that is to say – 'it befell me by CHANCE, or by ACCIDENT' – is absurdly saying – 'It befell by falling.'[12]

This reduction of language to the simple units of which, 'in fact', it was etymologically composed had the dual advantage of eliminating some of the more hazy parts of empiricist linguistics, and, at the same time, reducing most parts of speech to nouns. Tooke's 'discovery' and his etymological 'proofs' were to dominate sections of English philology for almost fifty years, and to earn the approval of such men as Noah Webster, James Mill, Hazlitt and Archbishop Trench,[13] and the project of creating a true etymological dictionary on Tooke's principles was taken up by a number of lexicographers.[14] Yet, even given this chorus of approbation, it is a little hard to see why Coleridge, of all people, with his strong sense of the complexity of human mental processes, should have been so taken by an essentially *reductionist* programme, and have found in it a liberation from the doctrines of Hartleian mechanism.

As late as 1809 we find an entry in his notebooks which, though it does not mention Tooke by name, is a classic example of the Tookean method in action – and, once again, the target is Hartley.

> it will be my business to set forth an orderly proof, that Atheism is the necessary Consequence or Corollary of the Hartleian Theory of the Will conjoined with his Theory of Thought & Action in general – Words as distinguished from mere pulses of Air in the auditory nerve must correspond to Thoughts, and Thoughts is but the verb – substantive Participle Preterite of *Thing* (So in Latin/Res, a *thing* – reor, I *think* – and observe the passive termination of the verb, which is a verb middle or deponent, i.e. an active–passive – an action upon a passive. *Res* = thing: res in praesenti = thinking, i.e. thinging or thing out of me = a thing in me – it is a

> thing-thing – *reata*,[15] res preterita, a thought – a thing representative of what was but is not present – thought is the past participle of thing – a thing acts on me but not on me as purely passive, which is the case in all *affection*, affectus, but res agit in co-agentem[16] – in the first I am *thinged*, in the latter I thing or think – Rem reor – reatam rursus reor.[17] If therefore we have no will, what is the meaning of the word? It is a word without a Thought – or else a Thought without a Thing, which is a blank contradiction. . . .   (*CN*, III, 3587)

It is difficult to gauge the exact tone of these jottings but the suspicion occurs that this parade of Tookean pseudoerudition is ironic. Even at the time he was first reading Tooke, Coleridge had commented impatiently on his 'charletannery' (*sic*) that 'makes such a mystery & difficulty out of plain palpable things' (*CL*, I, 559) and his irritation did not diminish with time. In later life he came to reject Tooke entirely.[18] Yet, for all his impatience with Tooke's manner and pretensions, there is no doubt that for a few years around and after 1800 Tooke performed a service of great value to Coleridge. He awakened him, as never before, to the science of etymology.

Tooke believed that he had shown the stable and unchangeable nature of words. Coleridge fell with delight upon his 'proof' and rapidly deduced the opposite: the flux and constant change of language. Hartley, like his mentor, Locke, had assumed a fixed relationship between words and ideas; in attempting to prune back all words to their roots, Tooke had shown Coleridge the astonishing diversity and luxury of the undergrowth that had sprung up, and raised the still more fascinating question, 'From where then did all this verbiage grow?' As Coleridge himself developed the metaphor in the already-quoted letter to Godwin,

> Are not words &c parts & germinations of the Plant? And what is the Law of their Growth? – In something of this order I would endeavour to destroy the old antithesis of *Words & Things*, elevating, as it were, words into Things, & living Things too.

To '*philosophize* Horne Tooke's System' in fact meant nothing less than standing it on its head.

For once Coleridge was as good as his word – or at least his exhortation. He did, in some sense, tackle the theme he had proposed to Godwin. In the *Philosophical Lectures* of 1819 we find the fruit of Coleridge's inversion of Tooke:

> let those who exclaim against jargon and barbarous terms and every new and original mind that appears before them, . . . recollect that the whole process of human intellect is gradually to desynonymize terms, that words, the instruments of communication, are the only signs that a finite being can have of its own thought, that in proportion as what was conceived as one and identical becomes several, there will necessarily arise a term striving to represent that distinction. The whole progress of society might be expressed in a dictionary, in which . . . might be expressed from the first and simplest terms which would satisfy all the distinction that occurred to the first men, while as they perceived that other things and yet other things, which they had grouped in one mass, had each their distinctive properties . . . and the whole progress of society . . . depends upon . . . the progress of desynonymizing, that is, the feeling that there is a necessity for two distinct subjects which have hitherto been comprehended in one.[19]

The ironic relationship of this passage to Tooke is, of course, underlined by the counter-proposal for a dictionary to demonstrate the unfolding process of 'desynonymy': in other words, for a purpose diametrically opposed to that of Tooke's. If further evidence of the way Coleridge had taken, used and reversed Horne Tooke's backward-looking etymology were needed, we have it in the explanatory footnote to chapter 4 of the *Biographia Literaria*, where the word 'desynonymise' is first used, where Coleridge cites (without acknowledgement) Tooke's idea that 'give' and 'if' were once synonymous.[20] Though *The Oxford English Dictionary* gives the coinage of 'desynonymy' to Coleridge in *Biographia Literaria* in 1817, there was nothing new about the concept of 'synonymy', and in the late eighteenth and early nineteenth centuries there had been a whole spate of works on 'English Synonymy'.[21] What Coleridge has done here, however, is to replace the mechanical metaphors of Hartley by the organic models advocated by Scots rhetoricians such as Thomas Reid and turn the etymological search not towards roots but towards a history of linguistic *development*. As an example of what he means, Coleridge cites the words 'compelled' and 'obliged', which were as late as Charles I's time 'perfectly synonymous' – thus enabling Hobbes to argue that there was no such thing as guilt.[22] Similarly, as late as the Restoration, 'ingenuous' and 'ingenious', like 'property' and 'propriety', were used as synonyms. In seeking to distinguish between 'imagination' and 'fancy' in *Biographia Literaria*, or in *Aids to Reflection* to anglicise Kant's distinction between 'reason' and 'understanding', Coleridge is himself serving the growth of our collective consciousness through the continuing progress of desynonymising.

One could say much more about Coleridge's theories of language. Yet even from this brief discussion we are in some position to try and see what Coleridge may have meant in the fragment quoted above on 'the language of nature' as a 'subordinate *Logos*'. The Greek word *logos* as used at the beginning of John's Gospel meant both 'word' and the thought or reason which is expressed in words. Greek philosophers, believing in an essentially rational universe, used *logos* to denote the rational principle by which it is sustained. Thus, not merely does the 'language of nature' speak of an active, creative and ordering principle – a divine immanence sustaining life throughout the whole chain of being – but there is also the intriguing suggestion that, so far from revealing of the great permanencies of its unchanging character popularly associated with Wordsworth, Coleridge's 'nature' is in a constantly changing relationship to man as its 'language' evolves and *desynonymises*.

There are a number of hints that Coleridge did in fact come to think of nature in precisely this way. To begin with, it accords very closely with his notion of an 'idea'. By the time of *Biographia Literaria* Coleridge had come to think of an idea in terms directly opposed to Locke – that is, as a Platonic 'form' which can only be apprehended symbolically in the material world.[23] Similarly, in *The Statesman's Manual* of the same year, he wrote, 'every living principle is actuated by an idea; and every idea is living, productive, partaketh of infinity, and (as Bacon has sublimely observed) containeth an endless power of semination'. The ultimate model for an 'idea', in this sense, is clearly the *Logos* itself: perfect and unchanging perhaps in the eyes of God, or in the world of absolute forms, but here dynamic and in a process of constant organic evolution so that it is analogous to the seed that contains within itself the whole history of its past and future growth at any given moment.[24] The opposition between 'words' and 'things' which he was worrying at seventeen years before in his letter to Godwin has been resolved, at least metaphorically, by this nexus of analogies linking language and nature by means of the *Logos*. 'For if words are not THINGS, they are LIVING POWERS, by which the things of most importance to mankind are actuated, combined, and humanized'.[25]

Yet the big question, of course, still remains to be asked. Languages are systems of communication: they do not communicate themselves, they are *about* something else. Granted that the 'language of nature' is one of progressive desynonymy by which new meanings and subtler shades of distinction are constantly coming into being, what does this have to *tell* us? What *is* this unfolding message?

The immediate answer of the Romantics is not difficult to discover. Wordsworth is at pains to spell out the message throughout his work, from the *Lyrical Ballads* through *The Prelude* to *The Excursion*. At its simplest, though by no means its crudest, it can be encapsulated in the famous lines from 'The Tables Turned':

> One impulse from a vernal wood
> May teach you more of man;
> Of moral evil and of good,
> Than all the sages can.

It was no doubt his endorsement of this belief that led Keble to give his version in the poem with which we began:

> The works of God above, below,
> Within us and around,
> Are pages in that book, to show
> How God himself is found.

It was perhaps confidence such as this that led Wordsworth to observe publicly that he admired *The Christian Year* so much that he wished he had written it himself – and so improved upon it – and, privately, that Keble's verse was inferior to that of Watts and positively 'vicious in diction'.[26] The 'message' of nature, of 'moral evil and of good' is never free from ambiguity for Wordsworth. Moreover, it is an ambiguity that is rooted deep in the perceptual process itself, below the threshhold of consciousness. One – and perhaps the most striking – example of how the Romantics saw the participation of the perceiver in each act of perception occurs in a short poem of Hopkins, written in 1864:

> It was a hard thing to undo this knot.
> The rainbow shines, but only in the thought
> Of him that looks. Yet not in that alone;
> For who makes rainbows by invention?
> But each a hand's breadth further than the next.
> The sun on falling waters writes the text
> Which yet is in the eye or in the thought.
> It was a hard thing to undo this knot.

For nearly all the Romantics, the rainbow had come to stand as a metaphor for man's creative participation in nature. Hopkins takes up this image and combines it with the tradition of 'linguistic' images we have been looking at to make the sunlight upon falling water into his 'text' to be 'read' by the perceiving mind – differently for each beholder, because each has a different standpoint. The biblical symbol of God's unchanging promise to mankind is now to be read as an exemplum of the ambiguous and therefore creative nature of perception itself. 'As a man is,' said Blake, 'so will he see.'

Yet if Coleridge's idea of desynonymy is to have any real part in his metaphor of the language of nature, we should also expect that the lasting depth of the process could only be discoverable by hindsight. His own examples are, significantly, all taken from the seventeenth century. By a strange irony most of his own attempts at desynonymy proved oversubtle and too complex to pass into the language. People with a literary education will know his distinction between 'imagination' and 'fancy', but it is by no means universally accepted; 'Reason' and 'understanding' reflect technicalities in philosophy rather than standard usage; and the carefully elaborated binaries of *Church and State*, such as 'opposite' and 'contrary', have not passed even into the technical vocabulary of dialectics, whose terms are more often from Germany and France. Certain of his coinages, such as 'existential' have stood the test of time.[27] Yet, if his contributions to the development of the English language have not been as significant as he no doubt hoped, it is arguable that his contributions to the language of nature were both more important and more enduring.

Contemporaries were well aware of the magnitude and significance of the shift in sensibility that had occurred with Romanticism. F. D. Maurice, arguably the most important Anglican theologian of the century, and a lifelong Coleridgean, wrote in 1838,

> From about the middle of the last century, we may trace the commencement of a poetry which had a much more direct and substantive reference to the outward universe than that of earlier periods. The doings of men, as well as the songs in which they were celebrated, had become artificial and conventional: those whom domestic habits had inspired with a dislike of the hollowness of general society, or whom their early cultivation had taught to desire something more living and permanent than the modes of a particular generation, took refuge in nature.[28]

More personal and dramatic was Hopkins's opinion of Wordsworth:

> 'There have been in all history a few, a very few men, whom common repute, even when it did not trust them, has treated as having had something happen to them that does not happen to other men, as having *seen something*, whatever that really was.'
> Plato is the most famous of these . . . human nature in these men saw something, got a shock; wavers in opinion, looking back, whether there was anything in it or no; but is in a tremble ever since. Now what Wordsworthians mean is, what would seem to be the growing mind of the English speaking world and may perhaps come to be that of the world at large / is that in Wordsworth when he wrote that [Immortality] ode human nature got another of those shocks, and the tremble from it is spreading. This opinion I do strongly share; I am, ever since I knew the ode, in that tremble. You know what happened to crazy Blake, himself a most poetically electrical subject both active and passive, at his first hearing: when the reader came to 'The pansy at my feet' he fell into a hysterical excitement.[29]

Hopkins, like Maurice, was a Coleridgean, and had had the added advantage, as a college friend of H. N. Coleridge, of having stayed in the Coleridge household and having had access to the unpublished letters and notebooks of his friend's famous uncle. He was familiar with the theory of desynonymy, which, as we have seen, was closely parallel to his own ideas.

But what of Coleridge himself? Let me try to answer that by quoting from one of the most learned, if most controversial, of his twentieth-century interpreters, Owen Barfield. Writing of the revolution in perception of nature that reached its climax with the Romantic movement, he calls attention to what he describes as 'a sharp divergence in the behaviour of two broad classes of words':

> Of those which refer to nature, or what we now call nature, we observe that *the further back we go*, the more they appear to connote sentience or inwardness. Of those on the other hand which refer to human consciousness, the opposite is the case, and their meaning, if I may put it so, becomes more and more outward. Nature, as expressed in words, has moved in the course of time from inwardness to outwardness; consciousness, as expressed in words, has moved from outwardness to inwardness.[30]

Earlier, in a stimulating little book entitled *Saving the Appearances*, he had sketched in the corresponding change of human consciousness that he saw accompanying this semantic shift:

> The elimination of original participation involves a contraction of human consciousness from periphery to centre – a contraction from the cosmos of wisdom to something like a purely brain activity – but by the same token it involves an *awakening*. For we wake, out of universal – into self-consciousness. Now a process of awakening can be retrospectively surveyed by the sleeper only after his awakening is complete; for only then is he free enough of his dreams to look back on and interpret them. Thus, the possibility to look back over the history of the world and achieve a full waking picture of his own gradual emergence from original participation, really only arose for man . . . in the nineteenth century.[31]

Coleridge's theory of language, with its stress on the evolving collective consciousness of the culture and the accompanying process of desynonymising words comes at a moment when this semantic shift from inner to outer in nature, and from outer to inner in consciousness, was just becoming observable. It constitutes one of the principal themes of his *Philosophical Lectures*. Consider, for instance, this passage:

> In the commencement of literature man remained for a time in that unity with nature which gladly concedes to nature the life, thought, and even purposes of man, and on the other hand gives to man himself a disposition to regard himself as part of nature. Soon however he must have begun to detach himself; his dreams, the very delusions of his senses which he became acquainted with by experience, must have forced him to make a distinction between the object perceived and the percipient.[32]

The basic model, of course, is similar to that of Vico, and, though there is no external evidence that he had read either Vico or Herder until a few years later, that resemblance alone must make it likely. Where he differs decisively from Vico, Herder and other putative predecessors is, of course, in knowing Wordsworth. The result is the second volume of *Biographia Literaria*: the most sustained attempt so far to understand the revolution in sensibility created by Wordsworth in the English language. There is a sense in which the *Philosophical Lectures* of 1819 are an extended footnote to that profound intuition – an attempt, as it were, to sketch the historical background to what he dimly perceives as being a watershed in human mental development. If we have come to identify that change in consciousness at the beginning of the nineteenth century with Wordsworth more than with any other single figure, I believe that we must give much of the credit for the realisation of the nature of that change to Coleridge.

To sum up, therefore: I believe we can distinguish in the development of Coleridge's thinking about language at least three phases. In the first, following Locke and Hartley he was willing to accept a fairly simple and essentially ahistorical view of the logical relationship between words and things. In the second, which we would associate with the influence of Horne Tooke, he became aware of the illogical complexities of etymology, and saw words primarily in relation to their supposed semantic roots rather than to external objects. In the third, he came to see language as a process of continual semantic change and evolution, with words related not so much to things as to changes in human consciousness itself.

We can, moreover, connect each of these phases with stages in the development of Romanticism – and, in particular, with the evolution of meaning in the word 'nature'. In the first phase, which we might associate with Locke's attempts to empiricise Newton, 'nature' is thought of largely in terms of the scientific or theological laws governing the material world – an extreme example would be the first book of Pope's *Essay on Man*. Hartley's *Observations* are, in effect, an attempt to extend this notion of 'mechanical' laws to cover the workings of the mind and the progress of the race. In the second, we find an awareness of nature in terms of history and therefore of origins. Wordsworth's interest in childhood, especially in his conception of the child as the 'best philosopher' in the Immortality Ode, and his primitivism in such matters as poetic diction would correspond to this stage. The third, while it retains a sense of historical origins incorporates them into the process and evolution of human consciousness – recognising the perceptual shifts inherent in such a process. In literary terms it anticipates some aspects of the nineteenth-century novel, and poems such as *In Memoriam* – and even, arguably, Darwin.

That, however, was in the future. Our quest has been the more limited one of tracing the development of the metaphor and its meanings to the Romantics through the well-documented prism of Coleridge's mind. It is to Coleridge, for instance, that we must turn if we wish to understand the pervasiveness of the metaphor from Keble through to Tennyson and Hopkins and beyond – of that tantalising and as yet inarticulate vision of which he could at one time despairingly comment, 'We understand nature just as if, at a distance, we looked at the image of a person in a looking-glass, plainly and fervently discoursing, yet what he uttered we could decipher only by the motion of his lips or by his mien'[33] – and yet still look forward to the time when 'the other great Bible of God, the Book of Nature, become transparent to us, when we regard the forms of matter as words, as symbols, valuable only as being the expression, an unrolled but yet a glorious fragment of the wisdom of the Supreme Being'.[34]

NOTES

1. John Keble, *The Christian Year*, 43rd edn (1851) Septuagesima Sunday, p. 80.
2. Ibid., p. 22.
3. See, for instance, 'Expostulation and Reply', 'The Tables Turned', or *The Prelude*, V.
4. Sampson Reed, *Observations in the Growth of the Mind* (Boston, Mass., 1826; repr. Gainesville, Fla, 1970) pp. 46–7.
5. Coleridge, 'On Genius and Public Taste' (fragment), *Shakespeare Criticism*, ed. T. M. Raysor (London, 1960) p. 185.
6. See Stephen Prickett, *Coleridge and Wordsworth: The Poetry of Growth* (Cambridge, 1970) ch. 2.
7. The usage is unique to Hartley: see *The Oxford English Dictionary*.
8. David Hartley, *Observations on Man, his Frame, his Duties and his Expectations* (London, 1749) I, 79.
9. I am indebted for the speculative background to this conclusion, to W. A. Krebs, 'The Study of Language in Scotland, 1760–1810' (unpublished PhD Thesis, University of Leeds, 1977).
10. Ibid., p. 297.
11. John Locke, *An Essay Concerning Human Understanding*, ed. J. W. Yolton (London, 1961) II, 10.
12. John Horne Tooke, *The Diversions of Purley*, 2 vols (London, 1798–1805) II, 19–20.
13. Krebs, 'The Study of Language in Scotland', p. 85; Hans Aarsleff, *The Study of Language in England, 1780–1860* (Princeton, NJ, 1967) pp. 73ff.
14. See, for instance, Charles Richardson, *Illustrations of English Philology* (1815): 'if the Dictionary of John Horne Tooke had been completed, the united labours of Samuel Johnson and Henry J. Todd might have been spared to warm the baths of Alexandria' (p. 18).
15. In English, 'thought', or 'having been thinged'.
16. In English, 'the thing acts upon the co-agent'.
17. In English, 'I think or thing – I think it again when I have thought it.'
18. Coleridge, *Table Talk*, ed. H. N. Coleridge (London, 1851) p. 66.
19. Coleridge, *Philosophical Lectures*, ed. Kathleen Coburn (London, 1949) pp. 173–4.

20. Horne Tooke, *The Diversions of Purley*, I, 102.
21. For instance, John Trusler, *The Difference between Words Esteemed Synonymous in the English Language, and the Proper Choice of them Determined*, 2 vols (London, 1766); and Hester Piozzi, *British Synonymy*, 2 vols (Dublin, 1794).
22. *Philosophical Lectures*, p. 174.
23. 'An IDEA, in the highest sense of that word, cannot be conveyed, but by a symbol' (*BL*, I, 100).
24. For a further discussion of this point, see Prickett, *Coleridge and Wordsworth*, pp. 197–8.
25. Coleridge, *Aids to Reflection*, 4th edn (London, 1913) p. xix.
26. Georgina Battiscombe, *John Keble* (London, 1963) p. 104; Mary Moorman, *Wordsworth: The Later Years, 1808–1850* (Oxford, 1965) pp. 479–80.
27. *Philosophical Lectures*, p. 48.
28. F. D. Maurice, *The Kingdom of Christ*, 3rd edn, 2 vols (London, 1891) I, 177–8.
29. *The Correspondence of G. M. Hopkins and R. W. Dixon*, ed. C. C. Abbott (Oxford, 1935) pp. 147–8.
30. Owen Barfield, 'The Nature of Meaning', *Seven*, II (1981) 38.
31. Owen Barfield, *Saving the Appearances* (New York, 1957) pp. 182–3.
32. *Philosophical Lectures*, pp. 343–4.
33. Coleridge, *Anima Poetae*, ed. E. H. Coleridge (London, 1895) p. 232.
34. *Philosophical Lectures*, p. 367.

9 Wordsworth and the 'Mystery of Words'

MICHAEL EDWARDS

I

A Christian approach to the poetics of poetry might well begin by considering the problems of writing poetry in a world that is fallen. This will involve reflecting on the sources of poetry, or inspiration, and on the power of poetry to change the world, or re-creation: on the difficult, and indeed perilous, engagement of poetry with transcendence. One of the poets from whom one has the most to learn along these lines, despite his by no means straightforward relation to the Christian faith, is, I believe, Wordsworth.

Consider the opening of *The Prelude*:

> O there is a blessing in this gentle breeze,
> A visitant that while he fans my cheek
> Doth seem half-conscious of the joy he brings
> From the green fields, and from yon azure sky.[1]

In this marvellous beginning, Wordsworth takes the ancient idea of an inspirational afflatus and relocates it, first, in a wind blowing in the north of England. Nature itself becomes the power moving on the poet, and the physicality of inspiration is strangely stressed. Since the breeze 'fans my cheek' (it 'beats against my cheek' in 1805), it also suggests another physical activity associated with poetry: that of the breath blowing inside the cheeks in the making and saying of verse. The whole poem begins, indeed, with the lips shaping as for breath so as to form 'O'. Even the later reference to an inner inspiration claims that this 'correspondent breeze' too was felt 'while the sweet breath of heaven / Was blowing on my body' (lines 33–5).[2] The physicality in itself need not surprise – a vivid passage in one of Wordsworth's letters runs, 'I have procured a pair of skates and tomorrow mean to give my body to the wind';[3] only the practice of the body as a channel for poetry need do so.

Yet there is still of course something more than natural in the wind, which contains a 'blessing', and which comes, in a detail absent from the 1805 text, as a 'visitant'. Without exactly being the Spirit or Breath of God, the wind alludes to him with a kind of 'as if'. When the sweet breath of heaven blows on Wordsworth's body, moreover, 'sweet' and 'blowing' and 'body' play against the other, religious meaning of 'heaven', to evoke an experience poised between the senses and the spirit, as if heaven – just at the moment when he refers to the inward breeze of creativity – were almost touching the body, or the body were almost in touch with heaven. Wordsworth intimates, I presume, a more than natural wholeness, where human feeling and imagination, a natural wind and also a spiritual wind, from both earth and sky, meet in a corporeal jubilation: a hint, it seems, of what the 'Prospectus' to his epic work names as the 'blissful hour', the 'great consummation' (lines 56–8).[4] He celebrates the interaction of one's body with the world's, and with something in the world beyond the bodily, as the source of poetry; and he offers, as access to an inspiration that is personal ('he') and that 'comes' with a 'mission' (line 5), specifically the sense of touch.

In these opening lines of *The Prelude* it is the urge to poetry itself that encounters a transcendence in the real; and their suggestiveness goes beyond the onset of inspiration, for the wind also alludes to the making and remaking of the world. A breeze occurring in the first line of a long poem clearly relates to the Spirit of God present at the very opening of the Bible (where he presides over an even vaster piece of writing to follow) as the agent of the Creation. The later comparison of the mind of the poet to a mother dove who 'Sits brooding' (line 141) quotes Milton's version, in the poem of *Paradise Lost*, of the same Spirit moving creatively on the face of the waters. And doesn't the exclamation, 'I breathe again!' (line 18), recall God breathing into Adam's nostrils the breath of life? The beginning of *The Prelude* is the beginning of a world. The reality to come is modified, however, by the famous reference, in 'The earth is all

before me' (line 14), to Milton's statement about Adam and Eve
as they leave Eden, that 'The world was all before them': it
advances Wordsworth a stage further, to being an Adam entering on a fallen world; while the fact that such an auspicious line
at the opening of his epic joins with another at the very end of
Milton's implies quite overtly that *The Prelude* is to be, if not his
Paradise Regained, his move towards it. The ensuing poem, inspired by the breeze, will be an attempt not to create but to
re-create the earth – or rather, a probing of the means of its
re-creation; and, since the origin of the poem is the experience of
a world both natural and more than natural, the paradise to be
aspired to is likely to be similarly poised between the two.

II

One sees why the wind is the border between realms. It is not
only that many languages play across 'breath', 'wind' and
'spirit', so that in the Bible, for instance (though I take it to be
the decisive instance), the Spirit is also the Breath or the Wind of
God, and Jesus, when likening the Spirit to the wind in the third
chapter of John's Gospel, uses, even according to the Greek
translation, the same word for each. The wind is surely a
threshold to the invisible world, since it is already invisible; it
almost belongs to that world through its invisibility, while it
belongs to this through its effects. Something of the genuine –
the natural – mystery of the wind is caught in the reference back
to the correspondent breeze and to the heavenly breath as the
inspirer of the poet, in the opening of book VII of *The Prelude*:

> my favourite grove,
> Tossing in sunshine its dark boughs aloft,
> As if to make the strong wind visible,
> Wakes in me agitations like its own,
> A spirit friendly to the Poet's task.
>
> (VII.44–8)

One senses nature straining through darkness to give entry to
the strong wind of the Spirit, the 'rushing mighty wind' of
Pentecost.

That initial exploration of the source of poetry is pursued in

the same and in later books in a number of passages that are
linked to each other as it were subliminally. A series of refocus-
ings, they show Wordsworth not expounding a theory but continually re-entering an experience, so as to search, develop and
deepen it. The first is the bird-nesting episode in book I:

> Oh! when I have hung
> Above the raven's nest, by knots of grass
> And half-inch fissures in the slippery rock
> But ill-sustained, and almost (so it seemed)
> Suspended by the blast that blew amain,
> Shouldering the naked crag, oh, at that time
> While on the perilous ridge I hung alone,
> With what strange utterance did the loud dry wind
> Blow through my ear! the sky seemed not a sky
> Of earth – and with what motion moved the clouds!
>   (I.330–9)

Not only does the wind recur (winds blow, of course, throughout
the poem), but the phrasing and the lineation of 'did the loud
dry wind / Blow through my ear' recall 'the sweet breath of
heaven / Was blowing on my body', as a kind of mnemonic. The
wind has changed utterly, but is still personal ('Shouldered')
and still mysterious; and the poet senses that mystery once again
through touch, as the blast suspends him in the air, or rather, in
his own very precise wording, suspends him 'almost (so it
seemed)'. The parentheses are not without interest. The text in
1805 read, 'almost, as it seemed / Suspended', and was already
doubly tentative; the parentheses add a further recession of
doubt, but they also add, along with an affirmation from the
present that it did seem so, an isolated pocket of consciousness
endeavouring to recapture how it felt. The doubt is not, moreover,
finally dismissive: it doesn't register, surely, the adult's realisation
that the fancy was appropriate to the scared boy but that we know
better. For one thing, the parentheses are followed, not preceded,
by what they question, and the supreme assertiveness of 'Suspended by the blast', along with the sustained alliterative confidence, runs counter to that questioning. The strangeness of the
wind also carries through, into its speaking, into a sky that,
admittedly, 'seemed' not to be a 'sky / of earth' (itself an
unwonted expression, emphasised by the line break), and into an

unknown motion in the clouds. The blast did not 'suspend' the boy in any ordinary sense, but then ordinary sense is not alone in operation here. One only needs to catch the excitement of the lines to know that Wordsworth is registering, in all seriousness, an intuition, not of a supernatural world quite different from ours, but of the real world become, to the senses of the imagination, astonishingly and overmasteringly other. The sky turns – almost – to heaven; the wind is the breath, as it were, of Spirit; and the mere movements of clouds, no longer a simple matter of fact, look as if they occur in a natural scene transfigured.

Whereas the earlier wind that met, in particular, his cheek was silent, the wind that now reaches 'through' his ear speaks with a 'strange utterance'. That strangeness derives of course from the unworldly quality of the breath that delivers it; what he hears is inarticulate speech from the earth and seemingly from beyond the earth, as he hangs on a 'perilous ridge' at the earth's end. And, although he is writing of himself as a nine-year-old, isn't poetry again in question? Unlike the natural 'voices' that he hears elsewhere as a child, the utterance of the wind or Spirit is almost a language to be reached for, remembered. Here is a further encounter with a source of poetry, where the body is once again the medium of inspiration; and the sense that makes him sensitive is now that of hearing.

This is not the only language that he hears, and to evoke the other he again rewrites the passage (I am not referring to the chronological order of composition), in the next book:

> I would walk alone,
> Under the quiet stars, and at that time
> Have felt whate'er there is of power in sound
> To breathe an elevated mood, by form
> Or image unprofaned; and I would stand,
> If the night blackened with a coming storm,
> Beneath some rock, listening to notes that are
> The ghostly language of the ancient earth,
> Or make their dim abode in distant winds.
> Thence did I drink the visionary power . . . .
>
> (II.302–11)

He is once more, though not surprisingly, alone; the wind returns, as does the rock; the strange utterance has become a ghostly language; a sky not of earth is recalled in stars above an almost equally unfamiliar 'ancient earth'. The language is again difficult to define. As a language of the earth it may hark back to notions of telluric oracles, such as that at Delphi. Is it possible, however, that 'ancient', especially when allied with 'ghostly', 'distant' and 'visionary', means, as in French, 'former' as well as 'old', and refers to Eden? We know from elsewhere in *The Prelude* of Wordsworth's belief in the availability, to special perception, of something surviving from an Edenic origin. When Coleridge goes to Sicily for his health, Wordsworth questions whether there may not be some place in the vale of Enna 'From the first play-time of the infant world / Kept sacred to restorative delight' (XI.420–1). It is notable that the unfallen earth resembles the unfallen child of 'Intimations of Immortality', being described as an infant, and that its function in a fallen world is to restore; it is also notable that the text of 1850 adds the line, 'When from afar invoked by anxious love', as if to emphasise the distance and the unease from which we perceive Eden. Indeed, it may be that a reference in the 1805 *Prelude* to 'breezes and soft airs that breathe / The breath of paradise' (XI.10–11) was removed because of the absence of any difficulty of access; while the lines, 'Earth, nowhere unembellished by some trace / Of that first Paradise whence man was driven' (III.111–12), were added for the 1850 text to confirm the presence of an Edenic 'trace' while acknowledging our exile from Eden itself. Without such glimpses of a 'first' paradise there would be no conceiving of a second, and without that exclusion there would be no incitement to achieve it.

If this is the language of Eden, the former earth, it is no doubt ghostly in part because it haunts the place as the language of paradise lost. It is also *geistlich* or 'spiritual', and so relates once again to the no-longer silent wind. As a language both ghostly and 'of the earth', moreover, it exists between earthiness and ghostliness, between matter and spirit; like the 'strange utterance' of the previous book, it is already at once real and transcendent. Not merely disembodied, it resembles the natural yet also unnatural 'distant winds' in being the passage to the invisible.

The passage is specifically, and curiously, sound. Sound is described here, by hyperbole and with some provocation, as creating a mood 'unprofaned' by form or image, as if sound were sacred, an elevation into a temple to which the merely visual has no access. Yet the ear does not withdraw from the rest of the body: hearing gathers into itself both sight, at the point where the latter fails, since the notes make a 'dim' abode in distant winds, and breath, since, through a bold adynaton, sound is said to have the power to 'breathe' an elevated mood. The suggestion seems to be that the body, listening to these rare sounds, itself changes rarely, so as to become a kind of transfigured hearing.

Sound and hearing, in fact, are often mysterious in Wordsworth, part of the broad mystery of matter and of the senses. In the well-known passage about stealing a bird from someone else's snare that immediately precedes the bird-nesting in book I, the boy Wordsworth hears 'sounds / Of undistinguishable motion, steps / Almost as silent as the turf they trod' (I.323–5). Invisible motion is perceived through sounds that are scarcely audible, steps that almost share the silence of the turf, 'low breathings' numinous for being on the brim of soundlessness. Extraordinarily sensitive to the body's relations, Wordsworth is concerned for the passing not only of the visible to the invisible but also, on this occasion at least, of the audible to the inaudible.

In the lines we are considering, sound is said, again provocatively, to afford 'visionary power', it being clear that vision is not physical seeing and may therefore be induced by another sense. It is accompanied, in fact, by an obfuscation of sight, in the 'dim' distance, and Wordsworth emphasises this in the following lines by figurative references to moods of 'shadowy' exultation (II.313) and to an 'obscure' sense of possible sublimity (line 317). The revision of the passage also carefully confined such experiences to the night, and added the allusion to the night blackening. Isn't this because darkness is the natural accomplice of vision? – and even of sight, if one considers how little of the universe is visible during the daytime. A darkness has already reverberated with sound earlier in the same book, when a wren was heard in the nave of a ruined church:

> So sweetly 'mid the gloom the invisible bird
> Sang to herself, that there I could have made
> My dwelling-place.
>
> (II.125–7)

(Wordsworth's poetry is deeply, it seems, a search for 'dwelling', for 'abode'.) One remembers the birdsongs of Eliot charged with similar meaning, and also, along with a change of sense, the equally liminal intuition, in 'The Dry Salvages', of the 'wild thyme unseen'. The wind is again present, and appropriately so, as 'Internal breezes' in the ruin, 'sobbings', and 'respirations from the roofless walls' (*Prelude*, II.122–3). In a passage that becomes more elusive and suggestive the more one attends to it, the wind, as a natural and also more than natural breath, 'touches' the place, and in particular the 'shuddering' ivy (lines 121, 124).

What Wordsworth hears, it seems, is a ghostly language of before the earth as we know it, and a strange utterance from beyond the earth, or from the beyond of the earth. Both are the speech of a spirit-like breath, blowing in a world momentarily transfigured, and entering a human body similarly wrought upon. One might again think of Eliot; but, whereas Eliot in *Ash-Wednesday* names, as the 'ancient rhyme' and the 'new verse', the two human languages – of paradise lost and of paradise regained – between which one's own language is inevitably strung as a kind of 'cry', Wordsworth listens to the signs of those languages in the natural world, discovering their source in the inspiring wind.

III

This authoritative knowledge of the mysteriousness of poetry, which took Wordsworth so far beyond Dryden and Pope, at least in their thinking about their art, continues into his reflection on words. For at the end of book V, of *The Prelude*, having meditated the origins of poetry and the languages that he hears, he considers the power of verse, when inhabited itself by the wind of inspiration, to effect changes in the world, and, in the terms of the 'Prospectus', to elicit paradise from the common day:

> Visionary power
> Attends the motions of the viewless winds,
> Embodied in the mystery of words:
> There, darkness makes abode, and all the host
> Of shadowy things work endless changes there,

As in a mansion like their proper home.
Even forms and substances are circumfused
By that transparent veil with light divine,
And, through the turnings intricate of verse,
Present themselves as objects recognised,
In flashes, and with glory not their own.

(V.595–605)

This is surely a crucial passage in the history of thinking about the relation of words to things. Yet again, it is the rewriting of a previous passage, the one in book II about the language of the earth. In each, one enters an obscurity, where the notes that one attempts to hear 'make their dim above' in distant winds, or 'darkness makes abode' in the words of poetry that try to capture those winds, while, perhaps as a mnemonic, a 'shadowy exultation' is recalled in a host of 'shadowy things'. What is in question in both cases is 'visionary power', in the first derived for the poet from a ghostly language and from distant winds, in the second present within the poem, in the workings of words and the motions of 'viewless winds'. 'Viewless', one of a number of pointed changes introduced into the 1850 text, marks the final stage in the winds' role. Already agents of vision in nature and on one's body, through being the frontier to the invisible, they now penetrate words to become the agents of vision in poetry.

In taking up and developing one of the earliest parts of *The Prelude* to be composed, the lines alter the focus, from an encounter in what the immediately previous lines call 'living Nature' to an experience of 'the great Nature that exists in works / Of mighty Poets'. And what they say apropos of those works is that verse transforms the world. As objects and their words enter poetry, and in particular the 'turnings intricate' of verse, they are modified, being caught up into a pattern of semantics, of sounds, of syntax. 'Turnings' is in fact a pleonasm, or a kind of etymological pun, since a 'verse' is already a turning, a furrow-like back-tracking from line to line; and the close attention to the word appears to have prompted a further pun, so that, as the lines turn technically, they also turn or convert the objects to which they refer.[5] The changes wrought on things are also reflexed in the changes, the exploratory ploys and plays, that are wrought on words. The insights of Mallarmé are anticipated here, and specifically his notion, in 'Variations on a Theme',

that a line of verse, in constituting a 'new word', alters the thing
that it connotes, so that 'the reminiscence of the named object
bathes in a new atmosphere'.

Verse is also being established as a special place, a 'there'
whose adverb is repeated for emphasis even more powerfully
than in the lines about the church and the singing wren ('there I
could have made / My dwelling-place, and lived for ever there'
– II.126–7); while the changes produced in it are, according to
another significant revision, 'endless'. They reflect continually
on one another, and, rather than presenting the world transformed once and for all, the poetry endlessly prosecutes the
changes of a world whose renewal into paradise is for the future.
The lines send one back yet again to the dimly heard language of
book II. Although it was recorded in an act of memory, and came
from a past of the world even more remote than the past of the
poet, because of Wordsworth's understanding of the creative
power of memory it too opened exhilaratingly to the future,
though to a future likewise withdrawing continuously from
attainment: through the growth of its faculties, he wrote, the soul
feels that 'whatsoever point they gain, they yet / Have something
to pursue' (lines 321–2). The lines also look forward to the
celebrated passage in Book VI (which is, indeed, another
rewriting[6]) where the imagination, revealing the invisible world,
reveals also that our 'destiny', being with 'infinitude', is with
'something evermore about to be' (line 608).

The process is also a traversing of darkness towards light. The
darkness is no doubt in part the puzzlement of the reader, his
necessary difficulty in penetrating the mystery of change; for the
light is described overtly as 'divine', and 'glory' has obvious
heavenly connotations, while forms and substances seem to be
'circumfused' as with an aureole or nimbus. Also perplexing is
the apparent reference, in the 'viewless winds', to Claudio's
speech, 'Ay, but to die, and go we know not where', in Shakespeare's *Measure for Measure*. Is it that Claudio's terror of what
may happen –

> To be imprison'd in the viewless winds
> And blown with restless violence round about
> The pendent world
>
>   (III.i.123–5)

– although it envisages winds quite different from those of Wordsworth, supplies the passage with the hint of death? If that is so, the objects of the world enter darkness so as to die metaphorically in the 'there' of verse, with a view to rising again into a heavenly light and being seen anew as if they were in paradise. The process, the most fundamental of all, would be of death and resurrection.

Because the winds are invisible, the poetry is visionary, and creates a power in the reader to pass beyond ordinary sight. Poetry, one might say, blinds the reader (as painting deafens and paralyses the viewer), so as to alter his seeing. The merely 'glittering' verse (*Prelude*, V.591) by which the young are attracted differs therefore from the 'light' of the highest poetry, since this enables one to see figuratively – to perceive, that is, not another world but this world transmuting. The transmutations are nevertheless profound. Although objects are 'recognised', since their reminiscence has entered the poem, and maybe since they are the shapes of the everyday and not the furniture of Arcady or Atlantis, they are also recognised in a more novel sense of the word – with a certain amazement and awe, through and despite their change, their newness – since the glory that invests them, according to yet another probing revision, is 'not their own'. Once again, however, the change is not final. Even if the recognition, as one might conclude from 'Intimations of Immortality', were of the celestial world of childhood or before, the objects of its ken present themselves not in the steady light of paradise but only in 'flashes'.

Verse is also described as a veil; and Wordsworth is surely right to imply that words veil rather than show, their role being not to describe a world merely given but, since it is a world excluded from Eden in expectation of Paradise, to conceal it in such a way as to change its appearance. 'Transparent veil' is in fact formidably precise: almost an oxymoron, it suggests both our no-longer quite seeing the object when poetry has intervened, and our seeing yet not seeing the object as transformed in the poem. As we look, not 'through a glass, darkly' but through a transparency, veiled, we catch, by flashes, a kind of other radiance. It may even intimate the veil of the temple. This was not transparent, to be sure, and at Jesus's death it was not made transparent but was rent. In Wordsworth's context, however, it does seem to mean that one might pass, through the veil of verse, if not to the holy of holies, at least to an earth become heavenly.

For, according to a related metaphor, verse is also a 'mansion', and a place, for the agents of inspiration that have come to dwell there and work their changes, 'like their proper home'. And what should that home be but heaven? – the Father's house, in Jesus's expression, where there are 'many mansions' (John 14:2). The poetry where they shed their light is therefore a similitude of heaven, and once more a locus for viewing familiar objects as if they were in paradise.

One senses here the large things that loom from small linguistic details, and human language as no less 'strange' or 'ghostly' than languages from the extremes of nature. And there is more. To add a final weave of complexity, doesn't the underlying figuration of the passage relate the activities of verse to a particular religious ceremony? That the winds should be 'embodied' hints at Incarnation, while the word 'mystery', through its association with 'sacrament', focuses that Incarnation in the Communion. The thought is strengthened by 'changes', despite the plural, and by 'substances', with its history in theological speculation about the substances and accidents of the bread and wine, especially when those substances appear with a 'glory not their own'. In such company, even the prefix in 'transparent', following close after, may call up 'transubstantiation', and 'host' evoke its Eucharistic homonym. The 'transparent veil', while not a biblical or theological term (though a transparent veil does cover the remains of the consecrated elements), insinuates the bread and the wine as veil for the body and blood of Christ. Death and resurrection are again in the shadows.

In this prodigious passage, therefore, Wordsworth seems to have used a Catholic-tinged doctrine of a miraculous changing of ordinary objects – objects, indeed, of 'the common day' – as a way of referring to his main theme here: the changing of the objects of the world in poetry. As he describes change, moreover, he inevitably effects it. The very elusiveness of the writing – the 'darkness' for the reader as he reaches for hints about the Communion and for moves in a complex poetic theory – is an index of the depths of both the mysteries, the religious and also the poetic.

This passage in book V, as it declares the mystery and intricacy of words, is itself intensely mysterious and intricate. (It repays the closest reading, even to significant sound effects such as 'Embodied . . . abode', and suggests that there is a density of writing in Wordsworth for which he is not always given credit, especially as the density here is different in kind from the allusiveness of the opening of book I.) We have encountered, indeed, recesses of strangeness in all Wordsworth's probing of inspiration and imagination, of a poem's rapport with the world at large and of its ability to rework that world; a strangeness which is partly corporeal. For the body that meets with wind also meets, over and again, almost with spirit, through touch, through hearing. Sight becomes vision, the literal merges into the figurative, and the senses 'sense' what is beyond them. To register a change in the world, the body itself changes; and one recalls a passage in 'Tintern Abbey', where Wordsworth refers, as if we all knew it, to

> that serene and blessed mood,
> In which the affections gently lead us on,
> Until, the breath of this corporeal frame,
> And even the motion of our human blood
> Almost suspended, we are laid asleep
> In body, and become a living soul . . . .
>
> (lines 42–7)

The body is not cast aside in this experience, so that the soul can achieve excarnation: one is still 'in body', and the motions of body, including those of the breath, have been not suspended but 'almost suspended' – have been taken, one might say, to the verge of the physical. One is 'laid asleep', and to be asleep is not to cease breathing but to breathe differently and more profoundly, and under the sway of something beyond consciousness. The quotation from Genesis – 'and man became a living soul' (2:7) – suggests indeed that if, in this suspension, 'We see into the life of things' ('Tintern Abbey', line 50), it is because there has been breathed into us, as into Adam, 'the breath of life'. Without actually saying so, and without even naming the divine breath, the lines hint at the possibility of the latter almost superseding, mastering, our own breath. They evoke a relation of body, mind and spirit, and they do so with a realism that one can find powerfully suggestive in terms of Christian practice. One also realises that the experience they so subtly enact might not be so different from death.

A work that explores its own origins, relations and powers, *The Prelude* is also greatly suggestive for a more specifically Christian poetics, beyond what I have already drawn out or implied. As is well known, Wordsworth secularised the theology of apocalypse so as to view the re-creation of the world as an act of imagination, in which the mind rises above a material reality by virtue of its more divine fabric. If one reasserts apocalypse within his perspective, what the imagination sees, or may see, is the world being remade from elsewhere, by God – becoming other and, more importantly, belonging to Another – as a foresight of the sudden and final remaking, the establishing of 'new heavens and a new earth' (2 Peter 3:13). It could be argued, in fact, that re-creative poetry can only exist because a Re-creation will in truth occur; and also that, without such a Re-creation, there is actually no substance to be given to the 'blissful hour', the 'great consummation', to which, for Wordsworth, writing is the prelude. It could even be maintained that only the Re-creation enables one to distinguish a real encounter with a transcendental change in the world beyond the self, entailing a real change within the self, from an encounter with the capacities of one's own imagination.

NOTES

1. All references to *The Prelude* are to *William Wordsworth: The Prelude, 1799, 1805, 1850*, ed. Jonathan Wordsworth, M. H. Abrams and Stephen Gill (New York, 1979). I quote the 1850 text unless otherwise stated.
2. See, M. H. Abrams, 'The Correspondent Breeze: A Romantic Metaphor', in *English Romantic Poets*, ed. M. H. Abrams (New York, 1975).
3. 24 December, 1799; and see *The Prelude*, I.453.
4. I refer to the end of 'Home at Grasmere', the only completed book of *The Recluse*, which Wordsworth used as a 'Prospectus' to his intended threefold masterwork of *Prelude*, *Excursion* and *Recluse*. I quote the line-numbering of the 'Prospectus' from *The Poetical*

Works of William Wordsworth, ed. Ernest de Selincourt and Helen Darbishire (Oxford, 1949) V.

5. Doesn't the overall shaping of *The Prelude* work similarly? It too turns this way and that, changing its materials by the new lights being thrown on them and changing its lines by rewriting them in different perspectives. The microcosmic 'turnings intricate' of verse are even implicitly related to the macrocosmic structure of the poem as a whole at the beginning of book IX, when Wordsworth (in a revision) describes what he has written so far as having 'Turned and returned with intricate delay' (line 8).

6. VI.599–602 –

> 'I recognise thy glory': in such strength
> Of usurpation, when the light of sense
> Goes out, but with a flash that has revealed
> The invisible world, doth greatness make abode,

– is a lacing-together of words and phrases from the end of book V of *The Prelude*.

10   Wordsworth and the Credo

J. R. WATSON

I

I begin with two passages of prose. The first is from John
Wesley, in this 1779 Preface to *A Collection of Hymns for use of the
People called Methodists* (1780): 'When Poetry thus keeps its place,
as the handmaid of Piety, it shall attain, not a poor perishable
wreath, but a crown that fadeth not away.'[1] The second is from
Wordsworth, from the second of his *Essays on Epitaphs* (published
in *The Friend*, 1810, when Coleridge was hard up for copy): 'ages
must pass away before men will have their eyes open to the
beauty and majesty of Truth, and will be taught to venerate
Poetry no further than as She is a Handmaid pure as her
Mistress – the noblest Handmaid in her train!'[2]

Both of these are concluding sentences. This gives to practis-
ing Methodists a definite sensation of *déjà vu* on reading the end
of Wordsworth's essay, although I have no evidence that he ever
read John Wesley or that he ever had an acquaintance with
Methodism. But the sentences are close, and in their closeness
lies their interest. They are saying almost the same thing in the
same way, but between Wesley's 'Piety' and Wordsworth's
'Truth' there is a crucial and tantalising distance. It is the
closeness and the distance which I intend to explore, as a
contribution to the study of the interacting relationship between
literature and religion. This relationship often seems very close,
but the closeness can mask a great distance; and it is this
oscillation between closeness and distance that I wish to study in
some poems of Wordsworth written in 1798, considering ways in

which he uses images, phrases, linguistic forms and verse structures that are common in traditional religious usage. How does
Wordsworth use such phrases? What are the implications for
Romanticism and religion of the way in which he writes? And
how do such moments affect the way we see the remainder of his
poetry? These are questions which I intend to address myself to,
not necessarily expecting definitive answers but hoping to understand more about the symbiotic relationship between literature
and religion in studying the work of a pivotal figure. Wordsworth is pivotal because he is the chief exemplar of what Harold
Bloom has called the 'faithless faith' of the Romantics:[3] he
operates at a point where doctrine gives way to experience,
where language is appropriated for new explorations, even for
new formulations of a belief. In his work we can see with
particular clarity the application of old formulae to burgeoning
ideas, ideas which transcend the limitations of previous attempts
to connect doctrine and experience.

II

A poem such as 'Tintern Abbey', for example, allows a movement from precision towards an indeterminate end. Its language
is supple and flexible, and it is this which allows the poem to
move so sweetly between inner and outer, between the specific
space–time continuum and the explorations of the internal
quest for selfhood and stability. Among Wordsworth's mature
poems, it is distinguished by the openness with which it uses
words which are normally applied to Christian mystical experience. To the landscape is owed

>   that blessed mood,
> In which the burthen of the mystery,
> In which the heavy and the weary weight
> Of all this unintelligible world,
> Is lightened . . . .

The contrast between the blessed mood and the unintelligible
world is the traditional antithesis which comes down from
St John's Gospel; immediately afterwards Wordsworth takes up
the idea and expands it:

> that serene and blessed mood,
> In which the affections gently lead us on,
> Until, the breath of this corporeal frame
> And even the motion of our human blood
> Almost suspended, we are laid asleep
> In body, and become a living soul . . . .

The word 'soul' comes at the end: the transition is a delicate one, the living soul emerging at the final stage of a gentle process which can be seen as leading indeed to a 'blessed mood'. In it the breath, the corporeal breath as Wordsworth is at pains to point out, is almost suspended; its preservation allows the individual to go on living, but it is the finer breath of the spirit which now occupies the space. The word 'spirit' begins at this point to play an important part in the poem: the poet's spirit turns to the river Wye twice in the space of three lines, and in the great passage which follows the poet finds not only 'a sense sublime' but

> A motion and a spirit, that impels
> All thinking things, all objects of all thought,
> And rolls through all things.

The poet has a spirit, and so does the visible universe: 'the spirit itself beareth witness with our spirit, that we are the children of God'. In such a way does Wordsworth pick up echoes of biblical language, and use them for his own purposes. So too in 'Tintern Abbey' he uses specific phrases of belief and trust: after his initial statement of pleasure and goodness derived from his memories of the landscape, he adds,

> Nor less, I trust,
> To them I may have owed another gift,
> Of aspect more sublime . . . .

He 'dares to hope' that there is life and food for future years; and he has found other gifts to replace the early raptures: 'for such loss, I would believe, / Abundant recompense'.

'Trust', 'hope', 'belief', 'feeling', 'blessing': these are the words which Wordsworth uses to transact states of changing and developing sensibility in 'Tintern Abbey'. Towards the end of the poem he is making a prayer 'Knowing that Nature never did betray / The heart that loved her', and he describes himself as one 'so long / A worshipper of Nature', who 'hither came / Unwearied in that service'. 'Prayer', 'worship', 'love', 'service': to these words must be added what, in this poem, are the equivalents of the fruits of the spirit: kindness, love, harmony, joy, quietness, beauty. All these, together with sweet sounds and harmonies, and the sense sublime, are the result of a power that is

> The anchor of my purest thoughts, the nurse,
> The guide, the guardian of my heart, and soul
> Of all my moral being.

The spiritual assurance of the poem is such that Wordsworth can claim that nothing can prevail against the power which he has invoked in prayer. Nothing can separate him from the love in nature, the source of energy, 'or disturb / Our cheerful faith, that all which we behold / Is full of blessings'.

Now the closeness of this to specific patterns of religious belief is extremely interesting. It helps, by its very evocation of parallels in St Paul, to emphasise the distance between the traditional object of worship and veneration and the new discovery of Nature as an all-sufficient source of strength. So does the inclusion in the poem of faith, hope and love: these are found both implicitly, in the progress of the poem's discovery of the self in its relation to others and to the outside world, and explicitly. Wordsworth is using the language of Christian devotion for his own intelligent understanding of the external world. He is asserting the right of the individual to fashion his deepest beliefs from his own experience and not from some doctrinal formula. The daring of this is substantial, the self-sufficiency characteristic: in 1812 Wordsworth told Crabb Robinson that 'perhaps' he felt no need of a Redeemer.[4]

III

If we begin thus with Wordsworth's unorthodoxy, we shall be in a better position to appreciate his closeness to traditional patterns of religious thought in other ways. In particular, we can recognise the kind of correspondence which is implied in the assumption that the letter killeth but the spirit giveth life. The suggestion could be made that Wordsworth was engaged in bringing life to ideas that had become attentuated and flaccid through conventional use. Equally, it could be argued that Wordsworth, by concentrating on his own experience, was merely reiterating a personal heresy that is meaningless in religious terms. The dilemma posed by closeness and distance is a crucial one: at what point does the individual interpretation of the external world become no longer relevant in religious terms, since it is merely an imaginative expression of the quest for the self?

Wordsworth is peculiarly interesting in this respect, because his expression of belief is found in more than one form. It occurs in the sinewy and complex syntax of 'Tintern Abbey', which has been much discussed and admired, and also in the robust hymn form of the 'credal lyrics' from *Lyrical Ballads*, which have been less discussed and less admired. Both of these forms contain statements of belief: the first tentative and experiential, the second assured and uncomplicated. In their different ways both are part of that quest for the self which characterises so much of Wordsworth's mature poetry, the quest for the self which is also the quest for the other, that beyond the self, the limits of self, the beyond in the self; which is found not in sterile self-inquiry but in the interaction of the spirit with the external world, and in what Gerard Manley Hopkins called 'his spiritual insight into nature':

> What I suppose grows on people is that Wordsworth's peculiar grace, his *charisma*, as theologians say, has been granted in equal measure to so very few men since time was – to Plato and who else? I mean his spiritual insight into nature; and this they perhaps think is above all the poet's gift?[5]

Hopkins did not think this to be the poet's gift, which he saw as rhetoric; but his understanding that Wordsworth had a peculiar grace (a phrase which he borrowed from Wordsworth's 'Resolution and Independence') is Hopkins's way of saying that Wordsworth was a prophet (as he certainly wished to be known) and that he had succeeded in communicating his prophecy to others. The religious presence becomes immediately evident: the prophet–poet has taught, communicated, inspired, handed down his 'spiritual insight into nature' (which is one reason why the Jesuit Hopkins is uneasy).

What has happened in the 'credal lyrics' is that Wordsworth has summarised his beliefs, his idiosyncratic faith, in a way that makes it credible to many readers; and in so doing he is living dangerously, as we shall see. The creed is stated so unambiguously that there is no escaping the consequences of reading it. This is why I want to examine it: there are many more rewarding parts of Wordsworth but none so naked and so perversely insistent. It is a kind of Wordsworthian fundamentalism, the prophet–poet at his most demanding. And since in the last few years it has tended to become neglected, passed over in favour of other Wordsworthian features, such as sensitivity to the use of language in expressing complex intuitions, it deserves to be revisited for its very plainness.

It is private because it is prophetic, and prophetic because it is private. Hopkins's use of the word 'charisma', which is also Max Weber's crucial word in defining the prophet, directs our attention to this; and according to Weber the prophet is a 'purely individual' bearer of charisma.[6] Wordsworth begins and ends *The Prelude* with the idea of himself as a prophet (a fellow prophet with Coleridge at the end); and it is the individuality of this vision which causes the problems. In Wordsworth's 'credal lyrics' we have, carefully and unequivocally stated, the fundamental articles of his belief. From these poems the circles spread out concentrically: the beliefs become more and more diffused, refined, accommodated to the subtleties of reason and feeling; accommodated, too, to the wider human concerns of joy and grief, to the general human condition of *grandeur* and *misère*.[7] The great tragic poems of Wordsworth are easily recognised as significant in a non-religious age; it is more difficult to make something of

> Through primrose tufts, in that green bower,
> The periwinkle trailed its wreaths;
> And 'tis my faith that every flower
> Enjoys the air it breathes.

The first of the 'credal lyrics' to be written is the one entitled 'To my Sister'. It describes a beautiful day in early spring, and attempts to define some magical quality that belongs to it:

> There is a blessing in the air

> Which seems a sense of joy to yield
> To the bare trees, and mountains bare . . .

At this point I wish to reinvoke the concepts of closeness and
distance, for the word 'blessing' arrives in the first line of this
verse charged with accumulated meaning: from the myth of
Jacob and Isaac onwards, the sense of blessing as the most
valuable gift which can be gained from a father by a son is
paramount in religious thinking, so that the Old Testament
stories of blessing prefigure the New Testament ideas of Christ
blessing children, which in turn becomes a symbolic act for the
blessing of God in Redemption, the Father blessing his children.
In 'Tintern Abbey' Wordsworth had professed a 'cheerful faith,
that all which we behold / Is full of blessings'; and now the
blessing is 'in the air': it seems to have no source, and Wordsworth is drawing on a religious tradition in order to subvert and
extend its meaning. In this case the blessing is active: it yields a
sense of joy to the universe, or rather it 'seems' to yield a sense of
joy. There is much virtue in that 'seems', as in Touchstone's 'if':
it allows the reader to preserve his own reservations about
whether it is really there or whether it exists only in the mind of
the poet. To this must be added the further meaning of 'seems' –
that is, 'appears': there appears to be a sense of joy, but it is up to
us to judge the reality, whether or not it actually exists. The poet
is apparently being simple in this verse, but actually he is being
devious – in the best possible way, allowing visions and revi-
sions: there appears to be a blessing in the air, yielding joy to all
things; there appears *to me* to be a blessing in the air. Again, it
'seems' in the sense of being the only possible conclusion that
can be drawn from the evidence. It seems, therefore, that the
first mild day of March is so beautiful that there must be a
blessing in the air, yielding joy. As the reader leaves such a verse
there remains in the air an unresolved sense of possibility,
together with the other vital element, the poet's private certainty. It is followed by the prophetic call to the poet's sister:

> My sister! ('tis a wish of mine)
> Now that our morning meal is done,
> Make haste, your morning task resign;
> Come forth, and feel the sun.

It is my wish, my will that you should come out: the poet is not just indicating that he would like his sister to join him outside, but he expects an immediate acquiescence: it is an amiable command. What follows is deliberately incongruous, a domestic version of the traditional patterns of liberty and bondage. Its use of 'come forth' connects it with certain biblical moments, such as the raising of Lazarus (John 11:43) and the release of Paul and Silas from gaol (Acts 16), both of which indicate the process of freedom from death and from slavery which it is the purpose of the Christian gospel to proclaim. These in turn are prefigured by the Old Testament descriptions of the God of the children of Israel leading them out of bondage, and the trust in God during the Babylonian captivity found in the chapters of Ezekiel. In this poem, however, the coming forth is for the purpose of 'feeling the sun' a participation in a life-giving, out-of-door natural experience instead of the routine of domestic life. The putting-on of the woodland dress also emphasises the way in which his sister is invited to join him in experiencing this moment of special time. She is to bring no book, for this would be a distraction from the absolute attention which she has to give to such time – an attention, paradoxically, of idleness.

Now if Wordsworth really had been reading John Wesley, which I think is unlikely, he would have known something of the ferocity with which that great man urged the importance of early rising, not wasting time, and not being idle. Wordsworth, in defiance of the ethic of rising capitalism, encourages or portrays idleness in all of the 'credal lyrics'. Here it is a natural response to the special time of the spring day:

> No joyless forms shall regulate
> Our living calendar:
> We from today, my Friend, will date
> The opening of the year.

The living calendar is, of course, set up in opposition to the dead mechanical calendar of January to December; this is (as I have argued elsewhere[8]) sacred time as opposed to profane time, and the meaningful response to such time is no more, and no less, than enjoying the fresh air and sunshine of the spring. Once again the suggestive language and the profound patterns enclose a very simple action, or rather inaction. It is a religious pattern of movement with nothing at the centre; or, if you will, with everything at the centre. Wordsworth certainly claims this in the verse that follows:

> Love, now a universal birth,
> From heart to heart is stealing,
> From earth to man, from man to earth:
> It is the hour of feeling.

The striking arrival of 'Love' in the poem is essential, because it questions the apparent simplicity of the idleness which precedes it. Now we learn that the business of sitting out-of-doors on a spring day is being present when the interchange of love is going on. It is a universal birth, which means, I take it, that it is a birth everywhere and also that it is a birth which originates from the universe itself, from the life of all created things. It seems to be a connective and enveloping force, an I–thou relationship, although it is from earth to man and from man to earth: it is a relationship between the individual and that which lies outside him, but not, we observe, from man to God and God to man but from man to earth. If it is 'the hour of feeling', then we have to presume that this feeling, whatever it is, is not for what is traditionally thought of as the numinous, but rather for some interactive power which Wordsworth wishes us to see as holy (it was Wordsworth's attachment to nature as numinous that upset Blake and made him ill).

Yet 'the hour of feeling' is extremely unsatisfactory as a definition of what is the central feature of this special time. It is characteristic of the fundamental slipperiness of a poem which at first sight seems to be so absolutely credal; the language of religious experience is employed on a more mysterious errand:

> One moment now may give us more
> Than years of toiling reason:
> Our minds shall drink at every pore
> The spirit of the season.

Again, there is a curious absence of particulars here. We discover only that this precious moment will result in 'silent laws' which will be made in our hearts, 'Which they shall long obey'.

The silence of these laws is significant: they seem to have been written within and never uttered or 'outered' (to use Terence Hawkes's play upon words). They are the private property of the feeling individual and not the unsilent laws of doctrine and authority: 'Lord have mercy upon us, and write all these thy laws in our hearts, we beseech thee.' The tradition of Christian thought and biblical authority is undermined by the privacy and silence of the laws. The closeness of the language masks the profound distance between inner and outer, between that which is subscribed to as part of an accepted code of belief and that which is the property of private experience and thought. For instance, in the verse which follows:

> And from the blessed power that rolls
> About, below, above,
> We'll frame the measure of our souls:
> They shall be tuned to love.

This sounds like Isaac Watts, but is actually far removed from his orthodoxy, determined as that is by his paraphrasing mind. The blessed power, is, like God, in all things, 'Him that filleth all in all' (Ephesians 1:23), or who 'worketh all in all' (I Corinthians 12:6) but it is clearly not God. Traditional religious language is being overtaken and subsumed into the primacy of individual experience. Thus we are returned to the dilemma: that doctrine without imagination, without the infused grace of the perceiving and interpreting mind, is formulaic; and, on the other hand, the speculations of the individual upon such matters may well lead to unorthodoxy, to heresy, or to the simply personal. On the difficult accommodation of these two things rests the crux of the relationship between literature and religion: at its most secure that relationship rests upon a corroboration of vision and event of the kind which is found in the rediscovery of Old Testament prophecies in the actions of the New Testament. Such a recalling of the Old Testament prophets gives significance to the New Testament events (because they are seen as part of a pattern of history) and gives substance and justification to the original visions. The unquestioned power of Old Testament prophets is one reason why the Romantics were so interested in Ezekiel and why Blake, for instance, claimed to have dined with Ezekiel and Isaiah. The problems come, as Blake undoubtedly realised, when the prophetic vision goes unheard, or unreflected in events; even more when the prophetic vision becomes uncontrollable, or antinomian, or plain daft, as it did with Joanna Southcott.

Wordsworth's credal lyrics may be the work of a prophet--poet, but they are also characterised by a private and domestic arrangement. The original title of 'To my sister' was 'Lines written at a small distance from my House, and sent by my little Boy to the Person to whom they are addressed', which immediately suggests an intimacy, and even a game, with little Basil Montagu acting as a go-between in the communication between the poet and his sister. It is instructive to notice in this respect how different Wordsworth's private confidence in his individual vision is from Coleridge's hectic oscillations at this time between orthodoxy and Unitarianism; only four weeks before the poem was written, Coleridge had come back from Shrewsbury, where he had preached six sermons and finally decided not to accept the minister's position.

Apart from this month when Coleridge was away, Wordsworth would have enjoyed Coleridge's company almost uninterruptedly since the previous summer; the 'credal lyrics' gain added significance if we understand them as the work of a man who had been exposed to many religious ideas, and who had considered with particular attention the interaction between religion and politics. He had known Thomas Holcroft and William Godwin; he possessed a copy of Coleridge's *Conciones ad Populum*, and he may have seen Coleridge's 1795 lectures on Revealed Religion, which (in Peter Mann's words) 'constituted a sustained and comprehensive attempt on Coleridge's part to "find himself"'.[9] *Conciones ad Populum*, in particular, wrestles with two things that Coleridge had found to be uneasy companions in a revolutionary situation: force and love. His last paragraph ends, 'Quit yourselves like Men! Be strong! Yet let all things be done in the spirit of Love.'[10] Before that he had looked to the distant future, to 'the perfectness of future Men'; and more immediately to a kind of person who, 'uniting the zeal of the Methodist with the views of the Philosopher, should be *personally* among the Poor'.[11] By the side of such engaged speculation, such agitated description of various kinds of unsatisfactory, wild and headstrong revolutionaries, and such futuristic vision, Wordsworth's poems seem a deliberate exercise in private authenticity.

In religious terms this makes his poetry more difficult to talk about because it is much more intuitive and private than Coleridge's attempts to apply doctrine and precept to the local situation.

We notice this in the second of Wordsworth's credal lyrics, 'Lines Written in Early Spring':

> I heard a thousand blended notes
> While in a grove I sat reclined
> In that sweet mood when pleasant thoughts
> Bring sad thoughts to the mind.

This is obviously a very private and even inexplicable experience, that blending of pain and pleasure which is unaccountable. The poem goes on to suggest at least one reason, the contrast between the sense of nature and the works of man:

> To her fair works did Nature link
> The human soul that through me ran;
> And much it grieved my heart to think
> What man has made of man.

The brooding of the last line becomes almost abstract when compared with Coleridge's agitated commentary on the political and revolutionary times in *Conciones ad Populum* and the 1795 lectures: in Wordsworth's phraseology it becomes a philosophical point, a commentary on the fallen world. He oscillates in this poem between human failure and natural goodness, between the actual and the ideal, between his own consciousness of himself as a human being and therefore part of the sad process, and his faith that there is a better existence:

> Through primrose tufts, in that green bower,
> The periwinkle trailed its wreaths;
> And 'tis my faith that every flower
> Enjoys the air it breathes.

'Nature's holy plan', as it is called in the final verse, is that all creatures shall have pleasure in their movements, their activities, their very existence. This, like the appearance of the old man in 'Resolution and Independence', is a belief that is 'sent from heaven'. If it is holy and sent from heaven, it ought to have some connection with a divine presence who sent it; and yet the poem has no apparent reference to any teaching of this kind, nor to any doctrine or traditional context of prayer and praise. Wordsworth has taken over words such as 'faith', 'heaven' and 'holy', and applied them to his own individual belief. This is not so much 'split religion', as T. E. Hulme characterised Romanticism, as an assertion of an alternative belief, given credibility by the authenticity of the poet's private experience. It is the forerunner of reinterpretation of Scripture, of existentialism and of unorthodoxy; to some, such as John Stuart Mill, it represented a new and vital spiritual truth.[12]

IV

These two short poems indicate something of the difficulty of using religious language in expressing the individual insights of Romantic poetry; or at least, the difficulty of using it without causing tensions between orthodoxy and unorthodoxy. Wordsworth is not just spilling religion: he is appropriating its language for his own religion. These poems, and others, are extremely interesting, and also difficult to engage with, because they suggest a shamanic communication with ideas and states that are beyond the powers of ordinary men. In this connection they may be compared with another composition of 1798, the lines entitled 'The Pedlar' which Wordsworth added to 'The Ruined Cottage' (written in 1797). In 1797 the poem had, it is believed, been a simple and unadorned tragedy; in 1798 Wordsworth added much of the description of the pedlar, in which we learn of his upbringing and his beliefs:

> He was a chosen son:
> To him was given an ear which deeply felt
> The voice of Nature in the obscure wind,
> The sounding mountain and the running stream.
> To every natural form, rock, fruit, and flower,
> Even the loose stones that cover the highway,
> He gave a moral life; he saw them feel
> Or linked them to some feeling. In all shapes
> He found a secret and mysterious soul,

> A fragrance and a spirit of strange meaning.
> Though poor in outward shew, he was most rich;
> He had a world about him – 'twas his own,
> He made it – for it only lived to him
> And to the God who looked into his mind.

The pedlar has his own world, for, like God, he made it; it lives only to him and to God, and the God who looks into his mind is clearly also the God who looks out of it, the creation of the sublime and awe-inspiring intellect. The world about him is created by him, in his own individual assumption of God-like activity. It is the process which Coleridge was later to distinguish by the name of imagination, whether primary or secondary, that repeats on earth the great creative activity of the infinite I AM. But, although this seems like repetition, it may not be, for no man has seen God at any time; and the problem remains that individual belief may take over the language of religion without its substance.

The pedlar is a case in point. His ability (described elsewhere in the poem) to suffer with those whom he saw suffer, and his tranquillity when faced with the tragic events of Margaret's life and death in the ruined cottage, suggest a mind that is scarcely human in its awesome philosophical grandeur. In the first version (MS B) the poem ends with Margaret's death – 'Last human tenant of these ruined walls'[13] – but, probably in 1798, Wordsworth added the conclusion which is found in MS D, in which the pedlar seems to find a calm which the tragedy scarcely justifies:

> My Friend, enough to sorrow have you given,
> The purposes of wisdom ask no more;
> Be wise and cheerful, and no longer read
> The forms of things with an unworthy eye.
> She sleeps in the calm earth, and peace is here.

At first sight this looks like a Sophoclean acceptance, and a belief that the peace of death is better than the uncertainty and misery of life. But its mixture of consolation and acceptance of so much avoidable misery is disquieting. It is followed by a description of the weeds and spear-grass all dewy and misted over, and the tranquillity which they conveyed:

That what we feel of sorrow and despair
From ruin and from change, and all the grief
The passing shews of being leave behind,
Appeared an idle dream that could not live
Where meditation was. I turned away
And walked along my road in happiness.

These are the final words of the pedlar. He turns away with a kind of serenity which is very difficult to comprehend: indeed it is the central and most mysterious difficulty of Wordsworth's poetry. In attempting to understand it, the reader is driven to consider certain features of the pedlar's life and character which, as it turns out, are related to the questions raised by this present inquiry.

In the first place, the pedlar is a chosen son. Like the children of Jacob his chosen, the pedlar is one of those who is close to God, one of the royal priesthood who is called, and chosen, and faithful. Secondly, the pedlar is a private man, communing with himself and with nature, solitary but not lonely, peripatetic but not devoid of intention and purpose. His rejection of a settled occupation (teaching) and his abandonment of a fixed home suggest the figure of a travelling prophet, and it is significant in this regard that Max Weber describes one of the characteristics of the prophet as the rejection of regular pecuniary reward and security.[14] The assumption of the shamanic role that goes with this is connected with the assumptions which lie behind the credal lyrics:

If this belief from heaven be sent
If such be Nature's holy plan,
Have I not reason to lament
What man has made of man?

In this verse the 'If's may be conditional, but they also carry a strong hint of 'Therefore' or 'Since' within them: the poet, convinced of the joys of the natural world, laments the misery of the human condition. He does so in a language which is curiously detached from it, which characterises the human suffering in terms of what man has made of man, not of what God has allowed to happen. So too the pedlar makes it clear that Margaret's suffering is owing not only to bad harvests and her husband's illness, but also to the absence of any provision for hardship by the community. Both the poet and the pedlar see from the position of a chosen son: each laments the miseries of man, and does so from a superior position, a place of the elect. To see these miseries from the point of view of a sufferer is a very different, as Hardy bitterly noted in a sidelong glance at the credal lyrics in *Tess of the d'Urbervilles*.[15]

This is what makes Wordsworth's credal poetry so difficult. He describes his beliefs, but he is, throughout, responding to the element within himself which is not natural but supernatural, shamanic, commanding, God-like. Coleridge's suggestion that the poet, 'described in *ideal* perfection, brings the whole soul of man into activity' is another formulation that contains the God-like image latent within it. Thus Wordsworth, who is a maker of prayers and a worshipper of nature in 'Tintern Abbey', is also, like his pedlar, self-sufficient and all-sufficient. When Michael Edwards, in *Towards a Christian Poetics*, discusses writing as re-creation, he reminds us that 'Writing really does re-create the world for us, but it is only a sign, and analogy, of Re-creation proper, which is in the power of God.'[16] In the process of such imitation, however, the visionary poet will take upon himself, like Wordsworth and his pedlar, an attitude to *grandeur* and *misère* in human life which is appropriately God-like:

> Have I not reason to lament
> What man has made of man?

Wordsworth is here both shaman and suppliant, giver and receiver, and the credal lyrics show his adoption of a mode which can include both states. Encouraged by Coleridge, he saw himself as a giant; guided by his memory and his conscience, he knew himself to be human. Yet he was capable of writing in 1798, about the great poem of which 'The Ruined Cottage' was to be a part, 'My object is to give pictures of Nature, Man, and Society. Indeed I know not any thing which will not come within the scope of my plan.'[17]

This is a most extraordinary sentence, and it indicates Wordsworth's confidence and boldness, the recognition of the God within him. It is a concept which has a fundamental reference to the credal lyrics, for whenever Wordsworth says 'my' it is an expression of a self that is both human and divine, a recognition of the power within him:

> And 'tis my faith that every flower
> Enjoys the air it breathes.

It is this which makes Wordsworth's idea of poetry so much nobler and more authentic than John Wesley's. Wesley saw poetry as the handmaid of piety; Wordsworth *knew* it as the handmaid of truth. He knew its truth because, being a god-–poet, he knew what the truth was. His *credo* was a belief in himself. I need hardly point out how dangerous this can be; but how necessary also, if religious experience is to advance beyond the simplest formula of belief or the most slavish adherence to authority. The vocabulary of the 1798 poems, in other words, is an indication of the uneasy relationship which exists between literature and religion, between unorthodoxy and orthodoxy, between imagination and authority, between a freedom that can be dangerous and a stability that can be unimaginative.

NOTES

1. *The Methodist Hymn Book* (London, 1933) p. vi.
2. *The Prose Works of William Wordsworth*, ed. W. J. B. Owen and J. W. Smyser (Oxford, 1974) II, 79.
3. Harold Bloom, *The Visionary Company*, rev. edn (Ithaca, NY, and London, 1971) p. 1.
4. *Henry Crabb Robinson on Books and their Writers*, ed. Edith J. Morley (London, 1938) I, 87.
5. *The Correspondence of Gerard Manley Hopkins and Richard Watson Dixon*, ed. C. C. Abbott (London, 1935) p. 141.
6. Max Weber, *The Sociology of Religion*, tr. E. Fischoff (London, 1965) p. 46.
7. Pascal's terms, as summarised in Michael Edwards, *Towards a Christian Poetics* (London, 1984) pp. 2–8.
8. See J. R. Watson, *Wordsworth's Vital Soul* (London, 1982) pp. 152–5.
9. Coleridge, *Collected Works*, I: *Lectures 1795 on Politics and Religion*, ed. Lewis Patton and Peter Mann (Princeton, NJ, 1971) p. liii.
10. Ibid., p. 49.
11. Ibid., p. 43.
12. John Stuart Mill, *Collected Works*, I: *Autobiography and Literary Essays*, ed. J. M. Robson and J. Stillinger (London, 1981) p. 151: 'I felt myself at once better and happier' (ch. 5).

13. Wordsworth, *'The Ruined Cottage' and 'The Pedlar'*, ed. James A. Butler (Hassocks, Sussex, 1979) pp. 3, 14.
14. Max Weber, 'The Sociology of Charismatic Authority', repr. in *Max Weber on Charisma and Institution Building*, ed. S. N. Eisenstadt (Chicago and London, 1968) p. 21.
15. Thomas Hardy, *Tess of the d'Urbervilles*, ch. 3: 'Some people would like to know whence the poet whose philosophy is in these days deemed as profound and trustworthy as his song is breezy and pure, gets his authority for speaking of "Nature's holy plan".'
16. Edwards, *Towards a Christian Poetics*, p. 150.
17. Wordsworth, *'The Ruined Cottage' and 'The Pedlar'*, p. 16 (letter of 6 Mar 1798).

11 Changing Sensibilities: the Puritan Mind and the Romantic Revolution in Early American Religious Thought

T. MARK LEDBETTER

The Puritan mind, influenced by John Locke and the Scottish institutionists, dominated the religious scene in America for well over 200 years. From Thomas Hooker, 'that great physician of the soul and a veritable doctor of the church', who led New England Puritanism in the seventeenth century, to the Yale divine Nathaniel Taylor, a strong and vocal Neocalvinist of the early nineteenth century, Puritan sensibilities were firmly established in the theological pursuits of the American intelligentsia. While Anglicans, Baptists, Lutherans and Quakers early on established religious communities in America, Sydney Ahlstrom points out that even as late as 1775 'the Puritans comprised seventy-five percent of the religious population in the United States'. With characteristic religious zeal and intellectual vigour, Puritanism established itself as a formidable foe to any religious or philosophical movement that threatened its spiritual tenets. Unitarianism posed little threat because the movement had too few converts until the nineteenth century. And, with surprising adaptability, the Puritans, who had always tended to emphasise an element of rationalism in their theological doctrines, incorporated many ideas of the Enlightenment into their own religious beliefs.

Not until the November of 1829 when James Marsh published Coleridge's *Aids to Reflection* in its first American edition, did there exist a viable alternative to Puritanism for the theologically minded liberals who had begun to make their presence known to the American religious scene. Certain that here must be a religious alternative to the Enlightenment other than orthodoxy, Marsh published the *Aids* with a long prefatory essay of his own. The publication gave new life to the nascent movement of Transcendentalism and established new religious sensibilities in America. A radical change took place in the Puritan consciousness that was so dominant on the American religious scene in the 1820s, a Romantic revolution that was led by James Marsh. With the publication of Coleridge's *Aids to Reflection* in 1829, Marsh provided a long-awaited alternative to Lockean philosophy and the Christian orthodoxy so prevalent in the churches and academies of particularly the northeastern United States. Marsh's alternative is best understood by a critical evaluation of the established Christian thought of the period with reference to its most outspoken proponent, Jonathan Edwards, followed by a critical explication of Marsh's response to the Calvinist tradition found in his prefatory remarks to the *Aids*.

The Edwardians were the strongest Puritan faction during the eighteenth century. They took their name from Jonathan Edwards (1703–58), their spiritual and intellectual leader. Edwards was a preacher firmly established in the New England Puritan tradition. Son of a minister and a graduate of Yale, Edwards worked hard to bring together the speculation of the Platonic tradition with the ever-increasing demands of modern science.[1] Influenced greatly by Isaac Newton and John Locke, Edwards attempted to combine the spiritual nature and the rigid self-discipline of the Puritans with the Enlightenment's emphasis on reason.

What did Edwards preach? He taught that Christian spiritual experience is analogous to sensory experience – straight from John Locke – and that such spiritual experience gives authentic knowledge of the divine.[2] Edwards writes, 'Those ideas are false that are not consistent with the series of ideas that are raised in our minds by, according to, the order of nature.'[3]

Edwards believed that there was a cause and effect for everything. Even the existence of God must be proved by discursive reasoning, and he scoffs at those who would talk of God by reference to intuition. Edwards claimed that it is an 'absurdity' 'not properly [to] come to the knowledge of the being of God by arguing: but our evidence be intuitive'.[4] Man proves God's existence *a posteriori* or from effects: 'prove by argumentation, not intuition' – 'from the proved necessity of his existence'. Simply put, things cannot exist without a cause and God is the cause. And there cannot be 'more in the effect than in the cause'.[5] The intuitive soul of the human being has no place in the theology of Edwards. The human creature is special because he possesses the power to reason in terms of cause–effect. In fact, the human species, according to Edwards, is a part of the cause–effect cycle. 'Those beings which have knowledge and consciousness are the only proper and real and substantial beings, inasmuch as the being of the other things is only by these.'[6] The human creature knows things 'as necessarily connected with others and dependent on them'.[7] While this appeared to make all living things equal (humans and animals), Edwards points out that human beings differ from animals because they have souls, and 'man's soul has an end in what it does'.[8] As a creature with the power of discursive reasoning, the human being with 'knowledge and consciousness' is aware of and can make sense of his place in the world.

Edwards best represented Puritan orthodoxy's views on free will and original sin. Concerning free will, Edwards believed that freedom existed as a metaphysical principle but only as a part of God's plan for the world. His reasoning again is cause–effect, and he couches his argument in an if–then corollary. If God does not foreknow the lives of all human creatures and the future of the world that he created, then 'God is liable to be continuously repenting what he has done'.[9] If the human being possesses free will, redemption is a product of God's 'own disappointment', and an attempt on God's part 'to mend and patch up, as well as he could, his system'.[10] And if a human being retained free will after redemption, how long would it be before God is 'disappointed a second time' in his creation?

Concerning sin, Edwards believed that all persons are tainted by sin: not by choice but by nature. Sin is self-love, and self-love 'belongs to our nature'.[11] In fact, self-love 'represents all those sinful inclinations which are in the corrupted nature of man'.[12] The human being does not choose corruption, but, because all human creatures are in direct descent from Adam, they share

Adam's corrupted nature. God dealt with Adam 'as the head of the whole body . . . from which it will follow, that both guilt, or exposedness to punishment, and also depravity of heart, came upon Adam's posterity just as they came upon him, as much as if he and they had all coexisted, like a tree with many branches'.[13] Sin is not the fault of Adam, but sin is a state of human nature. Adam is merely the first of an organism of which all human beings are a part.

The dominant philosophical position of American thought at the beginning of the nineteenth century was that knowledge is outside the mind, located in an object. One possesses a knowledge of objects, and these objects, in turn, inform the mind of truth. Marsh wished to move beyond this position to the philosophical stance that knowledge is of the mind itself and truths are beyond observation. What Marsh desired, writes Ronald Wells, was 'not primarily a theory of knowledge or a system of ethics, but an assertion of religious faith that was neither derived from natural science and natural rights and in that sense transcendental nor dependent upon ecclesiastical tradition and in that sense philosophical'.[14] Calvinistic orthodoxy adamantly opposed such a view, and for this reason Marsh found himself a transcendentalist.

Marsh believed that transcendentalism was capable of its own 'great awakening', and that the movement was the only viable alternative to orthodoxy. He writes, 'May we not venture at least without incurring the charge of arrogance and youthful presumption, to indulge a suspicion, that "there are more things in heaven and earth than are dreamed of" in the sensuous and empirical philosophy of the day.'[15] There is a difference between the natural and the spiritual, and the human creature must learn to appreciate the difference. Coleridge's *Aids* would inform this appreciation.

Coleridge's *Aids to Reflection*, writes Marsh, functions as the 'title imports'.[16] The philosophical work is an aid to the mental practice of reflection. There exist certain truths, philosophical truths, which one understands only by means of reflection. What constitutes reflection? Marsh explains that it is 'to turn the mind continually back upon the premises themselves – upon the inherent grounds of truth and error in its own being' (p. xxiv). He is echoing Coleridge, who describes reflection as 'the exercise of the reasoning and reflecting powers, increasing insight, and

enlarging views', and 'requisite to keep alive the substantial faith
in the heart' (p. 7). Truth and knowledge must be found 'in the
laws of our own being, or they are not found at all' (p. xxv).
Self-inspection leads to a higher plane of religious existence. And
once the individual understands his own being, he comes closer
to understanding the 'ground of all being' (p. xxv). For these
reasons, Coleridge's *Aids* would be a welcome sight on the
American religious scene, because, writes Marsh,

> Whatever indeed tends to awaken and cherish the power and
> to form the habit, of reflection upon the great constituent
> principles of our own permanent being and proper humanity,
> and upon the abiding laws of truth and duty, as revealed in
> our reason and conscience, can not but promote our highest
> interests as moral and rational beings.   (p. xxvi)

One of the major contributions of Coleridge's *Aids*, according
to Marsh, is the introduction of philosophy as a means by which
a person may pursue religious truths. He notes that at the time of
the publication of the *Aids*, 'a strong prejudice exists against the
introduction of philosophy in any form, in the discussion of
theological subjects' (p. xxxiii). Calvinists believed that philosophy deviates from the path of the traditional revealed religion
and that philosophy is not based in Scripture. Marsh is unwilling to accept the traditional view that philosophy cannot be
religious or that religion cannot be philosophical. It is not an
unthinkable matter to apply philosophy to the interpretation of
Scripture. What is important is the ultimate goal of philosophy.
The use of philosophy should be an 'endeavour by profound
reflection to learn the real requirements of reason, and attain a
true knowledge of ourselves' (p. xxxix). As Coleridge noted, 'He
that speaks against his own reason, speaks against his own
conscience' (p. 229).
    Marsh points out that there is a certain hypocrisy in the
opinion that philosophy does not play a major role in the search
for religious truths. What religious system can exist without at
least a minimal reliance on philosophy? Every writer today,
Marsh exclaims, claims to be guided 'only by common sense and
the laws of interpretation. But I should like to know how a man
comes by any common sense in relation to the movements and
laws of his intellectual and moral being without metaphysics'.

Thus the question is not, 'Do we use philosophy?', but 'Is it true?' 'We can have no right views of theology until we have the right views of the human mind: and that these are to be acquired only by labouring and preserving reflection' (p. xl). The preservation of reflection is a philosophical task, and therefore philosophy must be an integral part of the religious quest.

As one might expect, Marsh believed that the key to Coleridge's system and its value to the American religious scene was Coleridge's distinction between understanding and reason. Marsh believed that this important distinction explained the dichotomy between nature and spirit and 'boldly asserts the reality of something distinctively spiritual in man' (p. xxxi). Marsh's forerunners used the terms 'reason' and 'understanding' interchangeably. Reason or understanding was the means by which man comprehended the natural world and, in turn, God.

Yet Marsh, taking his cue directly from Coleridge, gives reason a unique role in man's spiritual pursuits. Reason differs in kind from understanding. While understanding is discursive and refers to an other, reason is fixed and stands on its own ground (p. 148). Reason becomes the basis for universal and necessary laws, and reason determines the conditions for understanding. 'Reason is the power of universal and necessary convictions, the source and substance of truth above sense' (p. 143). Understanding is a part of human experience, it is a part of Being, but understanding is not Being itself. As Coleridge explains, even 'beasts partake of understanding' (p. 144). Reason is Being and 'the end of Understanding is to lose itself in reason, which by definition is eternal'.

Marsh uses a common-sense approach to Coleridge's concept of reason to convince the common-sense philosophers of its superiority to the understanding. To claim that something is reasonable is to claim that it is not irrational. And one would not expect a spiritual truth to be irrational. 'Nay, I maintain', writes Marsh, 'that when we use the term [reason] in the higher sense [reasonable/rational reason – as opposed to absurd or irrational], it is impossible for us to believe on any authority what is directly contradictory to reason and seen to be so' (p. xxxiv). He continues that there is one reason and anything that contradicts that reason 'can not be received as a matter either of knowledge or faith' (p. xxxv).

Reason informs the intuitive insight of the human being, enlightening that person concerning 'certain moral and spiritual truths' (p. xxxiv). As Coleridge explains, Reason is the 'reference to actual truth' and 'the fountain of ideas' (p. 143). These truths, as part of the intuitive process submitted to the view of reason, are attributed to 'the Supreme Reason, to the Divine Mind' (p. xxxv), and, therefore, the individual must give to these intuitive truths, governed by reason, the same validity he gives to a mathematical equation. It is ludicrous and irrational to believe a proposition in philosophy and, at the same time, deny it in theology.

What Coleridge has done, to the delight of Marsh, is to establish that religious truth 'cannot be shown to contradict the unchangeable principles of right reason', and that, while a religious truth might be 'incomprehensible' to the understanding or the world of experience, such incomprehensibility is not 'an obstacle to our faith' (p. xxxviii).

Marsh does battle with the proponents of 'positive science and theoretical insight'. Such people wish to reduce the pursuit of religious truth to speculative knowledge. But speculative knowledge does not equate to a spiritual life. He quotes approvingly from Coleridge that 'Christianity is not a *theory* or a *speculation*, but a *life*. Not a *philosophy* of life, but a life and living process' (p. xlii). Marsh wishes to dismiss the notion of empirical knowledge as religious foundation. Rather, religion must be a form of being, 'a principle of unity and consistency in itself distinct from the unity and consistency or our theoretical views'. Important is what a person 'feels and knows spiritually' (pp. xlii–xliv).

Marsh had long awaited a spokesman of Coleridge's eloquence to speak in favour of free will. He thought it absurd to believe with the Edwardians that 'acts of the free-will are predetermined by a cause *out of the will*, according to the same law of cause and effect which controls the changes in the physical world' (p. xlix). If persons are under the control of the laws of nature, what happens to moral responsibility and the need for grace, forgiveness and redemption? Marsh fails to see any logic in the Lockean argument of cause–effect. Also, if individuals must conform to the physical laws of nature, they are no better than the 'brutes' that roam the earth (p. l), and, therefore, human beings are no more blameworthy for their acts than the animals. The belief in a cause–effect philosophy 'preclude[s] the very idea of a free-will, and render[s] the feeling of moral responsibility not an enigma merely, not a mystery, but a self-contradiction and an absurdity', and stands in direct contradiction to human reason (p. lii).

Self-approbation or remorse suggests that every human being possesses free will. Marsh suggests that it is a contradiction to claim that being is created under a law of nature yet possesses a feeling of moral obligation 'to fulfil a law above its nature' (p. liii). Nathaniel Taylor had suggested that, while a person must, according to the nature and the origin of sin, commit sin, there is a power to the contrary. But, if sin is a law of nature, writes Marsh in his Preface, there is no 'power to the contrary', and, if there is a 'power to the contrary', then there must be self-determined will (p. lvi).

The publication of Coleridge's *Aids to Reflection*, along with Marsh's prefatory remarks, made a radical impact on religious thought in America. The intelligentsia, mainly young theologians of the transcendental persuasion, hailed Coleridge's work as not only seminal but prophetic. James Freeman Clarke, a noted churchman, claimed that after reading the *Aids to Reflection*, he 'was born a transcendentalist'.[17] America's greatest religious mind of the period, Ralph Waldo Emerson, who claimed that he was 'tired and disgusted with the preaching' he had 'been accustomed to hear',[18] discovered in the writings of Coleridge the two elements that were to become central to his religious thought: 'the primacy of spirit over matter and the immediacy of God to the human soul'.[19]

All that I have said leads to perhaps more interesting questions and to the next essay to be written on this subject. Does Coleridge misread German idealism (and many believe that he does), and does Marsh pass this misreading on to his audience, helping to perpetuate transcendentalism as a religion based in part on philosophical simplification? But, even if such an assertion is true, it remains imperative to acknowledge the tremendous debt owed to James Marsh and Coleridge for their contributions to early American religious thought.

NOTES

1. *Theology in America*, ed. Sydney Ahlstrom (Indianapolis, 1967) p. 149.
2. H. Shelton Smith, Robert T. Handy and Lefferts A. Loetscher,

American Christianity: An Historical Interpretation with Representative Documents, I (New York, 1960) 340.

3. Jonathan Edwards, 'The Mind, No. 10', in *Theology in America*, p. 157.
4. Ibid.
5. Ibid., p. 158.
6. Jonathan Edwards, 'Of Being', ibid., p. 155.
7. Edwards, 'The Mind, No. 10', ibid., p. 159.
8. Ibid., p. 160.
9. Jonathan Edwards, 'Freedom of the Will', ibid., p. 169.
10. Ibid., p. 170.
11. Jonathan Edwards, 'Miscellanies', ibid., p. 172.
12. Ibid.
13. Jonathan Edwards, 'Original Sin', ibid., p. 173.
14. Donald Vale Wells, *Three Christian Transcendentalists: James Marsh, Caleb Sprague Henry, Frederic Henry Hedge* (New York, 1972) pp. 146–7.
15. Ibid., p. 22
16. Coleridge, *Aids to Reflection*, with preliminary essay by James Marsh, 4th edn (London, 1913) p. xxiv. Further references in text.
17. Smith, Handy and Loetscher, *American Christianity*, p. 121.
18. Ibid., p. 119.
19. Ibid., p. 120.

12 Tennyson, Newman and the Question of Authority

MICHAEL WHEELER

I

Of all areas of nineteenth-century English theology, none was more problematic and contentious than that concerning life after death.[1] The centrality of the subject in the Victorian period is reflected in the sheer quantity and variety of other kinds of writing on death, and in the fact that Tennyson, the leading poet of his generation, and Newman, the greatest English Christian apologist of the age, both wrote poems which directly addressed the subject of the future life, and which were well received by a wide variety of readers. *In Memoriam* (1850) and *The Dream of Gerontius* (1865) were welcomed by Victorian readers as helpful, and specifically hopeful, religious poetry, although their interpretations of the Christian hope of eternal life are very different. Tennyson's tentative expression of a vague 'larger hope' (*In Memoriam*, lv[2]) was later to become something of a rallying cry for F. W. Farrar, a leading churchman who, although not himself a 'universalist', was as hostile as Tennyson and F. D. Maurice towards what he called 'the common view' of judgement and everlasting punishment.[3] In contrast to Tennyson, the confident hope expressed in the Soul's final speech in the *Dream* is predicated on belief in Christ as both saviour and judge, and an idea of the pains of purgatory as 'The longing for Him, when thou seest Him not; / The shame of self at thought of seeing Him'.[4] In an age, however, increasingly troubled by the damnatory or 'fulminating' clauses of the Athanasian Creed (which, incidentally, Tennyson's father refused to read in church), and, in the second half of the century, by the idea of the majority of

185

mankind being condemned to everlasting punishment in the fires of hell, Newman's emphasis upon purgatory as sanctification rather than satisfaction, purification rather than punishment, made some Protestant readers highly receptive to the poem's teaching.[5]

In examining these poems in the context of nineteenth-century ideas on the nature of the future life, one is constantly brought back to the fundamental question of authority, and specifically the relationship between each work and its respective authorities, or authoritative sources. Tennyson, of course, inherited his Romantic precursors' respect for the authority of the heart, but not the authoritative voice of the Romantic poet as *vates*. The Prologue to *In Memoriam* (introductory stanzas written for the trial issue of March 1850) is in part an act of contrition – 'Forgive these wild and wandering cries'; and, in the lyrics that follow, Tennyson is acutely self-conscious in his acknowledgement of their therapeutic value for the 'unquiet heart and brain' (v). From the early lyrics of bereavement and loss, of the dark house 'where my heart was used to beat' (vii), through the central lyrics of doubt, where 'the heart is sick' (l), to the point at which

> My heart, tho' widow'd, may not rest
>   Quite in the love of what is gone,
>   But seeks to beat in time with one
> That warms another living breast
>
> (lxxxv)

the heart's pain is written out – in both senses – in a kind of diary form.[6] The poem is also a religious confession, however, and here the question of *religious* authority, with which I am principally concerned, comes into view.

For Bernard Ramm, 'Revelation is the key to religious authority.' Whereas the Roman Catholic Church bases its doctrine of authority and its claim to infallibility upon God's revelation (contained in the scriptures and in oral tradition) and his 'one true Church', the Protestant principle of authority is defined by Ramm as 'the Holy Spirit speaking in the Scriptures': 'there is an *external* principle (the *inspired* Scripture) and an *internal* principle (the witness of the Holy Spirit). It is the principle of an objective *divine* revelation, with an interior divine witness.'[7]

The antithesis between Catholic and Protestant positions was placed in a historical context by Friedrich Schleiermacher, the leading Protestant Romantic theologian of the early nineteenth century. For Schleiermacher himself, authority lies in religious experience, in what he defines as 'Feeling and Self-consciousness' – equivalent terms which he juxtaposes in order to avoid misinterpretation of his word 'feeling' as simply emotion, or even unconscious states, while the 'essence of piety' is defined by him as 'the consciousness of being absolutely dependent, or, which is the same thing, of being in relation with God'.[8] Hegel is reputed to have said that, if the essence of religion consists in the feeling of an absolute dependence, 'then the dog would be the best Christian'. Early in his career, however, Hegel himself had defined a 'religious man' as a one whose 'heart feels the activity, the awe and presence of the Godhead . . . he bows before Him, utters thanks and praise'.[9]

The appeal to the heart and to feeling in matters of religion has a venerable history, of course, from the Psalmist's 'harden not your heart' (Psalm 95) and St Paul's 'fleshy tables of the heart' (II Corinthians 3:3) to Pascal's *Pensées*: 'We know Truth not only through reason, but also by the heart; it is in this way that we have knowledge of first principles.'[10] It is in European Romanticism, however, a period of secular intellectual 'reformation', that the heart and feeling are apotheosised as the inner or internal authority in both theology and literature. For Coleridge, whose influence on Newman, F. D. Maurice and (through the Cambridge Apostles) Tennyson, was profound, the heart's function provides an analogy for the living principle of Christianity. The word *heart* recurs again and again in his *Aids to Reflection* (1825), where he writes, 'Too soon did the doctors of the Church forget that the *heart*, the *moral* nature, was the beginning and the end; and that truth, knowledge, and insight were comprehended in its expansion.'[11] For Coleridge, however, as for Schleiermacher, the hope of eternal life is firmly grounded in Christ, as both a model for this present life – Christians are to look to him as 'their Pattern both in doing and suffering, and drawing power from him for going through both' – and as risen Lord.[12] Schleiermacher writes on the future life,

all the indications [the Redeemer] gives are either purely figurative, or otherwise so indefinite in tenor that nothing can be gathered from them more than what for every Christian is so much the essential thing in every conception he may form of

existence after death, that without it such existence would be
mere perdition – namely, the persistent union of believers
with the Redeemer.[13]

The 'indefinite' quality of New Testament teaching on the
nature of the future life is the root cause of all doctrinal debate on
the subject. The story of the raising of Lazarus, for example,
raises more questions than it answers, as Tennyson himself
knew:

> Behold a man raised up by Christ!
>   The rest remaineth unrevealed;
>   He told it not; or something seal'd
> The lips of that Evangelist.
>   (*In Memoriam*, xxxi)

For Tennyson, however, speculation on what lies 'behind the
veil' (lvi) remained a lifelong obsession, and one which (in-
versely) probably shaped his interpretation of Scripture. A year
after the publication of *In Memoriam*, when he was living at
Twickenham, Tennyson told William Allingham that he could
not eat his dinner without a belief in immortality: 'If I didn't
believe in that [immortality, not his dinner], I'd go down immediately and jump off Richmond Bridge.' He would read any
book on theology, science or spiritualism, listen avidly to any
theory, that might throw light on the question. 'What I want', he
told Allingham in 1868, is 'an assurance of immortality.'[14] With
his yearning for assurance of immortality, and a belief in universal progress, went a liberal position on the question of hell, as his
son Hallam reveals in the *Memoir*:

> One day towards the end of his life he bade me look into the
> Revised Version and see how the Revisers had translated the
> passage 'Depart from me, ye cursed, into everlasting fire'
> [Matthew 25:41]. His disappointment was keen when he
> found that the translators had not altered 'everlasting' into
> 'aeonian' or some such word: for he never would believe that
> Christ could preach 'everlasting punishment'.[15]

Although in 1884 Tennyson referred Allingham to 'Farrar's
book', which 'proves from original sources that no such doctrine
[of everlasting damnation] existed in the early days of Chris-

tianity',[16] Farrar only confirmed what he himself had always felt
and thus believed. When Tennyson stated that 'everlasting
damnation' was 'not a right translation', Allingham answered,
'But it's the authoritative teaching of the Church.'

It is instructive to move from such reminiscences of Tennyson
to Newman's devastating note on liberalism in the *Apologia Pro
Vita Sua*, published a year before *The Dream of Gerontius*: 'Liberalism then is the mistake of subjecting to human judgment those
revealed doctrines which are in their nature beyond and independent of it, and of claiming to determine on intrinsic grounds
the truth and value of propositions which rest for their reception
simply on the external authority of the Divine Word.' Indeed,
the ninth liberal proposition which Newman 'earnestly de-
nounced and abjured' could be applied to Tennyson on the
Revised Version: 'There is a right of Private Judgment: that is,
there is no existing authority on earth competent to interfere
with the liberty of individuals in reasoning and judging for
themselves about the Bible and its contents, as they severally
please.' Newman's approach is diametrically opposed to the
liberal position, and he defends the Roman Catholic Church
against the accusation that 'an infallible authority destroys the
independence of the mind'.[17] Tennyson agreed with Newman on
the limits of human reason in matters of religion, and would, I
think, have understood the concept of the 'illative sense'; but
here the common ground between them ends. Newman's idea of
development, for example, is by definition quite different from
Tennyson's idea of the progress of the human race. Whereas
Tennyson's eclectic religious sensibility drew upon those aspects
of Christianity which he felt to be true, selecting, as it were, from
a position outside the Church and its doctrine, Newman writes
from within a Catholic faith which, while retaining (on his
argument) the possibility of independence of mind for the believer, rests on the authority of the Church, to which the believer
willingly submits. We must now consider these differences as
revealed in *In Memoriam* and *The Dream of Gerontius*.

II

Tennyson's plea for forgiveness which I quoted earlier – 'Forgive these wild and wandering cries' – comes at the end of a
'Prologue' which begins with the invocation, 'Strong Son of God,

immortal Love . . . Thine are these orbs of light and shade'. T. S. Eliot, who found the poem's faith 'a poor thing', but its doubt 'a very intense experience', commented on the fact that the '"Strong Son of God, immortal Love", with an invocation of whom the poem opens, has only a hazy connexion with the Logos, or the Incarnate God'.[18] Jerome Buckley goes further, arguing that, although the 'Prologue' addresses the Son of God, *In Memoriam* is seldom specifically Christian.'[19] Buckley's subsequent description of the generality and universality of Tennyson's religious position is borne out by the notable emphasis on God's ineffable nature in the poem, and on the inadequacy of human attempts to know and describe him:

> Our little systems have their day;
>   They have their day and cease to be:
>   They are but broken lights of thee,
> And thou, O Lord, art more than they.
>
> ('Prologue')

Christ is generally described in the broadest theological terms in *In Memoriam*, without the particularity that often marks devotional writing: 'the Life', in the account of Lazarus and his sister Mary (xxxii); 'the Word', where Tennyson refers briefly to Jesus's ministry (xxxvi); and, most significantly in terms of the poem's central theme, 'Hope', in the first Christmas Eve lyrics (xxx). Structurally, of course, the three Christmases marked what Tennyson called 'the divisions of the poem' after the death of Hallam.[20] Theologically, while foregrounding the Light and Hope of Christmas in the coming of the Christ child, Tennyson places little emphasis upon the life of Christ (unlike Coleridge); Jesus's authoritative teaching (in the Lazarus story, for example, where he proclaims, 'I am the *resurrection*, and the life' – John 11:25); the farewell discourses in John 14–16; Christ as saviour and judge; or, crucially, the death and resurrection of the Redeemer (the ground of hope for Schleiermacher). Thus Tennyson does not seem to look to what Ramm calls the external principle of inspired Scripture for his authority.

   To press the point a little further, the Christian piety of the 'Prologue' – 'I trust he lives *in thee*' [my emphasis added] – is inadequately supported in the main body of *In Memoriam*, where the raising of Lazarus is treated speculatively in a section of the poem which asks, 'How fares it with the happy dead?' (xliv) The various ideas of a future state which are explored in the poem do not convey the sense of Christ *as* heaven which is affirmed in the 'Prologue', but rather of heaven as either individual persistence or absorption into 'the general Soul'. Unlike most Victorian ideas of heaven, Tennyson's had no sense of place (and here, perhaps, his vagueness is to be welcomed), no angelic host, but above all no conception of a risen Lord.

The lyrics in *In Memoriam* concerned with the nature of the future life end with Tennyson's famous defence of his lyrical strategy ('If these brief lays, of Sorrow born' – xlviii), in which the unique quality of the poem is captured beautifully. Tennyson was free to draw upon Christian tradition analogically, and without sustaining a sense of a coherent cosmology, in his 'Short swallow-flights of song, that dip / Their wings in tears, and skim away'. Tennyson once remarked, 'They are always speaking of me as if I were a writer of philosophical treatises',[21] and his defence in lyric xlviii suggests that the 'little systems' which 'have their day' ('Prologue') can be taken to include not only the heritage of philosophy, theology and science, but also his own poem. The problem of faith is faced squarely, however, and is stated most explicitly in the famous lyric cxxiv. Having failed to find God in nature, through the argument by design ('I found Him not in world or sun'), and in theology, through reason ('Nor thro' the questions men may try'), when assaulted by doubt

> A warmth within the breast would melt
> 　　The freezing reason's colder part,
> 　　And like a man in wrath the heart
> Stood up and answered 'I have felt.'
>
> No, like a child in doubt and fear:
> 　　But that blind clamour made me wise;
> 　　Then was I as a child that cries,
> But, crying, knows his father near;
>
> And what I am beheld again
> 　　What is, and no man understands;
> 　　And out of darkness came the hands
> That reach thro' nature, moulding men.

The second stanza quoted here was not in the trial issue of March 1850.[22] In the first (June 1850) and later editions the effect of this modifying stanza is characteristic of the poem as a whole; in the very process of describing the moment when he at last found the grounds of belief in feeling, Tennyson qualifies his own (authoritative) statement. Yet in this case the qualification actually brings him closer to a Schleiermachian feeling of absolute dependence, in that Romantic image of the child whose wisdom is more precious than knowledge. The added stanza thus validates the renewed sense in the final stanza of a personal identity ('what I am') in contradistinction from God ('What is'). Tennyson's idea of God as father–creator ('The Power in darkness whom we guess') is necessary in order to define his sense of self.

The sequence I have traced in lyric cxxiv, of feeling and affirmation modified into a sense of dependence and issuing in a categorical separation between self and God, is unusual in *In Memoriam*, although we will examine a variation upon it in lyric xcv in a moment. Typical, however, is the use of opposites in the lyric: warm/freezing, man/child, what I am/what is. *In Memoriam* traces such oppositions within a world of light and shade, man and brute, death and life. The larger 'diastolic–systolic rhythm' which J. C. C. Mays finds in *In Memoriam* is registered through seasonal change, the passing of the years, and the stages of bereavement.[23] But Tennyson, who had a general knowledge of physiology, would surely have shared Wordsworth's interest in the physiology of the heart, its physical reality as well as its analogical potential.[24] A post-mortem examination of Hallam after the fatal apoplectic 'rush of blood to the head' of 15 September 1833 revealed 'a want of sufficient energy in the heart'.[25] Tennyson might naturally have consulted books on the subject in 1833, or later. Whether he did or not cannot be proved, and is of only marginal interest, although the nature of Hallam's death may be reflected in the structure of Tennyson's *In Memoriam* stanza. More significantly, Tennyson's heartfelt response to that death most certainly is. The ABBA stanza has been much discussed, and particularly the effect of the rise at the end of the third line and the dying fall of the fourth,[26] described by Charles Kingsley as a return to the 'mournful minor key'.[27] To my ear the most characteristic effect of the third line is one of filling, expanding or swelling to the anticipated second B rhyme.

Another way of describing this would be dilation (or diastole), and indeed the four-line stanzas are often not unlike the four-chambered heart in their systolic–diastolic movements. (Lyric xix provides a particularly striking example of this effect.) The most fundamental opposition in *In Memoriam* is the I–he relation of Alfred to Arthur: the beating, suffering 'unquiet heart' (v) in the 'labouring breast' (xv) of the 'I', and the 'dead calm in that noble breast / Which heaves but with the heaving deep' (xi) of the 'he'. In Romantic elegy the mourner displaces the mourned as the principal subject,[28] and it is the poet's heart's events which inform the *In Memoriam* stanza. Tennyson's *spiritual* yearning, however, is for renewed contact with Hallam, which would offer an 'assurance of immortality', both for his friend and for himself. In lyric xcv, where some kind of contact (or 'touch') is finally achieved, the question of authority becomes most critical and most problematic.

Left alone in the darkened garden, the 'I' of the poem turns to written testimony of his dead friend's past existence: 'The noble letters of the dead'. Hallam's 'silent-speaking words' are clearly authoritative for Tennyson, unequivocal evidence of the faith, vigour and boldness for which the poet himself so often strives. In the 'Lincoln MS' and all editions up to 1870, the lyric continues,

> So word by word, and line by line,
> > The dead man touch'd me from the past,
> > And all at once it seem'd at last
> His living soul was flash'd on mine,
>
> And mine in his was wound, and whirl'd
> > About empyreal heights of thought,
> > And came on that which is, and caught
> The deep pulsations of the world,
>
> Aeonian music measuring out
> > The steps of Time – the shocks of chance –
> > The blows of Death. At length my trance
> Was cancell'd, stricken thro' with doubt.

At the critical moment in which the poet is 'touched' (and we speak of being touched emotionally, in the heart), the discourse moves into a higher spiritual plane: 'His living *soul* was flash'd on mine'. This sequence is reminiscent of other literary epiphanies, such as the moment of grace in Coleridge's 'Ancient Mariner': 'A spring of love gushed from my heart, / And I blessed them unaware . . . . The self-same moment I could pray . . . .' A more important parallel, however, is the passage in the *Confessions* where, reading books by the Platonists, St Augustine passes in his meditations

> from bodies to the soul, and . . . thus with the flash of one trembling glance it arrived at THAT WHICH IS. And then I saw Thy *invisible things understood by the things which are made*. But I could not fix my gaze thereon; and my infirmity being struck back, I was thrown again on my wonted habits, carrying along with me only a loving memory thereof, and a longing for what I had, as it were, perceived the odour of, but was not yet able to feed on.[29]

Shatto and Shaw gloss 'that which is' in lyric xcv as 'an expression in Greek philosophy for the supreme Truth of things'.[30] But the close structural and verbal parallels between lyric xcv and Pusey's translation of Augustine, published three or four years before the lyric is thought to have been written (1841–2), suggest that the *Confessions* might be a specific source. Such a source might be regarded as a putative authority for Tennyson, against which he could assess his own experience, and place it in a specific Western mystical tradition. That the question of whether the Augustine passage is a source or a parallel must remain unresolved, there being no other evidence to support the source theory, is characteristic of problems of interpretation in the poem.

A similar problem arises with the much discussed crux, 'His living soul' (1850), and Tennyson's substitution in 1872 of 'The' for 'His'. Tennyson himself commented to Knowles, '*The* Living Soul, perchance the Deity – the first reading was His living Soul was flash'd on mine – but my conscience was troubled by "his". I've often had a strange feeling of being wound and wrapped in the Great Soul.'[31] Several possible explanations for the conscience-stricken emendation present themselves, including Tennyson's anxiety concerning the nature of his relationship with Hallam, and the danger that, read in 1872, twenty years after the spiritualism craze had been imported from America, the event described might have seemed like some kind of seance. Some critics argue that the version we now have ('The living soul') is preferable to the original, being suitably mysterious and ambiguous, and suggesting both Hallam and the Deity.[32] What none of the commentators has considered, however, is the question of the provenance of the collocation 'living soul'.

'His living soul' has considerable impact in the original version, being introduced at the critical turning-point of the lyric and in sharp opposition to 'the dead man'. 'Living soul' is often used in such a context in the nineteenth century, as in this simile of George Eliot's, for example: 'as futile as the embalming of the dead body in the hope that it may one day be resumed by the living soul'.[33] In popular usage, as in Mr Peggotty's 'I'm a going ... to ... sink it where I would have drownded *him*, as I'm a livin' soul' (Dickens, *David Copperfield*, ch. 31), the collocation is merely a familiar phrase which has little resonance. Although the context of Tennyson's usage ('His living soul') suggests a meaning closer to George Eliot's, the Dickens example reminds us that it could mean little more than personal identity. '*The* living soul', on the other hand, obviously refers to some higher reality, but one which may be specific and individual (Hallam's soul) or general and universal (the Deity, maybe). And in both cases – '*His*' and '*The* living soul' – we come up against a problem similar to that encountered in relation to Augustine, as possible sources crowd in upon us. In I Corinthians 15, the most important chapter in the New Testament on death and resurrection, and the basis for many passages in the Burial Service, St Paul writes of Christ as 'a quickening spirit', by whom 'shall all be made alive': 'And so it is written, The first man Adam was made a living soul [Genesis 2:7]; the last Adam was made a quickening spirit.' Coleridge commented on the 'living soul' in Genesis in *Aids to Reflection* – 'It was [man's] proper *being*, his truest *self*, *the* man *in* the man'[34] – and used the collocation in the much earlier 'Dejection' (1802): 'To her may all things live, from pole to pole, / Their life the eddying of her living soul!' Four years previously Wordsworth had written, in a famous passage which could well have been a source for Tennyson: 'we are laid asleep / In body, and become a living soul' ('Tintern Abbey'). As in the case of the *Confessions*, the presence of the Genesis text in lyric xcv would place Tennyson's experience in a specific religious tradition, although the emphasis on 'living soul' rather than 'quickening spirit' might again suggest an unwillingness to invoke the *Christian* hope of eternal life. In both cases, however, without reinforcing evidence elsewhere in *In Memoriam*, one is driven back to the position of saying that 'that which is' and 'the living soul' are commonplaces rather than allusions, features of a discourse which describes a higher reality – as 'deep pulsations', for example, signifies the cosmic equivalent of the beating of 'my heart'.

Tennyson, then, seems to write on the internal authority of his own heart, rather than invoking received, external religious or literary authority. The harmony of the 'Aeonian music', like the mixing of dusk and dawn, East and West, in the 'boundless day' of the last line of lyric xcv, is the product of felt experience rather than achieved certainty of belief. Physiology predominates over theology. The ambiguity of 'The living soul' which many readers value can also be read as an example of Tennyson's Romantic, demythologising substitutions: Hallam for Christ ('a noble type / Appearing ere the times were ripe' – Epilogue); Hallam's letters for St Augustine's Platonist books; the living soul for St Paul's quickening spirit; and assurance of immortality for a 'sure and certain hope of the Resurrection to eternal life, through our Lord Jesus Christ' (*Book of Common Prayer*).

III

Whereas Tennyson found it necessary to explain that *In Memoriam* was a 'poem, *not* an actual biography', and that '"I" is not always the author speaking of himself, but the voice of the human race speaking thro' him',[35] Newman's *Dream of Gerontius*, while 'intensely individualist' in its theology,[36] is dramatic in form, and thus far less personal than Tennyson's lyrics. The drama of the *Dream*, however, springs from feeling, albeit feeling generalised to the point of typicality, as in the poem's opening lines:

> Jesu, Maria – I am near to death,
>   And Thou art calling me; I know it now.
> Not by the token of this faltering breath,
>   This chill at heart, this dampness on my brow, –

(Jesus, have mercy! Mary, pray for me!)
    'Tis this new feeling, never felt before,
(Be with me, Lord, in my extremity!)
    That I am going, that I am no more.

                                   (p.314)

Later in the *Dream*, Gerontius's own life, death and post-mortem
existence are related to Christ's saving act of 'innermost abandonment' in the 'double agony' of 'the garden' and 'the cross'
(p.355). In this opening passage, however, Gerontius calls upon
Jesus and Mary in undisguised terror. The counterpoint of these
early lines, marked by the use of parentheses, establishes a
pattern which is to recur throughout the work, as Gerontius in
his frail humanity first invokes and finally experiences the power
of God as saviour and judge.

In the opening section of the poem this power is celebrated by
the Assistants, friends of the dying man, and representatives of
the Church militant. The enfeebled Gerontius's request, 'So
pray for me, my friends, who have not strength to pray', is
answered in words from the Mass for the Dead: the Kyrie, and
the invocation to Mary, all holy Angels, the saints and martyrs
of Holy Church. In contrast to *In Memoriam* and the indetermi-
nacy we have noted in its intertextual relationships, the authoritative words of the liturgy are interpolated in Newman's text.
The ultimate authority to which the liturgy and Scripture point
is also invoked, as in the Assistants'

> By Thy birth and by Thy Cross,
> Rescue him from endless loss;
> By Thy death and burial,
> Save him from a final fall . . . .
>   (*Dream*, p.317)

It is, however, in the counterpoint between faithful affirmation
and a feeling of mortal terror in Gerontius's speeches that the
poem's main interest lies. Having made his Creed in the first
section ('Firmly I believe and truly' – p.318) Gerontius again
breaks down. From the received public discourse of the Mass, he
modulates into the experiential and individual discourse of
personal emotional crisis in a passage which anticipates Hopkins's terrible sonnet 'No worst, there is none':

> I can no more; for now it comes again,
> That sense of ruin, which is worse than pain,
> That masterful negation and collapse
> Of all that makes me man; as though I bent
> Over the dizzy brink
> Of some sheer infinite descent;
> Or worse, as though
> Down, down for ever I was falling through
> The solid framework of created things,
> And needs must sink and sink
> Into the vast abyss.

Out of profound despair, and following his first intimation of the
'bodily form of ill' which is later reified in the Demons (p.334f),
Gerontius repeats his opening prayer to Jesus and Mary in an
impassioned tone. Immediately the Assistants pray for him
('Rescue him, O Lord, in this his evil hour'), citing Hebrews 11,
and the host of those rescued by faith: Enoch and Elijah from
death, Noah from judgement, Isaac from sacrifice, Daniel from
the lions, and so on. In the crisis of death, reference to the
catastrophic nature of these saving acts meets a spiritual need in
Gerontius, who commits himself into his Lord's hands, and is
sent forth upon his journey by the Priest, 'in the Name of God /
The Omnipotent Father', who created him (p. 321). Both the
Assistants and the Priest, then, invoke the authority of the
Church triumphant in their ministry to the dying Gerontius,
who in the future life is to encounter the angelic host directly.
   The first speech of the Soul of Gerontius is a variation on the
theme of 'new feeling' in the opening lines of the poem, quoted
earlier:

> I went to sleep; and now I am refresh'd,
> A strange refreshment: for I feel in me
> An inexpressive lightness, and a sense
> Of freedom, as I were at length myself,
> And ne'er had been before.
>
>   (pp. 322–3)

Far from losing individual identity – a fear which Gerontius
formerly shared with the 'I' of *In Memoriam* – he gains it,
through the loss of the very form (his body) which in earthly life

is thought to express our individuality. This sense of identity, however, is stated rather than achieved in the poem, for the Angel's central speech (*Dream*, p.327) and the later exchanges between the Soul and the Angel in this second section convey no sense of a unique life history. Whereas Tennyson interprets Hallam's unique gifts as evidence of 'a noble type / Appearing ere the times were ripe', Newman's emphasis falls upon the repetition of the historic pattern of fall and redemption embodied in his representative figure of Gerontius. And the Angel's answers to the Soul's inquiries – like Gabriel's responses to Adam in *Paradise Lost* – have the authority of God's messenger, reflected in direct statement and unquestioning assertion: 'Thou art not let', 'Not so with us in the immaterial world', and so on (*Dream*, pp. 331–2). Drawing on examples from among the saints, such as St Francis (p.343), the Angel leads the Soul – both literally and metaphorically – towards his dramatic spiritual encounter with the Agony of Christ. In contrast to lyric xcv in *In Memoriam* and Tennyson's blurring of Hallam's soul and the 'Deity maybe', the Angel directly describes the 'eager spirit' flying 'to the dear feet of Emmanuel' (*Dream*, p.357). The Soul's own purgatorial song – 'my sad perpetual strain' (p.358) – is taken up into Psalm 90, a *community* lament:[37] 'Lord, Thou hast been our refuge: in every generation; Before the hills were born, and the world was: from age to age thou art God.'

Newman's achievement in *The Dream of Gerontius* is described by Geoffrey Rowell as the removal of eschatology 'from mechanical interpretations into the realm of the personal relationship between man and God': it thus 'spoke profoundly to the needs of the nineteenth century'.[38] This personal relationship, however, is generalised, made typical, by placing it in the context of the whole Judaeo-Christian scheme of history, and of Christ's one, full, perfect and sufficient sacrifice, for the sins of the whole world. The limitations of the *Dream* as a work of literature are closely associated with its heavy reliance upon liturgy and Scripture, and the authority of the Church. By narrowing his focus to a single soul approaching the gates of purgatory (here an ante-chamber of heaven), who knows that, in the words of the Angel, he 'cannot now / Cherish a wish which ought not to be wish'd' (p.330), Newman allows no area of freedom or 'possibility' in his treatment of the human condition. The corollary to this is obvious enough: the success of *In Memoriam* as a work of literature is at least partly attributable to the freedom which Tennyson exercises in his handling of religious and literary traditions. For Tennyson, the demands of the imaginative enterprise that is literature predominate over religion's demand for external authority.

NOTES

1. See, further, Geoffrey Rowell, *Hell and the Victorians: A Study of the Nineteenth-Century Theological Controversies Concerning Eternal Punishment and the Future Life* (Oxford, 1974).

2. Tennyson, *In Memoriam*, ed. Susan Shatto and Marion Shaw (Oxford, 1982) p. 79. All quotations from *In Memoriam* are from this edition. References in text, by lyric number.

3. See Frederic W. Farrar, *Eternal Hope: Five Sermons Preached in Westminster Abbey, November and December, 1877* (London and New York, 1904) pp. v, xxix–xxxii.

4. [John Henry Newman], *Verses on Various Occasions*, 2nd edn (London, 1869) p.351. All quotations from *The Dream of Gerontius* are from this edition. Further references in text, by page number.

5. See Geoffrey Rowell, '*The Dream of Gerontius*', *Ampleforth Journal*, 73 (1968) 184–92.

6. Cf. T. S. Eliot, 'In Memoriam' (1936), in *Selected Essays*, 3rd edn (London, 1951) pp.333–4.

7. Bernard Ramm, *The Pattern of Religious Authority* (Grand Rapids, Mich., 1957) pp.20, 63, 28, 29.

8. See Schleiermacher, *The Christian Faith*, ed. H. R. Mackintosh and J. S. Stewart (Edinburgh, 1928) pp. 103, 6, 12.

9. See James C. Livingston, *Modern Christian Thought: From the Enlightenment to Vatican II* (New York and London, 1971) p. 145.

10. *Pascal's Pensées*, tr. H. F. Stewart (London, 1950) p. 345.

11. Coleridge, *Aids to Reflection*, 4th edn (London, 1913) p. 126.

12. See ibid., p. 203; Schleiermacher, *The Christian Faith*, p. 713.

13. Ibid., p. 702.

14. *William Allingham's Diary*, intro. Geoffrey Grigson (Fontwell, Sussex, 1967) pp. 62, 185.

15. [Hallam Tennyson], *Alfred Lord Tennyson: A Memoir* (London, 1899) p. 270.

16. *William Allingham's Diary*, p. 328.

17. John Henry Newman, *Apologia Pro Vita Sua: Being a History of his Religious Opinions*, ed. Martin J. Svaglic (Oxford, 1967) pp. 256, 261, 238.

18. Eliot, *Selected Essays*, pp. 336, 334.

19. Jerome Hamilton Buckley, *Tennyson: The Growth of a Poet* (Cambridge, Mass., 1960) p. 127.
20. *Tennyson: A Memoir*, p. 255.
21. Hallam Tennyson, *Materials for a Life of A. T.* (privately printed, n.d.) II, 17; quoted in *The Poems of Tennyson*, ed. Christopher Ricks, Annotated English Poets (London and New York, 1969) p. 861.
22. See *In Memoriam*, ed. Shatto and Shaw, pp. 137, 283.
23. J. C. C. Mays, '*In Memoriam*: An Aspect of Form', *University of Toronto Quarterly*, 35 (1965) 22–46; repr. in *Tennyson, 'In Memoriam': A Casebook*, ed. John Dixon Hunt (London, 1970) pp. 267–8.
24. Cf. John Beer, *Wordsworth and the Human Heart* (London, 1978) p. 11.
25. See *Remains, in Verse and Prose, of Arthur Henry Hallam* [ed. Henry Hallam] (London, 1834) pp. xxxiv–xxxv.
26. See Alan Sinfield, *The Language of Tennyson's 'In Memoriam'*, Language and Style series, ed. Stephen Ullmann (Oxford, 1971) pp. 178–9.
27. Kingsley's comment of 1850 is quoted in Christopher Ricks, *Tennyson*, Masters of World Literature series, ed. Louis Kronenberger (London, 1972) p. 228.
28. See Eric Smith, *By Mourning Tongues: Studies in English Elegy* (Ipswich and Totowa, NJ, 1977) pp. 56–7.
29. *The Confessions of Saint Augustine*, tr. E. B. Pusey, Everyman's Library, 200 (London and New York, 1907) pp. 138–9. The similarity between lyric xcv and this passage is briefly noted by Percy H. Osmond in *The Mystical Poets of the English Church* (London, 1919) pp. 309–10; cited by Buckley in *Tennyson*, pp. 123, 276.
30. *In Memoriam*, ed. Shatto and Shaw, p. 255.
31. Cited ibid.
32. See, for example, Alan Sinfield, 'Matter-moulded Forms of Speech: Tennyson's Use of Language in *In Memoriam*', in *The Major Victorian Poets: Reconsiderations*, ed. Isobel Armstrong (1969) p. 63; Carlisle Moore, 'Faith, Doubt and Mystical Experience in *In Memoriam*', *Victorian Studies*, 7 (1963) 155–59, repr. in *Tennyson, 'In Memoriam': A Casebook*, p. 251.
33. *Essays of George Eliot*, ed. Thomas Pinney (New York and London, 1963) p. 29.
34. *Aids to Reflection*, p. 4.
35. *Tennyson: A Memoir*, p. 255.
36. Rowell, '*The Dream of Gerontius*', *Ampleforth Journal*, 73, p. 192.
37. See Artur Weiser, *The Psalms: A Commentary*, tr. Herbert Hartwell, Old Testament Library (London, 1962) p. 66.
38. Rowell, '*The Dream of Gerontius*', *Ampleforth Journal*, 73, p. 192.

13 Contrary Imaginings: Thomas Hardy and Religion

IAN GREGOR

I

It seems appropriate, in the present surroundings, to begin with a text, or, more extravagantly, with two texts. The first is brief and comes from an entry in Hardy's autobiography for 29 January 1890: 'I have been looking for God for 50 years, and I think if he had existed, I should have discovered him. As an external personality, of course, the only true meaning of the word.' The tone is reminiscent of that of a detective wearied in search of a missing person – confident in the nature of his search, robustly honest in recording the bleakness of its outcome.

My second text is rather different in mood and rather longer. It comes from Ford Madox Ford's book of recollections *Mightier than the Sword*:

> I think one of the most memorable occasions of my life occurred when before the fair-sized house-party at Mr Clodd's at Aldeburgh, Thomas Hardy made the curiously shy avowal that he was a practising and believing communicant of the Church of England. It fell, I believe, on all the rest of the party with a little shock of surprise.
>
> The party itself has, I believe, been made famous by another writer. Mr Clodd had invited some representative English people for a long week-end with the purpose of ascertaining to that extent the complexion of the religious belief of the country at the time. Mr Clodd had been in the eighties a

202

militant leader of the agnostic wave that swept over the world after the publication of *The Origin of Species*, and Mr Hardy's shyness at making his confession arose from his dislike of hurting the feelings of his old friend. It was indeed a bad day for Mr Clodd. Of the nine people present, five of us announced ourselves as Roman Catholic at least in tradition and turn of mind – all being writers of a certain position. A very distinguished Professor of Greek at Oxford professed belief in some form of spiritualism that included somewhere a black velvet coffin. There was another spiritualist or theosophist present, the only agnostic besides Mr Clodd being a relative of his. The agnostic pendulum seemed indeed to have swung back.

In such a body Mr Hardy's confession might well come as a shock since neither Catholics nor Spiritualists – nor yet indeed Agnostics – are inclined to regard the Church of England as anything but a social Institution . . . .

Taken together, the two texts suggest something of the treacherous terrain this paper seeks to cover, and, if my subject seems difficult to define, then I would suggest that the elusiveness is integral to the enterprise. If words such as 'apparently' and 'seemingly' seem to recur rather often, then this tentativeness echoes Hardy's own, in his lifelong insistence on the nature of his philosophical attitudes. The tone is sufficiently caught in this almost random selection:

7 March 1917. Like so many critics Mr Courtney treats my works of art, as if they were a scientific system of philosophy, although I have repeatedly stated in prefaces and elsewhere that the views in them are seemings, provisional impressions only, used for artistic purposes, because they represent approximately the imprecisions of the age and are plausible till somebody produces better theories of the universe.[1]

Unadjusted impressions [a favourite Hardy word] have their value and the road to a true philosophy seems to lie in humbly recording diverse readings of its phenomena as they are forced upon us by chance and change.   (Preface, *Poems of the Past and Present*, 1901)

And finally, most famously, the sentence from the Preface to *Jude the Obscure* (1895) which describes the novel as 'an endeavour to give shape and coherence to a series of seemings, or personal impressions, the question of their consistency or their discordance, of their permanence or their transitoriness, being regarded as not of the first moment'. The persistence of these observations – and they last a lifetime – suggests that something rather more is at stake here than keeping the demarcation lines freshly drawn between an artist's view of his task and a philosopher's.

For instance, a clue as to why this issue mattered so much to Hardy can be seen in the reply he made to 'his invidious critics', as he referred to them, who had applied a series of labels to him – agnostic, atheist, heretic, immoralist, infidel, pessimist (to arrange a selection in alphabetical order) – but 'never thought of calling him what they might much more plausibly – churchy'. It is a remark designed to shock, in the same way that 'the shy confession' did on the occasion of Mr Clodd's house party. What is Hardy up to on these occasions? It seems to be that he is making clear that for him 'belief' of any kind – Christian, agnostic, atheistic – finds expression not in a set of abstract propositions, but rather in areas of feeling, intimately related to ways of living. There is a moment in *Jude* which is illuminating in this connection. It occurs when Jude is setting fire to his religious books and pamphlets, and experiencing a great sense of relief at no longer being a hypocrite. Hardy remarks, 'He might go on believing as before, but he professed nothing . . . .' It overlooks, with a variation, the territory occupied by Newman's celebrated distinction between 'notional' and 'real' assent.

There would seem to be two ways of developing a discussion about Hardy's attitude to religion. The first might be loosely described as biographical. That is to say, it would be concerned with pointing out the dominant role played by the Church in his youth; the ambition, retained until about the age of twenty-five, to be ordained; the strict practice of church-going, so that, as he says, he knew the morning and evening services by heart, 'including the rubrics'; his intense admiration for Keble's *The Christian Year*, which he punctiliously annotated in the early 1860s. It was at this period of his life that he read Newman's *Apologia Pro Vita Sua* with pleasure and, as he records in his autobiography, 'with a great desire to be convinced by him . . . his logic really human, being based not on syllogisms, but on converging probabilities'.

With this background we have no difficulty in seeing why, in later life, Hardy should describe himself as 'churchy'. Curiously, it was not a background that was to be disturbed by the reading he began to do in the 1860s and 1870s, which created within him that agnostic disposition which, at a later date, the critics of his poems and novels described in terms that he found so objectionable. That reading consisted of a classical course in the development of Victorian agnosticism – Darwin's *Origin of the Species*, *Essays and Reviews*, Mill's *Liberty*, Arnold's essays, notably *Culture and Anarchy* and *Literature and Dogma*, and then, more singularly, the essays of Leslie Stephen, in which he found 'a perfectly fresh and original vein'. The significance of this reading, though Hardy refers to it in some detail, does not seem to have led in his case to any crisis of belief. There is nothing in his autobiography, for instance, that could remotely be called 'a dark night of the soul'. It is tempting to think in terms of chronology, of the Christian belief of his youth being quietly replaced by the agnostic belief of his middle and late years. But that suggests something much too clear-cut. There is a strange coexistence between Hardy the intellectual, at home in and taking for granted the world view of Victorian agnosticism, and Hardy the artist, drawing not only on the pieties of his past, but juxtaposing them with the present in order to point up its unrest and bleakness.

I said that there were two approaches to developing a consideration of Hardy and religion: the biographical is one, the literary-critical is the other. It is the second approach I have adopted for this essay. That is to say, I should like to show Hardy's imagination at work in a number of precise contexts; to try and get close to the phrase 'contrary imaginings' in a way that will reveal the kind of tension that is present when Hardy is not formulating an opinion, but responding to the pressures of artistic creation. To begin with I should like to look at *Tess of the d'Urbervilles* and *Jude the Obscure*, where religious issues are most overtly present; then to consider a small group of poems; and, finally, to offer a perspective which will provide a suggestive way of looking at the general issues that would seem to emerge from specific contexts.

By way of overture, I should like to look at the famous last paragraph of *Tess*, which expresses, in miniature, the general argument I wish to pursue:

'Justice' was done, and the President of the Immortals, in Aeschylean phrase, had ended his sport with Tess. And the d'Urberville knights and dames slept on in their tombs unknowing. The two speechless gazers bent themselves down to the earth, as if in prayer, and remained thus a long time, absolutely motionless: the flag continued to wave silently. As soon as they had strength they arose, joined hands again, and went on.

How often the opening sentence of that paragraph has been quoted in isolation and made to serve as 'the conclusion' to the novel, when in fact Hardy, true to his practice, makes his conclusion multiple in emphasis. The first sentence is a sombre acknowledgement of forces in the world over which we should seem to have little or no control. It is followed by a sentence which shifts from metaphysics to history, proclaiming the serene indifference of the past to the present. These two sentences are followed by two others which indicate contrary possibilities. We see an intimation of human resilience in 'the speechless gazers' who seek in the earth itself – in the conditions of man's terrestrial existence, notwithstanding his mutability – hope and not despair. In the last sentence, hope turns into strength, strength to affirm the human bond and to give direction to action: 'they . . . joined hands again, and went on'. It is a sentence which recalls, in its rhythm, the sadness – and the resolution – present in the final lines of *Paradise Lost*:

> They hand in hand with wandring steps and slow,
> Through *Eden* took their solitaire way.

It would be as foolish to isolate Hardy's last sentence, and see the final emphasis of the novel lying there, as it would be to isolate the first. For him, it is the four sentences taken together which constitute a human truth, by catching in varying lights our condition, flux followed by reflux, the fall by the rally; it is this sense of continuous movement which suggests that the fiction which records it should be described as 'a series of seemings'.

But we cannot leave it quite there, simply because an open-ended pespective can be as determinist as any other; plurality, as much as resolution, can come to be something deliberately worked-for and imposed. All these perspectives need to be related back to a unifying voice: it is the distinctiveness of that voice that gives coherence and direction to the constantly shifting and interrogating tones within it.

II

Some years ago I wrote an essay under the title 'What Kind of Fiction Did Hardy Write?'[2] and in the course of it I remarked, 'If Hardy is predominantly a philosophical novelist then it is remarkable how little gets into the fiction of such 19th Century intellectual concerns as the clash between science and faith . . . Matthew Arnold's doubts are not aired in Wessex.' This provoked an American critic, David de Laura, to remark that I had been 'curiously incautious' and there followed an article '"The Ache of Modernism" in Hardy's Later Novels',[3] with particular reference to *Tess of the d'Urbervilles*, in which he demonstrated the extent of my 'incaution'.

The only point of recalling this exchange now is that it raises a still pertinent critical issue about the existence of ideas in Hardy's art. Of course, de Laura was right that Hardy was much concerned about ideas – or, more precisely, his characters were – in that a great deal of rumination and reflection takes place. But, rereading his article the other day, I felt I knew why I had made my remark, and to that extent, was unrepentant. Despite the fact that there is a great deal of talk, it is surprising how little it touches upon the imaginative heart of the novel – Tess herself. The Shakespearean epigraph to the novel expresses for me its most pervasive feeling: 'Poor wounded name! My bosom as a bed / Shall lodge thee.'

Hardy clearly has strong feelings about Angel as 'a sample product of the last twenty five years', about Alec's swift conversion both into and out of Evangelical preaching, and, most poignantly of all, the Vicar's insistence that Tess's baby be buried not in consecrated ground, 'but in that shabby corner of God's allotment where all unbaptised infants . . . and others of the conjecturally damned are laid'. But the latter is moving precisely because it affects Tess, and other matters, though of consequence, exist in its margins.

Let us examine more closely what I see as the imaginative

centre of the novel and see what implications it has for the general theme of this essay. That centre lies, I want to argue, in the middle sections of the novel – 'The Rally', 'The Consequence' and 'The Woman Pays'. I think now, that the novel is so well established that we are inclined to forget the huge risk that Hardy took in attempting to make a tragedy, epic in scope and intention, out of such a subject. It could so easily have declined into the tragic adventures of a milkmaid. As Polanski's film shows, once the narrative is isolated and taken away from the informing authorial voice, then it diminishes alarmingly in scope. That voice, so compassionate in its tone, is continually seeking to relate and enlarge the narrative we glimpse through it, the outlines of a primal narrative – that of Paradise Lost. There is plenty of evidence in the novel to suggest that this epic was consciously in Hardy's mind, but I don't want to illustrate what I mean in the present context by the exhumation of references, but rather to indicate two subterranean streams of feeling which take the narrative beyond the immediacies of its realistic detail.

I locate these feelings in two passages – though they are not, of course, confined to those two – which have in common that they express well what Virginia Woolf indicated as giving us particular satisfaction in our reading of Hardy: 'the margin of the unexpressed'. The first passage occurs in 'The Rally' and is Tess's recital of the Benedicite:

> The irresistible, universal, automatic tendency to find sweet pleasure somewhere, which pervades all life, from the meanest to the highest, had at length mastered Tess. Being even now only a young woman of twenty, one who mentally and sentimentally had not finished growing, it was impossible that any event should have left upon her an impression that was not in time capable of transmutation.
>
> And thus her spirits, and her thankfulness, and her hopes, rose higher and higher. She tried several ballads, but found them inadequate; till, recollecting the psalter that her eyes had so often wandered over of a Sunday morning before she had eaten of the tree of knowledge, she chanted: 'O ye Sun and Moon . . . O ye Stars . . . ye Green Things upon the Earth . . . ye Fowls of the Air . . . Beasts and Cattle . . . Children of Men . . . bless ye the Lord, praise Him and magnify Him for ever!'[4]

' . . . irresistible, universal . . . to find sweet pleasure somewhere which pervades all life', this celebration of nature which turns into a hymn of thanksgiving is integral to the exuberant life that goes into the novel. The Benedicite is as much the utterance of the novelist, at this point in the narrative, as it is his character's. I prefer to say the novelist rather than the author, because the term serves as a reminder of the closeness of the artist to his creation in the process of its unfolding. Hardy had an extraordinary ability to enter into, to become absorbed by, the tale, so that we are always aware of his distinctive presence. There is a limpid quality about his art which allows it to speak for itself.

For him, Tess's life in the Valley of the Great Dairies released the bounty that is in nature; it becomes paradisal – 'the spectral, half-compounded, aqueous light which pervaded the open mead, impressed them with a feeling of isolation, as if they were Adam and Eve'. The fact that these half-lights are also eloquent of what is to come does nothing to discount the intensity and exuberance of feeling present at this stage of the novel. Hardy's writing in these pages is immensely assured, and in our dissolving memory of the novel it is these pages that continue to haunt the memory. The general point I am contending for is that no one who did not possess a profound feeling for the congruence of man with his habitat, so that to talk of paradise is not exorbitant, could have written this section of the novel. It is precisely because Hardy can give such authenticity to 'the invincible instinct towards self delight' that, when that instinct is thwarted and destroyed, its loss is so acutely realised. In this way Hardy unobtrusively enlarges our sense of Tess, so that she becomes an embodiment of an unfallen world: 'She was no longer the milkmaid, but a visionary essence of woman . . . .' Angel's perspective has been made ours. But so too is Tess's, when she resists this extravagance and pleads for particularity: '"Call me Tess", she would say askance; and he did.'

My second passage presents 'the blighted world' which, years before, Tess has foreseen in talking to her brother Abraham. Taken from the section 'The Woman Pays', the scene depicts a very different aspect of nature, Tess having now been deserted by Angel:

Every leaf of the vegetable having already been consumed, the whole field was in colour a desolate drab; it was a complexion without features, as if a face, from chin to brow, should be only an expanse of skin. The sky wore, in another colour, the same likeness; a white vacuity of countenance with the lineaments gone. So these two upper and nether visages confronted each other all day long, the white face looking down on the brown face, and the brown face looking up at the white face, without anything standing between them but the two girls crawling over the surface of the former like flies.   (pp. 363–4)

Imaged in terms of an expressionless face, the world is presented now as irretrievably indifferent to the fate of human beings, so that they are reduced to 'flies crawling over its surface'. Work, suffering, deprivation become their destiny. But in Hardy we continually have to remember that, just as 'The Rally' is succeeded by this scene of total alienation, so it, in its turn, will be succeeded by a scene less harsh. 'So do flux and reflux – ', Hardy writes at the end of one of the novel's concluding chapters, 'the rhythm of change – alternate and persist in everything under the sky.'

My purpose here is not to analyse the shifting moods of the novel, or to become involved in the literary-critical issues raised by these shifts, but simply to record that, for me, the dominant mood that emerges is one of elegy, but an elegy so intensely imagined that it brings with it its own vitality, amounting almost to exuberance. That may seem a strange word to use about a novel so tragic in its import, but, when we say that, we have in mind the abstract plot, rather than what it feels like to read. Now and again Hardy is tempted into authorial statements which make the novel seem more bleakly determinist than it is, and on occasions this gets into the narrative, as when Dairyman Crick plants his knife and fork on the table 'like the beginning of a gallows', where the real hand that does the planting belongs to Hardy rather than the dairyman.

But I come back to my two passages which I find supremely expressive of the polarities of feeling present in the novel, both involving Tess in the most direct way. This dialectic suffuses the deep imaginative structure of the novel, a dialectic which can be described, if the tense equilibrium between the two words is kept and maintained, as paradise/lost.

'Jude is only Tess turned round about', D. H. Lawrence writes. 'Instead of the heroine containing the two principles, male and female, at strife within her one being, it is Jude who contains them both. . . . Arabella is Alec d'Urberville, Sue is Angel Clare. These represent the same pair of principles.'[5] This kind of remark suggests what happens when you become too involved with the extraction of 'principles', because, in fact, *Tess* and *Jude* are two very different kinds of novel, and the distinctiveness of *Jude* in Hardy is made truly obscure if it is considered too resolutely in the terms which Lawrence proposes.

An economical way of suggesting the nature of that distinctiveness would be to say that, unless *Tess* had been written, *Jude* would not have been possible. There was still unfinished business in Wessex, and, without that long backward glance involving old pieties, ballads, Eden, it would hardly have been possible to write a novel which, in dramatic mood, if not in narrative detail, belonged to the present, and contained intimations of the future.

Nowhere does the contact with *Tess* emerge more sharply than in the opening section of *Jude*, 'At Marygreen'. The impression made is that it is acting as a prelude to the main novel. It is usual for Hardy to begin his novels in a very positive, but unhurried, way, but the pace with which *Jude* opens is quite remarkable. We have Aunt Drusilla reminding us of Jude's luckless existence – 'poor useless boy'; there is Jude deserted by his only friend, the schoolmaster, thrown out of a job by the local farmer and hopelessly deceived by an itinerant salesman of books. He then meets Arabella, who tricks him into marriage; they have a brutally short life together, and she leaves him. It comes as no surprise that, having known only the most fleeting moments of happiness in his young life, Jude should take himself out to the centre of a frozen pond and seek to drown himself. And at this point in the Wessex edition we have just reached page 82! A couple of pages later, Jude is on his way to Christminster and the novel really begins. Why did Hardy risk such a compression of incident in the opening section? I think we can speculate that he was anxious to write a novel about the contemporary scene, but to begin it in such a way, verging almost on parody, that the reader is made dramatically aware that the compulsion 'to move on' is Hardy's no less than Jude's.

Wessex, for so long a source of imaginative energy, has no further role to play, either to provoke a Benedicite or as a universe indifferent to man's fate; it is simply a place to leave

behind: 'The site whereon so long had stood the Ancient Temple
to Christian divinities was not even recorded on the green and
level grass plot that had immemorially been the churchyard, the
obliterated graves being commemorated by eighteen penny
cast-iron crosses warranted to last five years.'[6] The place of
Wessex is taken by Christminster, which Jude sees from afar as
'the heavenly Jerusalem':

> 'It is a city of light', he said to himself.
> 'The tree of knowledge grows there' he added . . . .
> After this figure he was silent a long while, till he added: 'It
> would just suit me'.   (pp. 30–1)

Paradise now? The novel is a quest for its occupation, and in
exploring it *Jude* is to realise itself as a distinctively modern
novel. That is to say, it is articulated with a new self-consciousness on Hardy's part. Christminster is as much a city
of the mind as a city built in stone, and the responses to it will
take place as mental attitudes, no less than bodily relationships.
If Hardy's involvement with Jude and Sue is quite different from
his involvement with Tess, this is to do not so much with the
differences in their individual characters as with the fact that in
Jude the protagonists enable the author to examine *his* aspira-
tions, *his* puzzles, *his* doubts. That contributes to the intensity of
the novel as much as the tale it tells.

A way of describing the relationship that Hardy has with *Jude*
would be to say that we encounter the reader of Matthew Arnold
most fully: not simply in the way that the novel offers itself as
preoccupied with certain Arnoldian preoccupations – the division between Hebrew and Hellene, the notion of 'imaginative
reason' – but more intimately than that, more dramatically. It
is present in the epigraph which Hardy gives to the novel, 'The
letter killeth.' That intimates the dialectic of *Jude* – letter and
spirit – which is fused into the imaginative structure of the
novel. How modern man should understand and interpret the
Pauline injunction is the unspoken question behind the novel.

As Jude is dying, his dog-eared Greek Testament lies beside
him covered with stone-dust. The closed book is a comment on
how little it has been able to affect his life. At the beginning it
had all seemed to be very different when, to pursue his dream of
learning, he had sent to Christminster for some Greek and Latin
grammars:

> Ever since his first ecstasy or vision of Christminster and its possibilities, Jude had meditated much and curiously on the probable sort of process that was involved in turning the expressions of one language into those of another. He concluded that a grammar of the required tongue would contain, primarily, a rule, prescription, or clue of the nature of a secret cipher, which, once known, would enable him, by merely applying it, to change at will all words of his own speech into those of the foreign one. . . . He learnt for the first time that there was no law of transmutation, as in his innocence he had supposed . . . .   (p. 35)

'He learnt for the first time that there was no law of transmutation' – this is a lesson which was to preoccupy Hardy, no less than Jude, throughout the novel. There is no law in which one kind of experience can be literally translated into the terms of another; there is only 'a series of seemings'. Aunt Drusilla's fatalism, Sue's idealism, Arabella's pragmatism – all exhibit a worship of the letter, a sense that these attitudes reveal definitively the way that things are. There is no need of further annotation. In the case of Jude himself, the matter is rather more complicated.

At the beginning, he trusted absolutely in appearances: Vilbert, Arabella, Christminster – even, in the case of the last, seeking admission by wandering the city and using as a selection procedure for college admission the physiognomies of their principal officers. A more complex instance of the same kind of naïveté occurs when, moved by the Easter hymn 'At the Foot of the Cross', he feels that the composer of such a work must have an insight into his problems. Characteristically, he arranges to meet him, to find that he is interested only in royalties and has turned to the wine trade for greater financial comfort. But, as the novel develops and goes into its second half, Hardy's interest swings away from Jude to Sue, and in fact he becomes an authorial commentator on her behaviour, and sees clearly enough the effects of 'The letter killeth.'

Hardy's attitude to his modernist thinkers had always been equivocal – Clym in *The Return of the Native*, Fitzpiers in *The Woodlanders*, Angel in *Tess*. Although all were afforded a measure of sympathy (in Angel's case a very small measure indeed), the dominant impression they all give is of a myopic self-centredness. It is curious to note that, as Hardy's fiction darkened, and

increasingly left behind the pieties of Wessex, it also acquired a
much sharper cutting-edge with regard to those who represented
'the modern spirit'. Of these later figures, it was Sue Bridehead
who was most keenly analysed.

'Save his own soul he hath no star': Swinburne's lines are
applied to Jude, but they could be applied even more tellingly to
Sue. There is something very attractive about the degree of
intellectual vitality, and when she proclaims herself to be a
follower of John Stuart Mill we are not in need of persuasion.
From one point, Sue is presented with a sympathy absent from
Hardy's other portraits of intellectuals; but, from another, her
destiny is more uncompromisingly tragic than theirs. Sue is also
distinctive among Hardy's female characters, who are presented
largely as victims, either of their temperaments or of the times in
which they live, in that she brings about her own destruction.
The will, which marked out her intellectual independence, stif-
fens into slavish adherence as she feels she has to honour a bond,
which exists in name only. Jude goes to visit her when she has
resumed her life as Phillotson's wife, and pleads with her, 'Don't
then be unmerciful. Sue! Sue! we are acting by the letter; and
"the letter killeth".' Hardy seems to be implying that the degree
of independence she sought was exorbitant – any relationship
was to be on *her* terms – and that remains true to the end, when
the last of her contracts is made, not with Phillotson or with
Jude, but with her own unrelenting will. It is this that leads to
what Hardy describes as 'the self sacrifice of the woman on the
altar of what she was pleased to call her principles'; as Jude
recognises, 'the ultimate horror has come . . . her enslavement to
forms'.

Although we are far here from the world of *Tess*, with the sense
of a paradise lost, there is a continuity with the ealier novel, in
that the question of how paradise can be regained exists in the
margins, at least, of *Jude*. Is secular idealism a sufficiently
positive aim? Hardy's treatment of Sue would seem to say
emphatically no, and yet are we not here falling into the very
same trap as I suggested Lawrence did, of pursuing principles at
the expense of particularities? Sue's destiny is tragic enough, but
is that the same as saying that her ideas, formed by her reading,
are put at a discount? Are there not other more individual factors
at work – her psychosexuality, for instance? In other words, Sue
must be responded to as an individual, certainly the most

complex in Hardy's fiction, not as an embodiment of abstract ideas. Having said that, there is clearly a sense in which 'ideas' are part of the imaginative substance of *Jude* in a way they are not in any other of Hardy's novels.

So we are not surprised to see Hardy's ambivalence about what he believed reflected in his novel. Intellectually, he, no less than Sue, was a follower of Mill, and generally speaking, as I remarked earlier, he shared the outlook of the major Victorian agnostic writers. This was made complex by his strong feelings for what Wordsworth described as 'natural piety', his profound feeling for the past and for human continuity. But what matters to us about Hardy is not that he was a thinker, but that he was an artist of genius. What is of consequence is what happens to this kind of thinking when it seeks and finds expression in art. Lawrence provides us with the necessary reminder here. 'Every work of art', he writes, 'adheres to some system of morality. But if it be really a work of art, it must contain the essential criticism of the morality to which it adheres. And hence the autonomy, hence the conflict necessary to every tragic conception' (*Study of Thomas Hardy*, p. 185). Literary thought is generated by the energy between the contraries.

III

I have tried to suggest something of the way this imaginative movement is present in *Tess* and *Jude*. I should now like to alter course and look at a small group of poems. Unlike the novel, where reference can only be allusive, a poem is able to present us much more directly with what is at issue and I shall take the opportunity this provides to make more explicit Hardy's attitude to religion.

The first poem I want to consider is 'Afternoon Service at Mellstock' (c. 1850)

> On afternoons of drowsy calm
>   We stood in the panelled pew,
> Singing one-voiced a Tate-and-Brady psalm
>   To the tune of 'Cambridge New'.

> We watched the elms, we watched the rocks,
>   The clouds upon the breeze,
> Between the whiles of glancing at our books,
>   And swaying like the trees.
>
> So mindless were those outpourings! –
>   Though I am not aware
> That I have gained by subtle thought on things
>   Since we stood psalming there.

In the *Life*, Hardy gives the general provenance of the poem: 'Thomas was kept strictly at church on Sundays as usual, till he knew the Morning and Evening Services, by heart, including the rubrics, as well as large portions of the New Version of Psalms. The aspect of that time to him is clearly indicated in the verses "Afternoon Service in Mellstock" . . . ' (*Life*, p. 23).

The theme of the poem is straightforward enough: the fading of religious faith and hope, expressed in terms of a church service recalled from his youth, into the agnostic temper of his age. But it is a change of attitude which has brought with it little satisfaction. In the first verse we are presented with a simple descriptive recall, with 'one-voiced' intimating the communal solidarity of belief. In the second verse the poet shifts his stance and from being an onlooker enters into the spirit of the congregation, and gradually the movements of the singers become one with the view that can be glimpsed through the windows, 'swaying like the trees'. The third verse records an abrupt switch of mood: the gentle inattention of the singers is seen now as 'mindless' outpourings; but then the pendulum swings back and 'subtle thought' has not brought its consolations. The poised equilibrium with which the poem ends is present in the phrase 'stood psalming', which contains both the mood of the present, looking back, kept at distance, and the mood of the past, wholly absorbed and intent upon that moment so many years ago. The poem is written out of the unresolved tension between 'now' and 'then'.

The second poem is 'The Impercipient (At a Cathedral Service)':

> That with this bright believing band
>   I have no claim to be,
> That faiths by which my comrades stand

> Seem fantasies to me,
> And mirage-mists their Shining Land,
> Is a strange destiny.
>
> Why thus my soul should be consigned
> To infelicity,
> Why always I must feel as blind
> To sights my brethren see,
> Why joys they've found I cannot find,
> Abides a mystery.
>
> Since heart of mine knows not that ease
> Which they know; since it be
> That He who breathes All's Well to these
> Breathes no All's-Well to me,
> My lack might move their sympathies
> And Christian charity!
>
> I am like a gazer who should mark
> An inland company
> Standing upfingered, with, 'Hark! Hark!
> The glorious distant sea!'
> And feel, 'Alas, 'tis but yon dark
> And wind-swept pine to me!'
>
> Yet I would bear my shortcomings
> With meet tranquillity,
> But for the charge that blessed things
> I'd liefer not have be.
> O, doth a bird deprived of wings
> Go earth-bound wilfully!
>
> *   *   *   *   *
>
> Enough. As yet disquiet clings
> About us. Rest shall we.

As in the first poem, there is within the poem the copresence of contrasting moods – a response to the affirming belief of the assembled congregation and the poet's own feeling of isolation. That conflict inheres in every detail of the poem and shapes the form it takes: 'mirage-mists their Shining Land', 'He who breathes All's Well to these / Breathes no All's Well to me'. We see Hardy looking about for an ending that will be true to his irresolute feelings. He tries several tones: the Romantic, plangent, 'Alas, 'tis but yon dark / And wind-swept pine to me'; personal fortitude – 'Yet I could bear . . . But for the charge'; a tremor of self pity – 'O, doth a bird deprived of wings / Go earth-bound wilfully!' Finally, he offers a perspective that frames both 'the faithful', and 'the impercipient', without resolving the conflict they embody. 'Enough', in the penultimate line, expresses the mood in which the poem is concluded – or, more precisely, abandoned. When Hardy's poetry is praised for its 'honesty', 'The Impercipient' is an admirably illustrative text.

My next poem is 'Nature's Questioning':

> When I look forth at dawning, pool,
>   Field, flock, and lonely tree,
>   All seem to gaze at me
> Like chastened children sitting silent in a school;

> Their faces dulled, constrained, and worn,
>   As though the master's ways
>   Through the long teaching days
> Had cowed them till their early zest was overborne.

> Upon them stirs in lippings mere
>   (As if once clear in call,
>   But now scarce breathed at all) –
> 'We wonder, ever wonder, why we find us here!

> 'Has some Vast Imbecility
>   Mighty to build and blend,
>   But impotent to tend,
> Framed us in jest, and left us now to hazardry?

> 'Or come we of an Automaton
>   Unconscious of our pains? . . .
>   Or are we live remains
> Of Godhead dying downwards, brain and eye now gone?

'Or is it that some high Plan betides,
　　As yet not understood,
　　Of Evil stormed by Good,
We the Forlorn Hope over which Achievement strides?'

Thus things around. No answerer I . . .
　　Meanwhile the winds, and rains,
　　And Earth's old glooms and pains
Are still the same, and Life and Death are neighbours nigh.

This is a poem not so much about an inexplicable universe, but more about why questions of 'explanation' should have been raised at all. The poem when it was first published in *Wessex Poems* was prefaced with the line drawing of a broken key.

The first verse begins, as it were, within inverted commas, with the kind of romantic rhetoric that we associate with such sentiments as 'Let Nature be your teacher.' There is a touch of whimsy as if 'the master's ways' of tireless questioning had eventually worn out his pupils. Verses four to six give various kinds of 'answers' to the riddle of the universe. Not that we are meant to linger on these, for the poem is more concerned to dramatise what 'an answer' looks like. The seventh verse opens with the key phrase of the poem, 'No answerer I . . .' – not because the poet hasn't got an attitude but because he is profoundly sceptical of this mode of philosophic inquiry. Nature and man are irretrievably other, and to assume that nature is there as a pupil for its master is profoundly mistaken. The title 'Nature's Questioning' expresses not so much an interrogation *by* man, as an interrogation *of* him. What might seem, on first reading, to be a bitter poem, turns out to be much more agnostic about its feelings: 'No answerer I . . . .'

My fourth poem is 'New Year's Eve':

'I have finished another year,' said God,
　　'In grey, green, white, and brown;
I have strewn the leaf upon the sod,
Sealed up the worm within the clod,
　　And let the last sun down.'

'And what's the good of it? I said,
　　'What reasons made you call
From formless void this earth we tread,

> When nine-and-ninety can be read
>   Why nought should be at all?
>
> 'Yea, Sire; why shaped you us, "who in
>   This tabernacle groan" –
> If ever a joy be found herein,
> Such joy no man had wished to win
>   If he had never known!'
>
> Then he: 'My labours – logicless –
>   You may explain: not I:
> Sense-sealed I have wrought, without a guess
> That I evolved a Consciousness
>   To ask for reasons why.
>
> 'Strange that ephemeral creatures who
>   By my own ordering are,
> Should see the shortness of my view,
> Use ethic tests I never knew,
>   Or made provision for!'
>
> He sank to raptness as of yore,
>   And opening New Year's Day
> Wove it by rote as theretofore,
> And went on working evermore
>   In his unweeting way.

The strategy of 'New Year's Eve' is not unlike 'Nature's Questioning' in that Hardy is concerned to dramatise the human impulse to question – 'You may explain / Not I' – rather than speak directly of an inexplicable universe. Of course, the poem is undeniably tragic in the general import, but there is an element at work in it that enables us to see what Hardy meant when he referred to it as 'a fanciful impression of the moment' (*Life*, p. 409).

Tone and rhythm have a crucial role to play in our response to the poem, and nowhere is this more evident than in the part assigned to God. In the first verse he is shown in a way that recalls an exemplary housekeeper, having just satisfactorily completed another year's domestic duties, together with a little painting, a little embroidery. The quizzical and familiar tone is reminiscent of Emily Dickinson, with the same scruple over language. 'And what's the good of it?' catches the tone of the exasperated moral inquirer (in the second verse), but by the penultimate verse this tone has given way to rueful musing on the part of the 'Deity and in 'ordering' and 'provision' we are reminded of the figure we met at the opening of the poem. It ends by resuming the process of serene, unheeding work and the quizzical mood emerges in the unlikely coupling of 'theretofore' with 'evermore'. Let me make clear my point here: it is not that 'New Year's Eve' is not a 'serious' poem, but through the wryness of imagery and rhyme Hardy gently detaches himself from the 'I' of the poem, who has angrily come to file a complaint about divine neglect. The poem, as it proceeds, creates a space between the colloquy that gives the poem its substance and the art that composes it into order.

The process of disengagement, hinted at in the poetic strategy of 'Nature's Questioning' and 'New Year's Eve', becomes the subject matter of one of Hardy's most celebrated poems, 'Afterwards'. It is a poem that could well have been subtitled 'Contrary Imaginings'.

When the Present has latched its postern behind my tremulous
    stay,
  And the May month flaps its glad green leaves like wings,
Delicate-filmed as new-spun silk, will the neighbours say,
  'He was a man who used to notice such things'?

If it be in the dusk when, like an eyelid's soundless blink,
  The dewfall-hawk comes crossing the shades to alight
Upon the wind-warped upland thorn, a gazer may think,
  'To him this must have been a familiar sight.'

If I pass during some nocturnal blackness, mothy and warm,
  When the hedgehog travels furtively over the lawn,
One may say, 'He strove that such innocent creatures should
    come to no harm,
  But he could do little for them; and now he is gone.'

If, when hearing that I have been stilled at last, they stand at the
    door,
  Watching the full-starred heavens that winter sees,

Will this thought rise on those who will meet my face no more,
  'He was one who had an eye for such mysteries'?

And will any say when my bell of quittance is heard in the
    gloom,
  And a crossing breeze cuts a pause in its outrollings,
Till they rise again, as they were a new bell's boom,
  'He hears it not now, but used to notice such things'?

The motive that prompts it is a familiar one – the need to get
out of ourselves, see ourselves as others see us. The neighbours
express themselves in blunt, colloquial phrases: 'He was a man
who used to notice such things'; 'To him this must have been a
familiar sight.' The preceding lines create 'such things', such
'familiar sights' as the poet's eye observed them. This is an
interrelationship between the verses, so that the poem moves
from light into darkness, from May into winter, from the wind-
warped upland thorn to the 'full-starred heavens', from 'such
things' to 'such mysteries'. But the most striking thing about the
poem is the sense of detachment that it conveys, as if Hardy were
already a ghost haunting the world he used to know. The rhetorical strategy is to create a distinction between Hardy as creator of
the poem and Hardy as its ostensible subject.

The title is rich in meaning. On one level, it is an epitaph by
the poet for himself; but in a curious way it is impersonal too,
creating within the poem the imagination which marks out the
poetic eye. The poem is a striking instance of empathy and
detachment, at once completely personal and quite impersonal.
To be able to view one's life in that way is to go beyond the
visual and factual, and reveal a moral poise.

It would be appropriate to think of 'Afterwards' in the way
Leavis considered 'After a Journey': 'It is a case in which we
know from the art what the man: we can be sure, that is, what
personal qualities we should have found to admire in Hardy, if
we could have known him.' This is not so much a biographical
tribute, as a tribute to the self which Hardy reveals in his art,
and which gives authenticity to his 'contrary imaginings'. 'Afterwards' takes us to the point in which we can return finally to the
link between the dialectic which his imagination so habitually
sought and 'the series of seemings' present in his religious belief.

IV

In 1907, shortly after completing 'New Year's Eve', Hardy set about making some notes for an article to be titled 'The Hard Case of the Would-be Religions', in which, despite 'his shy avowal' at Mr Clodd's house party, he made some familiar assertions: 'the days of creeds are as dead and done with as days of Pterodactylls'; 'Required: services at which there are no affirmations and no supplications'; 'We repeat the words (of church services) from an antiquarian interest . . . solely in order to keep a church of some sort afoot – a thing indispensable.'

We have seen in a succession of examples what these attitudes and counter-attitudes look like when they come to life in his art. The question remains, 'What effect does the existence of such work have on our understanding of faith and doubt in the latter part of the nineteenth century?'

Hardy once said of nature that it was 'played out as a Beauty, but not as a Mystery'. It is that sense of the mystery of religion that Hardy's art keeps alive; as John Coulson puts it, 'Victorian writers kept alive in their imaginations what their reason could no longer explain or profess'.[7] Hardy had a profound sense of the numinous, and throughout his life he was continually looking for a language in which to express it. He found the language of nineteenth-century scepticism as alien as the language of nineteenth-century belief – and for the same basic reason. They were too absolutist in their conclusions. Only, in fiction and in poetry – through story, symbol, and metaphor – did Hardy feel able to exemplify the provisional mood which the grammar of his convictions led him to, and within that art he articulated his beliefs through the articulation of contraries. He found no resolution, but by bringing to bear all the resources of language he made it possible for *us* to know, in a precise and human context, what it means to talk of the affirmations of doubt.

NOTES

1. Thomas Hardy, *The Life and Works of Thomas Hardy*, ed. Michael Millgate (London, 1984) p. 406.
2. Ian Gregor, 'What Kind of Fiction Did Hardy Write?', *Essays in Criticism*, 16 (1966) 290–308.

3. David de Laura, '"The Ache of Modernism" in Hardy's Later Novels', ELH, 34 (1967) 380–99.
4. Thomas Hardy, *Tess of the d'Urbervilles*, Library Edition (London, 1949) p. 134.
5. D. H. Lawrence, 'Study of Thomas Hardy', in Anthony Beal (ed.), *Selected Literary Criticism* (London, 1967) p. 198.
6. Thomas Hardy, *Jude the Obscure*, Papermac (London, 1966) p. 16.
7. John Coulson, *Religion and Imagination: 'In Aid of a Grammar of Assent'* (Oxford, 1981) p. 103.

14 The Impasse of Coleridge and the Way of Blake

KEVIN LEWIS

By way of explaining my title, I offer the view that, while William Blake is effectively a Modern, Coleridge remains an Ancient whose thought, for that reason, remains effectively unavailable for any appropriately modern enterprise of theological reformulation. I am in complete agreement with those who believe that the philosophical–theological contribution of Coleridge has yet to be assessed adequately and duly celebrated. But I believe that Blake is the Modern (and therefore one of *us*) while Coleridge, of these two, is the Ancient, and therefore, though an equally distant forbear and a kindred spirit, not at all one of us, and, therefore, unusable as a guide through the most challenging issues of contemporary philosophical theology.

Paul Ricoeur distinguishes what he calls the 'hermeneutics of suspicion', notable exemplars of which in modern times would be Feuerbach, Marx, Nietzsche, Freud and post-structuralist literary theory, from what he calls the 'hermeneutics of restoration'. The task of the latter is to restore religion, through reinterpretation, to the place of value it once held in the life of the mind before modernity cast over it the shadow of suspicion. I call upon this distinction in order simply to insist that it is now Blake and not Coleridge who is equipped to move the 'hermeneutics of restoration' forward. And this is the case especially where the epistemological issue of the role played by imagination in religion is concerned. It is Blake on the imagination who will help us achieve what Ricoeur calls generally the 'second naïveté', that state of restored religious consciousness which beckons from beyond the state of critical suspicion which, for most of us, has supplanted the 'first naïveté' of childlike single vision. Today, the nature and function of the religious imagination demand special attention, description and, more important, analysis. The place of religion in the modern mind will be secured, I believe, by the forging of a cogent theory of the religious imagination *as* imagination – that is, by the adoption of a hermeneutics grounded upon an adequate, modern epistemology of imagination.

But, before elaborating further upon this thesis, a caution. The American literary and cultural critic Lionel Trilling has written, echoing George Santayana, that a modernist is one who 'has ceased to be a Christian to become . . . a connoisseur of Christianity', and that the expression of this connoisseurship is 'the love of all Christianity in those who perceive that it is all a fable'. Those of us who press for a philosophy of religion framed upon a theory of imagination in the modern, post-Kantian context, inevitably risk falling into such a connoisseurship. Or we risk being *perceived* as having fallen into it. This is a delicate matter, not only for one's dialectic but also for one's spirit when expressed in a commitment of faith. I wish to protect this delicacy and guard against succumbing to such a connoisseurship.

Now I claim as my own the Romantic Protestant theological heritage whose great original spokesman is Schleiermacher. And I think it wise, at this juncture in the theological discussion, to risk proposing for sympathetic reinspection the concept and practice of fideism. But I have learned enough from the Church Fathers, the Barthians and from my own experience in the faith to keep a wary inner eye open for the creeping connoisseurship which is *my* great risk, as creeping idolatry is the risk of the sacramentalist. With this caution, I take the position that the adoption of a Coleridgean philosophical approach would effectively betray true religion for the modern by restoring nothing more than a frail support for the childlike 'first naïveté' of Ricoeur, whilst adoption of a Blakean point of view, suitably modified, will strengthen true religion as it frames the conditions for a genuinely modern 'second naïveté'.

But allow me to explain briefly what amounts to my prejudice against Coleridge. It is the prejudice of a 'born-again' empiricist who has found peace of mind (*and* of religious faith) in an epistemological dualism of a kind that is content with rendering unto scientific reason what can be verified or falsified by the established means and with rendering unto religious vision what the ecstatic imagination by graceful compulsion may construct. What I meet in Coleridge is the ancient, prescientific ascription to reason of the power to establish, by authority, unity of mind, of mind with nature, and of mind with God, of whom the claim is accordingly made that he can be 'known' with cognitive certainty. In the post-Kantian dispensation under which we moderns move and reflect upon our being, Coleridgean idealistic metaphysics remains a lumbering, discredited anachronism. As a modern dissenter from the church of the perennial philosophy (*qua* philosophy), my mental experience and the lights by which I see it compel me to reject the grounds of intuitive reason upon which Coleridge asserts the vision of unity. Experience compels me to reject his reasoned unity of all three sorts: that of the mind with God, of the mind with nature, and of the mind itself. The vision of unity itself is compelling, powerful and true, for some. But the language in which it is asserted, and the grounds upon which it is asserted and argued, I believe, are not at all compelling. To put it simply, Coleridge wants reason to do the work of imagination, and thereby to compete with what has now become of philosophy proper. The time is long past when he might have succeeded.

Let me put this another way. Coleridge's language is indeed a symbolic language. And, for the empirical side of the modern mind, reference is indispensable to cognitive meaning and truth. So far, no adequate theory has been presented which can show how non-scientific symbolic expressions refer to realities and can be verified. The reference of Coleridge's symbolic perception of unity cannot be verified. Indeed those 'realities' can and have been disputed by perceptions of contrary 'realities' equally compelling on similarly aesthetic grounds. Epistemologically, Coleridgean metaphysics will not do. I state this position simply to remind us that Coleridge's language, though it may differ in certain respects from that of precedent metaphysics, does not differ enough, and therefore cannot overcome the objections raised by rational empiricists. Coleridge does not succeed in recapturing reason from the scientists and the empiricists. I state this strongly to underscore the belief that for us there is no going back to the mind of the ancients to meet the form of our present needs.

In great part, our need is not new. Theologians characteristically have wanted to protect the special status of religious language. 'What has Athens to do with Jerusalem? What has the

Academy to do with the Church?' expostulates Tertullian, continuing, 'Away with all attempts to produce a Stoic, Platonic, and dialectic Christianity!'[1] Many of us appreciate the line of thought upon which Newman was advancing, especially in *The Grammar of Assent*, where a distinction is clearly drawn between *believing*, which depends upon one kind of warrant, and *having faith*, which depends upon disposition, feeling, choice and imagination. In his study *Religion and Imagination* (1981), John Coulson provides a stimulating survey of this theme in Newman and in subsequent theologians and writers of poetry and fiction in England who can be said to have *enacted* or at least to have provided a sort of commentary upon the consequences of the willing alignment of religious vision with unreasoning constructive imagination.

Our need for an adequate means of grounding and guarding religion *in* imagination is addressed in Gordon Kaufman's recent book, *The Theological Imagination: Constructing the Concept of God* (1981). This is a work of philosophical or 'fundamental' theology in which the modern search looks for more solid ground upon which to defend and promulgate the truth and value of religion among the cultured despisers. Kaufman is of special interest because in his influential, evolving thought revelation is becoming totally and irrevocably identified with imagination. In Kaufman, imagination is edging revelation, traditionally understood, out of the theological vocabulary. Only *now*, he argues, have theologians become able willingly to acknowledge how fully their work is rooted in 'human imaginative construction'. And he is willing to ascribe some truth to Feuerbach's claim that theology is no less but no more than disguised anthropology.

Kaufman is a Kantian who believes that, since the appearance of *The Critique of Pure Reason* (1781), Christian theology has been effectively avoiding direct confrontation with the challenge therein laid down. That is, mainstream liberal theology has wanted to avoid facing the implications of the radically critical and self-critical perspective Kant made incumbent upon all who acknowledge that knowing, as far as we can know it, is an active, interested, constructive enterprise, an enterprise of making, whether voluntary or involuntary. It has fallen to Kaufman to draw the inevitable conclusion that the emperor is wearing no clothes, that God-talk, theologically as well as philosophically speaking, is nothing but imaginative projection. And, the sooner those who talk of God critically embrace this simple modern finding, that theologians are entitled only to frame those imaginative constructs which express a human need for a fundamental 'orientation which will bring true fulfilment and meaning to life', the sooner the enterprise will discover (or rediscover) its legitimacy *vis-à-vis* other enterprises of the mind. The sooner the theologian stops trying to establish means of 'knowing' God and shifts to the task of reimagining constructively what a God that is truly God could be, the sooner theology will enjoy the respect previously accorded it. For it will then be doing, with a belated critical modern self-consciousness, the job it has always done. For Kaufman then, revelation cannot be reckoned with by the Christian theologian *qua* critical philosophical theologian. The actual God must remain for ever radically transcendent, radically transconceptual – that is, elusive to the grasp of reasoning and hence of 'knowing'.

Like his teacher, H. Richard Niebuhr, Kaufman has identified idolatry as the greatest danger against which theology must continually struggle. At the same time that he urges production of updated God-constructs, he believes that *any* concept of God that a theologian can reconstruct, no matter how subtly framed with checks and balances, will remain, for all *we* can know, inadequate. But, where Karl Barth wants always to talk about the actual identity and action of God, in spite of the inability of the finite mind ultimately to know fully that reality and its purpose, Kaufman has apparently banished from theological discourse this kind of talk, and on grounds that theology must now resist any temptation to speak *in* symbolic language (lest it fall into idolatry) – it must only speak about it. Theologians must no longer lapse into that sort of God-talk which risks leaving the impression that they remain unaware that God-talk is *only* an imaginative construct. This contrasts with Barth's position that, while our concepts of God, providence and everlasting life may indeed be illusions, the God in whom we are entitled to believe, when we experience him through grace, can be trusted to fill *our* illusions with *his* truth. There is nothing of this dialectic in Kaufman's new writings. His concept of imagination seems as earthbound as his implied modern concept of reason, and as positivistic.

My question then is this. Can a way out of the Kaufman dilemma be found without throwing out imagination altogether, and without returning to some sort of premodern assertion of our ability to *know* the actual God through some despairing retrieval or reconstruction of a premodern 'reason'? That is, can another, more helpful way of assigning imagination a crucial role in the religious mind be found?

I want to suggest a response to this by proceeding to William Blake by way of Hans Vaihinger. There is, for us, one particularly interesting way in which the heritage of Kant's first *Critique* has been applied to philosophical theology, the possibilities of which have yet to be fully explored. A word here about the curious possibilities of fideism. Apparently, fideism has rarely, if ever, been considered a legitimate strategic departure for philosophical theology. Who, since Vaihinger in his *The Philosophy of 'As If'* (1911), has ever given fideism serious attention? To do so, of course, invites the charge of connoisseurship. But this neglect is none the less surprising in a theological climate growing every year more favourable to imagination and the role it might be understood heuristically to be playing in the epistemology of faith. Even to court the fideistic position seems not within the accepted range of possible strategies open to theologians.

Vaihinger, however, reminds us simply that, for Kant, all 'knowing' is an imaginative activity, whether of a primary or secondary order, and that it gives us no secure hold on reality, of whatever order. Towards the end of the presentation of his 'System of the Theoretical, Practical and Religious Fictions of Mankind' Vaihinger blithely recommends the religion of 'as if' first promulgated by Fichte's contemporary Forberg in an essay of 1798, 'The Development of the Concept of Religion'.[2] He suggests that a modern religious person need only, out of moral and social duty, embrace religious vision 'as if' it were true: 'as if', for example, divine revelation were, rather than in fact is, mediated to the faithful by Scripture or by personal experiences of grace. He recommends that sort of post-Kantian, critical self-consciousness which must rule out any direct or even indirect apprehension whatever of the reality or the order of things proposed by religion.

To the extent that this proposal is made by a self-acknowledged positivist and pessimist, surely no traditional theologian can take it up simply as it is. For Vaihinger is entirely without an appropriately subtle theology of the mediating symbol. He is without a theology of supervening grace. He is without a theory of imagination. Nevertheless, as he directs us to understand self-consciously our gestures of assent or acts of willing belief as compelled not by reasoned assent to a cognitively 'known' truth but rather by aesthetic and moral assent to what *ought* to be the case, his approach, I believe, offers more than seductive therapy for the intellectual frustrations and betrayals that prey upon the religious who reflect upon warrants for their faith claims.

Vaihinger's theme, to these ears, flows like a muted undersong through the dissonant music of theological reflection in the past century and a half. It flows like a Siren song resisted, too dangerous to be voiced but always too hastily dismissed. His theme *would* attract renewed interest if we could find in a palatable epistemological dualism the means of restoring through a theory of imagination what is given away by positivist reason. For then might both transcendence and revelation be restored, albeit on shifted grounds. Within the arena of formal theological discourse, the cry is going up, 'Discover and follow imagination.' But no contemporary philosopher of religion has yet presented us with the hermeneutics we need. The task remains.

Nevertheless Liberal Protestant theology as we know it is a child of the Romantic period, a period which gave rise to ebullient theories of imagination. These theories come down to us as a culmination of a long tradition of biblical and literary exegesis in which we descry a steadily evolving enterprise of discriminating the powers of fantasy, fancy, imagination, vision and 'divine imagination'. In this literature, the problematic relation of the inspired poetry and narratives of the Bible to subsequent works of the religious, visionary and secular imaginations is adjudicated in the shifting terminologies of successive historical contexts. This is precisely the body of literature which theologians such as Kaufman, Ricoeur, David Tracy and others with a similar professed interest in imagination ought to be consulting. I particularly suggest that the attention of modern theologians and literary scholars should be directed to the rewarding hermeneutics proposed through dramatisation in the form of visionary myth by our true contemporary among the Romantics, William Blake.

To that end, I move toward a conclusion by reflecting on the possibilities that lie ahead for a theology of imagination if and when the position of our greatest antinomian, modernist theologian is taken into consideration together with certain elements basic to the fideist position.

How can we make use of what is usable and distinctive in Blake while at the same time remaining obedient to revelation, and perhaps even to the arguably outworn notion of an 'orthodox' rule of faith? Blake, I insist, is a modern and a usable prophet–theologian, the appearance of his Gothic-inspired pictorial art, his often outlandish rhetoric, and his occasional heterodoxy notwithstanding. Leopold Damrosch's recent study *Symbol and Truth in Blake's Myth* (1981), makes this quite clear. Damrosch shows that Blake is especially our contemporary in his sensitivity to and engagement with the problem of 'a truly critical religious hermeneutics' and of meaning itself. Blake, too, digested Lockean epistemology and Newtonian science, and spat them out. In certain of his contexts, Blake's answer to the Enlightenment was, in a word, to surrender reason totally to the rational empiricists, and, like the Muggletonians, then to view the usurping faculty of reason, in its overweening arrogation of power, as the 'right Devil' of the age.

But, finally, for Blake, imagination becomes not only that faculty in us alone capable of serving as vehicle for revelation in this our fallen state (cf. *Jerusalem*), but in this age the only truly human life, for which the mortal body and the other, mortal faculties serve as but distracting, temporary appurtenances, as constant reminders of our fallen state, and as obstacles to the recovery of human life fulfilled through the imagination, which he variously calls Eternity, the Golden Age or the Divine Vision. Blake, it is true, wants to bring us into Eternity as quickly as possible. He has no patience with this material world other than as a *felix culpa*, the only source of vehicular imagery for his ambitiously didactic, prophetic art. This impatience in Blake is a mark of his integrity but often a stumbling-block to our appreciation of what he really accomplished for philosophical theology. He is incautious, unscholarly, excessive, and for at least three generations he was believed to have been mad. But he now appears more sane, wise and appealing the more we know him. And what is theologically usable in his thought is precisely this initial move, in a time of trouble, of surrendering reason to the narrow but commanding assumptions of the rational empiricists, coupled then with the building of a Romantic Christian theory of visionary imagination as the sole agency in us through which, by grace, we apprehend revelation. 'I know of no other Christianity and of no other Gospel than the liberty both of body and mind to exercise the Divine Arts of Imagination', he writes in the 'Address to the Christians' at the head of the fourth chapter of his culminating work, *Jerusalem*. His times, like ours, were troubled, and for Blake it is the personification of imagination, the figure Los, who keeps the Divine Vision in a time of trouble, not Urizen, not reason.

After Descartes, Bacon, the British epistemologists and Kant, the game is up for reason as a faculty capable of providing knowledge of God. I applaud Kaufman for voicing this state of affairs with honesty, even if, in light of Tertullian, Blake and Barth, Kaufman's manoeuvre seems paltry and incomplete; for he fails to give us what Blake gives and what we need: a forceful, triumphant, consistent theology of imagination, discoverable to any who digest his writings. That is, Blake the theologian rightly urges us to separate and to reconfigure the independent powers that are great within us, nominating imagination the greatest of all, and leaving these powers to war naturally with each other. (One comes to value Blake's epistemology the more one is compelled to discriminate the independent activities or functions within what we loosely called the mind.)

Obviously, each of us will choose his or her own way of defining and valuing reason. Upon one's definition and valuation of reason will depend whether reason will or will not be assigned special privileges in one's philosophical theology. I am not a philosophical idealist, although the philosophical theologian by whom I have been most influenced over the years, Paul Tillich, *was* confessedly an idealist. The dualistic, Blakean, fideistic solution I am testing would fall under Tillich's label 'metaphysical schizophrenia', a label I now willingly embrace. Of course a philosopher must speak and write discursively, logically, consistently. He must be 'reasonable' in order to make any sense. But the philosophical theologian cannot reasonably demonstrate the validity or truth of the Christian revelation or any other, at least as *I* understand the determination of what is 'reasonable'. One can make reasoning discriminations within a system of thought, or within a myth. But that system of thought or that myth will be based upon unreasoning premises and postulates. One can reason about the implications of a hypothetical revelation, but one cannot reason revelation. We can only imagine revelation, where imagination is an unreasoning but powerful use of the intellect, prompted by powerful forces within the *Gestalt* of the self. We must take the consequences of so concluding. We apprehend transcendence categorically through this earthbound, Romantic faculty of imagination at work fantasising, feeding, constructing, envisioning.

Hence religious vision, to our reason, is but a heuristic scheme, or but one lens among many possible others through which we may choose to focus ('as if' it were thus) the world. To our imagination, when quickened by grace, religious vision is the fulfilment of human life itself, explaining and redeeming everything. To this kind of fideistic dualism, grace will be experienced, if at all, through imagination and not through reason. For we have made a bargain with the world: we have surrendered the usurper reason, and it was no loss. We have done so in order to consolidate the equanimity which is already ours in virtue of religious faith which, though *in* the world, is not of it, and in order to encounter and speak the language of scepticism without an anxiety unworthy of us. We have opened our reasoning embrace only to what *is*, empirically, in the world, bracketing what is *not*.

This reconstructed fideist–dualist would be a Christian prophet in the line of the Reformers, urging us to banish the idolatrous and impractical god of the usurper reason, and then to embrace the true God approachable only through the vehicular activity of personal and obedient visionary imagination. This kind of reconstructed fideist–dualist would remain conversant with *both* modernity *and* the mysteries uncompassed by modern reason. This is the task – of rethinking creatively the difficult epistemological issues to which Kant, the analytic tradition and Wittgenstein have brought only partial, still inconclusive, answers.

NOTES

1. Tertullian, *De Praescriptione Haereticorum*, 7, quoted *A New Eusebius* ed. J. Stevenson, (London, 1960) p. 178.
2. Hans Vaihinger, *The Philosophy of 'As If'*, tr. C. K. Ogden, 2nd edn (London, 1935) p. 321.

Index

Aids to Reflection (Coleridge), 36, 48–52, 55, 134, 177, 179–83, 187, 195
Allingham, William, 188–9
Arnold, Matthew, 205, 207, 212
Athenaum, 108
Augustine, St, 194

Barfield, Owen, 138
Barth, Karl, 1, 104, 107–8, 229, 233
Beveridge, William, 54
Biographia Literaria (Coleridge), 16–17, 26, 32, 37, 45, 53, 66, 74, 133, 134, 139
Blake, William, 4, 43, 136, 166, 167, 225, 231–3
Boehme, Jakob, 44, 54, 59
Butler, Bishop Joseph, 44–5

Carlyle, Thomas, 62
Christian Faith, The (Schleiermacher), 99–100, 108, 110, 118–20
Christian Year, The (Keble), 126–7, 135, 204
Clough, Arthur Hugh, 49–50
Coincidentia oppositorum, 109, 111, 114
Coleridge, Samuel Taylor, vii, 1, (theory of imagination) 16–39, (religious thought) 41–63, (and 'aesthetic') 66–78, (language) 128–40, 158, 168, 171, 173, (and America) 176–83, 187, 194, 195, 225, 226–7
Conciones ad Populum (Coleridge), 168–9
Confessions (Augustine), 194, 195
Constitution of the Church and State, The (Coleridge), 28, 136
Cottle, Joseph, 49–50
Coulson, John, 228

Creation, The (Haydn), 14

David Copperfield (Dickens), 195
Defence of Poetry, A (Shelley), 40
Descartes, R., 18–19, 20
Desynonomy, 133–8
Dewey, John, 39
Dilthey, Wilhelm, 83–122
Diversions of Purley, The (Tooke), 130–1
Dream of Gerontius, The (Newman), 185–200
Dryden, John, 98, 150
Durham, 45

Edwards, Jonathan, 177–9
Edwards, Michael, 173.
Eliot, George, 195
Eliot, T. S., 58–9, 62, 150
Emerson, Ralph Waldo, 183
Empson, William, 44
'Eolian Harp, The' (Coleridge), 44
Eroica (Beethoven), 1–2
Essay Concerning Human Understanding, An (Locke), 130
Essay on Man (Pope), 140

Farrar, F. W., 185, 188–9
Faust (Goethe), 4
Fish, Stanley, 91–2
Frank, Manfred, 83, 85–6, 88–9, 92, 93, 96
French Revolution, 1–2, 5, 8–11, 12
Friedrich, Caspar David, vii–viii, 2
Friess, H. L., 121

Gadamer, Hans-Georg, 81–2, 85, 86, 87, 89, 92, 93
Goethe, J. W. von, 2–7, 9, 12

235

Habermas, Jürgen, 87, 93
Hallam, A. H., 185–200
Hardy, Thomas, viii, 173, 202–23
Hartley, David, 128–32, 133, 139,
    140
Hazlitt, William, 44
Hegel, G. W. F., 1, 8, 18, 22, 25, 28,
    30, 86, 187
Heidegger, Martin, 39
Hermeneutics, 81–95
Hermeneutik und Kritik
    (Schleiermacher), 83
Herz, Henriette, 108, 115
Hölderlin, Friedrich, 1, 7–14
Hooker, Thomas, 177
Hopkins, G. M., 127–8, 136, 137,
    140, 162
Hume, David, 19, 45
Hutchinson, Sara, 41, 43, 44–8
Hyperion (Hölderlin), 8, 10, 12, 14

Imagination, Coleridge on, 16–40
In Memoriam (Tennyson), 185–200
Iser, Wolfgang, 91–2

Jacobi, Friedrich, 99
John, Gospel of St, 90, 128, 145,
    154, 159, 190–1
Jude the Obscure (Hardy), 203–4, 205,
    210–15

Kant Immanuel, 2, 3, 4, 5, 8, 9, 15,
    18, (and Coleridge) 20–30, 39, 45,
    68, 106, 111, 113, 228, 230, 233,
    234
Kaufman, Gordon, 228–9, 231, 233
Keats, John, 13
Kimmerle, Heinz, 82, 83
Kingsley, Charles, 192

Lawrence, D. H., 210–11, 215
Leavis, F. R., 222
Leighton, Archbishop Robert, 55,
    57–8
Locke, John, 19, 39, 45, 130, 134,
    139, 176, 177
Luther, Martin, 97
Lyrical Ballads, The (Wordsworth/
    Coleridge), 135, ('credal lyrics')
    162–70

Mallarmé, S., 151
Marsh, James, 177, 179–83
Maurice, F. D., 62–3, 137, 184, 187
Measure for Measure (Shakespeare),
    152
Mightier than the Sword (Ford Madox
    Ford), 202–3
Mill, J. S., 170, 205, 215
Milton, John, 144–5
Moravians, 59, 106–7, 122

Napoleon, 1, 2, 6, 11
Newman, J. H., 101, 185–200, 204,
    228
Newton, Isaac, 177
Nietzsche, Friedrich, 11, 13
Novalis (Friedrich von Hardenberg),
    108, 112

*On Religion: Speeches to its Cultured
    Despisers* (Schleiermacher), 109–
    10, 112–13, 115
Otto, Rudolf, 104–5
Oxford Movement, 55

Paradise Lost (Milton), 144–5, 199,
    206
Paul, St, 94, 161, 187
'Pedlar, The' (Wordsworth), 170–2
Pensées (Pascal), 187
Philosophical Lectures, The (Coleridge),
    38, 133, 139
Philosophy of 'As If', *The* (Vaihinger),
    230–1
Pietism, 105–7, 108
Pope, Alexander, 140, 150
Prelude, The (Wordsworth), 53, 135,
    143–57

Redeker, M., 121–2
Reed, Sampson, 127–8
Reid, Thomas, 133
Richards, I. A., 17
Ricoeur, Paul, 87–9, 92, 94, 96, 225,
    226, 231
Rousseau, J.–J., 2

Santayana, George, 226
Schelling, F. W. J. von, 1, 29
Schiller, Friedrich, 2, 3, 9

Schlegel, Friedrich, 111, 112, 113
Schleiermacher, Friedrich, viii, 1, 5,
  8, 59–60, (hermeneutics) 81–95,
  (translation and interpretation)
  97–103, (*sensus numinis*) 104–23,
  187–8, 226
Shakespeare, William, 3, 152, 207
Solger, Karl, viii
Spinoza, Baruch, 22
Statesman's Manual, The (Coleridge),
  35–6, 38, 134
Swinburne, A. C., 214

Taylor, Nathaniel, 176, 183
Tennyson, Alfred Lord, 140, 185–
  200
Tertullian, 227–8, 233
Tess of the d'Urbervilles (Hardy), 173,
  205–11
Theism, 76–7
Tillich, Paul, 108, 109
'Tintern Abbey' (Wordsworth), 155,
  159–61, 164, 195
Tooke, John Horne, 129–33, 140

Translation, 97–103
Tulloch, John, 50
Turner, J. M. W., 2

Unity, and Coleridge, 70–3, 77–8
Utopianism, 2–14

Vaihinger, Hans, 230–1
Vico, Giambattista, 139

Warheit und Method (Gadamer), 81–2,
  85, 92
Watts, Isaac, 167
Weber, Max, 163, 172
Wesley, John, 158, 165, 174
Wittgenstein, L., 234
Woolf, Virginia, 208
Word of God and the Word of Man, The
  (Barth), 60
Wordsworth, William, viii, 44, 46,
  48, 53–4, 126–7, 135, 137, 139,
  140, ('mystery of words') 143–57,
  158–74, 195